Inside the
Android™ OS

Android™ Deep Dive Series

ANDROID CONCURRENCY — G. Blake MEIKE

ANDROID DATABASE BEST PRACTICES — Adam STROUD

EMBEDDED PROGRAMMING with ANDROID — Bringing Up an Android System from Scratch — Roger YE

INSIDE the ANDROID OS — Building, Customizing, Managing and Operating Android System Services — G. Blake MEIKE

Visit informit.com/android for a complete list of available publications.

The Android™ Deep Dive Series is for intermediate and expert developers who use Android Studio and Java, but do not have comprehensive knowledge of Android APIs and want to bolster their knowledge of fundamentally important topics.

Each book in the series stands alone and provides idioms, frameworks, and engineering approaches. They provide in-depth information, correct patterns and idioms, and ways of avoiding bugs and other problems.

Inside the Android™ OS

Building, Customizing, Managing and Operating Android System Services

G. Blake Meike

Larry Schiefer

✦Addison-Wesley

Boston • Columbus • New York • San Francisco • Amsterdam • Cape Town
Dubai • London • Madrid • Milan • Munich • Paris • Montreal • Toronto • Delhi • Mexico City
São Paulo • Sydney • Hong Kong • Seoul • Singapore • Taipei • Tokyo

Library of Congress Control Number: 2021940286

Copyright © 2022 Pearson Education, Inc.

ISBN-13: 978-0-13-409634-6
ISBN-10: 0-13-409634-7

1 2021

Editor-in-Chief
Mark Taub

Acquisitions Editor
Malobika Chakraborty

Development Editor
Sheri Replin

Managing Editor
Sandra Schroeder

Senior Project Editor
Lori Lyons

Copy Editor
Paula Lowell

Production Manager
Aswini Kumar/ codeMantra

Indexer
Ken Johnson

Proofreader
Donna E. Mulder

Compositor
codeMantra

❖

Blake: For my siblings: Rusty, Annemarie.
Mercy, and Roger. One!

Larry: For Aidan and Ian. Don't ever stop
exploring and learning.

❖

Contents at a Glance

Contents

Preface

I started this book nearly 10 years ago. At the time, it seemed obvious to me that Android would be important in the burgeoning Internet of Things (IoT) world. Both Larry and I taught the Android Internals course for the great Marakana (later, New Circle). That class was so popular that both of us got to see a lot of the world while teaching it. I was certain that a book that described the general process of customizing Android for a new device without getting bogged down in details could be a hit.

On the other hand, I recall sitting in the restaurant in Grand Central Station with the editor of one of the books I co-authored (a man I very much respected) as he laid out comparable titles and explained in inexorable detail the chances that such a book would succeed. They were not good.

Sometime later, my co-author on O'Reilly's *Programming Android*, Zigurd Mednieks, proposed the *Android Deep Dive* series to Addison-Wesley. The idea was a series of small, replaceable titles, none of which had the overhead of a large book. If a volume became obsolete, it could be replaced or updated without impact to the rest of the series. In this lower-risk environment, my book made sense. It was green-lighted, and I started work on it.

Somewhere around the time I got the first few chapters written, Laura Lewin (the series editor at that time) and Zigurd pitched another book to me. That pitch turned into *Android Concurrency*. I am very proud of that book, but it took several years to write and completely stalled work on this one.

When I finally returned to this book, I was no longer teaching Internals. Cyanogen had shut down, and both Android and I had moved on. When I picked up the book again, I discovered that Android had changed so much in the interim (ART, Treble, and SE Linux) that each time I caught up, it had already moved on. The book was nearly canceled.

I had the great luck to have Larry Schiefer on board as a technical reviewer. When I finally conceded that the project was swamped and on the verge of drowning, our superstar editor Malobika Chakraborty suggested I take on a co-author. Talk about luck: Larry volunteered! He pulled the book out of its hole, laid down some fantastic knowledge, and made this project relevant again. I'm gonna buy him a t-shirt with a big yellow "S" on it.

Before you dig into the first chapter, let me offer a gentle reminder: This is *not* a cookbook. The book contains code examples, and they are all available online. They have all compiled successfully and run at least once. That, however, is no guarantee that they will compile and run for you (though we hope they do!). Tool chains change. Android changes. Devices change. Things that work today may well not work at all tomorrow. Our intention is that the content here is a guidebook, not a map.

Good luck!

Blake Meike, May 2021

Example Code

Most of the code shown in examples in this book can be found on GitHub at
https://github.com/InsideAndroidOS.

> **Note**
>
> Sometimes a line of code will be too long to fit on one line in this book. The code continuation symbol (➥) indicates that the line continues from the previous line.

Register Your Book

Register your copy of *Inside the Android OS* at informit.com for convenient access to downloads, updates, and/or corrections as they become available. To start the registration process, go to informit.com/register and log in or create an account. Enter the product ISBN 9780134096346 and click Submit. Look on the Registered Products tab for an Access Bonus Content link next to this product and follow that link to access any available bonus materials. If you would like to be notified of exclusive offers on new editions and updates, please check the box to receive email from us.

Acknowledgments

Blake: Many people contributed to this book over the years. Author and colleague, Zigurd Mednieks, made it possible as part of a series of small, replaceable titles. My agent, Carol Jelen, helped me pitch it, and the original editor, Laura Lewin, guided it during the first years. Adnan Begovic and Gil Zahaiek kept us honest technically, and Sheri Replin is our maven of prose. The incredibly patient Malobika Chakraborty supported the project through some very dark days. Lori Lyons and Aswini Kumar carried it over the finish line. Most of all, though, thanks to my co-author, Larry Schiefer, whom I was thrilled to score as a tech reviewer and who rescued this book from oblivion, breathed new life into it, and made it worth reading. You absolutely rocked it, Larry.

Larry: I would like to start by thanking my amazing wife, Shannon. Your never-ending patience and encouragement were essential to making this project happen. I could not have done it without you. I also want to thank my sons, Aidan and Ian, for your understanding when Dad was distracted or spending long hours writing. I love the three of you more than you'll ever know.

I'd like to thank my co-author G. Blake Meike for the opportunity to work with you on this project. Writing a book was something I've always wanted to do, but I never knew how to get started or had the courage to take the first step. This has been a great experience, and I'll be forever grateful.

A technical book like this is very challenging to write, especially for a moving target like Android! I would like to thank our technical reviewers for your hard work and feedback. Adnan Begovic and Gil Zahaiek, your insight as Android experts was invaluable. To our editors, Malobika Chakraborty and Sheri Replin, thank you for your understanding, patience, and a good prodding when needed. Through all the challenges, you both have stood steadfast in making sure this book happened, and I'm grateful for both of your insights and efforts.

About the Authors

Blake Meike is a passionate engineer, code poet, and veteran of more than 10 years of Android development at organizations including D2, Realm, Twitter, and Cyanogen. As a teacher, he has trained hundreds of new Android developers. He is author of several books on Android development, including O'Reilly's bestselling *Programming Android* and Addison-Wesley's *Android Concurrency*. He holds a degree in Mathematics and Computer Science from Dartmouth College and lives in the Pacific Northwest.

Larry Schiefer is the CTO and co-founder of HIQES, LLC, a mobile platform and app engineering services company. He has made a career out of creating software solutions for mobile, embedded, and desktop systems. He started his career at Motorola working on large area telecommunications systems then moved to startups in the telecommunications, networking, and embedded spaces. Digging into Android's internals was a natural progression with his background in telecommunications, embedded systems, and Linux kernel work. He has traveled around the world training engineers at Intel, Qualcomm, Bose, and others about the internal workings of Android. In addition to being an entrepreneur and technical leader, he continues to stay involved with the development of new software and platform solutions.

Why Android?

Android was built for small. It has scarcity designed deep into its DNA.

It was created in the early 2000s, a time when mobile devices were divided into categories like "smart phone" and "feature phone"; when flash drive program/erase cycles were counted in tens of thousands; and when 64 megabytes was a lot of RAM. The idea at Android's very core—that because there is no backing store to which to swap running programs, when memory gets tight the operating system has no choice but to terminate them—is the inescapable legacy of its fixation on frugality.

Modern smart phones have all the capabilities that laptops had at that time. Were it designed today, Android would likely be a very different thing. Although battery life is still a subject of much concern, a modern mobile OS could swap to flash memory as effectively as a modern laptop swaps to its SSD. Modern Android developers are supplementing—even replacing—the simple, frugal libraries built into Android with new and powerful but much more resource-intensive libraries such as GSON and RxAndroid.

At the same time that mobile phones, the original target of the Android OS, are outgrowing its architecture, a new and possibly larger opportunity is appearing: the Internet of Things and the smart devices that comprise it. In much the way that even small companies found, around the turn of the century, that they needed a web presence to compete, so many of the same companies are now discovering that their *products* need a web presence to compete. From medical devices and on-board systems in cars, to homes, appliances, and even clothes, all sorts of products are being supplemented with built-in intelligence. Many of these devices have substantial constraints on the processor they can support. Price, design, and flexibility make Android an excellent choice for powering these types of devices.

Adopting Android

There are a lot of reason that Android might be a good choice for a new smart device.

Full Stack

The Android OS addresses the full stack of product requirements. From hardware and the kernel to stereo audio and displays on multiple screens, Android offers flexibility and provides a wealth of options. One can think of Android as similar to a distribution of GNU/Linux such as Mint or CentOS. It transforms a device from a warm piece of silicon to a useful computer with basic functionality.

Broad Acceptance

Perhaps the most obvious reason for choosing Android for a hardware project is that it is ubiquitous. Some versions of Android run out of the box on nearly any common chipset. In fact, most SoC (system on a chip) vendors provide reference hardware kits with a version of Android and a backing Linux kernel. At least as important is that many developers are familiar with the Android system. Building a team, from front-end application and UI experts to those with the deep understanding of Android necessary to modify its core, should not be an impediment.

Beautiful UI

The Android system is capable of producing stunning user interfaces, which is perhaps its most important feature. Support for most popular audio and video media is baked right in and is relatively easy to use. Offering full lighting and shadowing, the tools for animation and 3D display are top-notch. One has only to look at some of the simply gorgeous applications such as Feedly or Weather View to grasp the nearly unlimited potential of the Android design palette. When the existing Android UI framework is not enough, the system supports both Open GL ES and Vulkan for low overhead, high-performance 3D graphics.

Linux Based

The Android operating system is based on the Linux operating system. Linux is one of the most popular and widely used of all operating systems. It is everywhere. Whether a chip is ARM-based, Intel-based, or something radical, nearly every chipset manufacturer provides a version of Linux that runs on their device. Bear in mind, however, that Android is officially only available for ARM- and Intel-based processors (both 32 and 64 bit.) This means the Android Open Source Project (AOSP) tree's build system, pre-built tools, test suites, and the publicly available native development kit (NDK) only support these architectures. That is not to say Android cannot run on some other architecture, just that the toolchains and build systems for those architectures are not supported.

While simply getting Linux ported and running on a new board is an important first step, quite a bit of work may well be necessary to get all the hardware accessible to software. Frequently, because the Linux kernel is licensed with the GNU Public License (**GPL**), the custom code necessary to support a particular sensor, display, or port will already be available for free online. Even if this is not the case, a large community of developers exists that is very familiar with the process of building new drivers for Linux. Accommodating a new board or a new device is, if not always simple, at least fairly straightforward.

Powerful Development Environment

The Android toolchains are quite powerful and are undergoing constant improvement. Both toolchains—that for building Android's infrastructure and that for building Java applications that run on top of Android—are based, largely, on common off-the-shelf tools.

The Android source code, the Android Open Source Project (**AOSP**), is well supported. Creating a build of the version of Android used in this book, API 29, is relatively straightforward on recent OSX and Linux platforms. The build system with its directory-based mechanism for per-hardware customizations was originally based on GNU make. With the Nougat release, the soong build system replaced make. Soong uses two additional tools, kati and ninja, to make the build much faster than it was using make. Existing makefiles continue to work as-is alongside the new soong build files.

Most of the development for an Android system—even most of the system-level programming—is done in Java. Android Java developers will use tools like Android Studio (a fork of IntelliJ's IDEA IDE) and Gradle, the standard build tool for Android applications. Gradle is very definitely sufficient for building, testing, and packaging even system applications with native components.

As mentioned previously, as of about 2014, several new, interesting, and powerful development frameworks are available for use in Java Android application. Although some are large and all are a trade-off in battery life, tools such as Realm DB, RxAndroid, and Retrofit can drastically improve the effectiveness of a development team.

One of the most important advancements in Android development was the announcement of Kotlin as a first-class supported language in May of 2017. Kotlin is clear, succinct, powerful language that seamlessly integrates with existing Java and even native code. Although it is not widely used within AOSP's core (yet), it can be used by applications written for a custom Android platform.

Open Source

Building an embedded device necessarily involves negotiating a minefield of legal issues. This book is technical, not legal. We are not lawyers and nothing in this or any of the subsequent chapters should be interpreted as legal advice. If you intend to attempt marketing your own device, you will need the help of a qualified lawyer. That said, some broad generalizations might help a budding device developer to understand the moving parts. Figure 1.1 is a very high-level model of code ownership in the Android system.

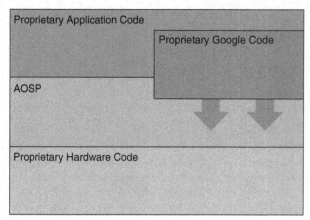

Figure 1.1   Android Code Ownership

At the bottom of the stack is proprietary hardware code. It is usually obtained from the hardware vendor, who may license it at no cost or, perhaps, impose some kind of fee. This code is frequently not open source. It is essential, but it may be delivered as pre-built binaries and possibly with strict legal injunctions about reverse engineering. Quite possibly you will never see the source and even the documentation for it might not be very good. Android's primary interface to this code is the Hardware Abstraction Layer (HAL), discussed in Chapters 8 and 10.

At the top of the stack are applications. These are things like the controller for a proprietary home-entertainment system or the Facebook and Twitter apps. Apps are also likely to be proprietary and, again, unless they are apps you develop yourself, you may never see their source code. If your platform needs specific applications, you will either have to make agreements with their owners or provide some kind of service (a store or marketplace) from which an end user can acquire them.

In between these two proprietary layers is the code base for Android itself, the Android Open Source Project (AOSP). It is completely open source. You can read it, copy it, customize it, and use it pretty much as you like. Nearly all of it is protected with licenses that even allow you to redistribute only pre-built binaries, should you choose to do so. You can take as little or as much as you need.

People are frequently confused about the openness of the AOSP code base, because Google strictly controls contributions. It is true that you are unlikely to be able to contribute a change to the canonical AOSP codebase as you could with most other open-source projects. What you can do, though, is create a fork of the relevant code repository, change it in any way you choose and use it wherever you want.

Although the AOSP code is truly open source, it is not necessarily free of legal encumbrances. Many of the technologies built into Linux and the Android services based on top of it have been the subjects of large and small legal battles. Among the technologies that you might need to license are things such as Wi-Fi, Bluetooth, multimedia codecs, and other more esoteric things (like a file system!).

What makes this even more confusing is the AOSP tree includes software implementations of some of these components (such as multimedia encoders and decoders) as placeholders. They do not come with any kind of patent or license grant from Google or the intellectual property (IP) holders. When you build a new device, these third-party components must be carefully examined to ensure the device is in compliance with technology-specific licenses.

Microsoft, in particular, has a portfolio of patents that it has successfully used in strong-arming an estimated $1 billion in license fees from various Android device manufacturers. The exact contents of this portfolio were a closely held secret for many years. In 2014, however, the Chinese government leaked the contents of the portfolio, and you can now easily find it online.

AOSP and Google

Google holds its control over the Android OS in two ways. First, most consumer Android-labeled systems contain a feature-rich, proprietary Google platform that is not part of AOSP. This platform includes things such as Google Play Services, Google Maps, and the Play Store.

Second, to install any of these proprietary services—or even, for that matter, to label the system as an Android™ system and adorn it with the Android robot icon—a device manufacturer must ensure the device complies with the Android Compatibility Definition Document (CDD) and passes the Android Compatibility Test Suite (CTS) and the Vendor Test Suite (VTS). After a device is verified as compliant, Google Mobile Services may be licensed for the device, allowing it to ship with Google's proprietary add-ons.

These constraints—the Google proprietary code, the licensing agreement, compliance with the CDD, and passing the CTS and VTS—do not affect the use of the AOSP codebase. Developers and device creators are free to use and adapt the AOSP code as long as they neither label the resulting device as "Android" nor need the Google proprietary code and its associated function-ality (marketplace, cloud services, and so on).

Several examples exist of forks of the AOSP codebase. Perhaps the best known of these is Fire OS, used on Amazon devices such as the Kindle, Fire TV, and the Fire Phone. Many, if not most, applications built for Android will run on Fire OS. Nonetheless, Fire OS cannot be labeled as Android, cannot include the Google Play Store, and does not support Google Play Services.

Both Samsung and LineageOS (formerly CyanogenMod) also maintain operating systems that are heavily modified versions of the AOSP codebase. Both of these forks, though, have managed to pass the CTS and stay on Google's good side. Both are labeled as Android.

Many other examples of AOSP code in non-Google devices exist, from popular phones and tablets in China and India to the UI for Comcast's Xfinity service. Although each of these devices has its own legal story and its own legal concerns, the use of the AOSP codebase is not, in itself, a problem for any of them. Depending on whether a manufacturer feels that it can provide an alternative to the Android label and the accompanying Google proprietary services, it either does or does not invite Google into its AOSP-based product. The devices it creates using AOSP code do not need be visible to Google in any way and do not need any permission or participation from Google.

Where it gets complicated is devices in the middle ground between the two ends of the spectrum just described: a device that does not need or want the Android label but on which the manufacturer wants to include apps with which users are familiar but are provided by Google. For example, consider a kiosk for renting movies that is powered by Android. The manufacturer would like to bundle YouTube so that users can view video trailers. Google's position is this arrangement is not supported. The manufacturer needs either to ensure the device is CDD/CTS compliant or find an alternative way of providing the desired functionality.

Other Choices

The number of products with embedded systems may be exploding but the idea of embedded computing itself is nothing new. Many alternatives to Android are available as the intelligence for an IoT device; Real Time Operating Systems (**RTOSs**), some much older than Android and some newly developed.

An even better alternative, though, might be no OS at all.

Micro-Controllers

Even with the falling prices and increasing power of single-board computers (**SBCs**), at the time of this writing, a board that can run Android will cost something in the $20–$50 range. It will also occupy around 20 cubic centimeters of space. That can be a lot of overhead for a small device.

When cost and space are of paramount importance, a micro-controller like the wildly popular Arduino may be an attractive alternative. Most micro-controllers are not full-fledged processors and cannot support multiple simultaneous processes, Linux, or a flashy UI, let alone Android.

At the time of this writing, so-called "mini" micro-controllers are a full order of magnitude less expensive than SBCs and may require less than a single cubic centimeter of space. Over time, certainly, the line between SBCs and micro-controllers will blur. SBCs will get smaller, micro-controllers will become more powerful, and RTOS capabilities will scale linearly with the hardware. Even now, though, it is possible to accomplish some very impressive magic with one or more small, simple micro-controllers.

An important limitation of micro-controllers, to be considered before choosing one as the brains for a project, is its upgradeability. While it is certainly possible to update a microcontroller-based system over the air, it can be difficult and might require additional specialized hardware. If over-the-air (**OTA**) updates are part of your device strategy, you might need a full-fledged OS.

Simplicity is a double-edged sword. A system that can be updated can be hacked. Hacking a micro-controller is entirely possible. Think Stuxnet. However, doing so is probably difficult and not interesting to an attacker. A simple read-only memory (**ROM**)-based micro-controller that is just sufficient to power your project may save you from a substantial security budget and keep your product out of the headlines during the next distributed denial of service (**DDoS**) incident.

Other RTOSs

The list of operating system alternatives to Android is long. Each of them solves some set of problems and introduces others.

QNX

QNX was the most popular embedded OS in the world before the advent of Android. Originally called QUNIX, it is a micro-kernel-based system and was developed by two students at the University of Waterloo. It was released in 1984 as QNX to avoid trademark infringement. Since that time it has been rewritten several times, and sold, first to Harman International and then to Research In Motion, now Blackberry. Shortly after Blackberry acquired QNX, it restricted access to the source.

VxWorks

If your device needs the kind of reliability and dependability that powers the Martian probes and military aircraft, you should consider VxWorks. VxWorks is a proprietary OS originally developed by RTOS pioneers, Wind River. Wind River is now a wholly owned subsidiary of Intel.

The VxWorks kernel is monolithic (unlike QNX), but the system is nicely modularized and the toolchain well developed. All of this, of course, comes at a price: Vxworks is proprietary and closed source. Wind River also produces Wind River Linux, a hardened kernel with a custom build system.

Android Things

Android Things is Google's version of Android stripped down for IoT. Codenamed Brillo, this stripped down version of Android was designed to be used by low-power IoT devices with significantly less RAM (as low as 32 MB) while still including Bluetooth Low Energy (BLE) and Wi-Fi support. Android Things requires manufacturers to use supported single-board computers (SBCs) or System on Modules (SoMs). Such devices would automatically receive OS and security updates from Google. Additionally, Android Things included a standard framework for developing custom hardware interfaces without requiring changes to the underlying kernel or Android framework. This approach allowed IoT manufacturers to focus on their specific purpose and not worry about the underlying OS, its security, or system-level updates.

Unfortunately, in early 2019 Google announced that Android Things had been refocused on smart TV and smart speaker systems and that broader long-term support is at end of life.

Others

Windows CE has been a very popular embedded OS as is evidenced by the blue screens of death on everything from subway and traffic signs to vending machines and museum kiosks. Microsoft recently introduced a successor to CE, called Windows 10 for IoT.

Nucleus RTOS, from Wind River's long-time rival, Mentor Graphics, found a home in a number of Samsung, LG, and Motorola phones. Riot OS, Arm Mbed OS, and Green Hills Integrity are all also players.

Nearly all of these popular RTOSs are proprietary and closed source. Free and open-sourced RTOSs are out there, though—FreeRTOS, MontaVista, and Contiki, to name a few—but none of them has the kind of history and support that Android has.

Summary

You can find many alternatives to Android. Few, however have the collection of features and support that make it such a great choice for an IoT project:

- It is free. Take as much or as little as you like; use it as you please.

- It is portable. Android can be made to run on virtually any type of hardware. Getting any operating system running on a new device can be very difficult. Android is no exception. There is, though, a lot of existing code and a large community with lots of experience with porting it.

- It is adaptable. Plumbing support for new peripherals into the Android framework is a straightforward and usually simple task. Doing so is the subject of the rest of this book.

- The toolchain is good. The low-level C and C++ code use standard tools augmented with a baroque but useful build system. Most of the code—high level and written in Java—is supported by Gradle, a couple custom plug-ins, and Android Studio. All of these tools are undergoing constant improvement.

- It supports reactive and beautiful UIs. Android can handle a variety of media, both audio and video. It has powerful tools for animation, and supports three-dimensional layouts and both touchscreen and D-pad input.

2

Booting Acme

Let's get started! Consider a project: customizing Android for a new device, the *Acme* device. The hardware engineers for the Acme project have, fortunately, chosen hardware that turns out to be fairly similar in architecture to a HiKey960. That means the Acme project will be based on the well-supported HiKey variant of AOSP and gradually modified to suit the project goals.

> **Note**
>
> The code and examples in this book were built and run on a HiKey960, using the release tag `android-10.0.0_r33` for the Android AOSP source tree and compiled on a Linux Ubuntu 16.04. While, of course, this is not a guarantee of reproducibility, it is some guarantee of consistency.

Even for developers who are not so fortunate as to have such a lucky choice of hardware for their project, the general strategy described in this chapter should be completely applicable. The absolute pre-requirements for the development process described in the rest of this book are a code-base that

- Is under source control and can be reproduced exactly
- Can be built with a stable, available toolchain to create a flashable image
- Produces an image that successfully boots into Android

Bringing up a device is work for wizards; it can be frustrating, time consuming, and unique to a particular device. It is unlikely that any book could describe it. Even if such a book did exist, it would be obsolete by the time it got to the printer.

> **Note**
>
> Developers at the interface between hardware and software call the process of getting a basic operating system running on a new device as "bring up." Bringing up a board is, usually, an iterative process, first getting some small simple code running and then using it to bootstrap a boot loader and, eventually, an operating system.

Although this chapter is a skeleton for the process, there is some wild hand waving: This is not a cookbook. Being able to get from source to running Android, however, is absolutely a prerequirement for proceeding. To follow the topics discussed in the rest of this book, a developer must be able to test incrementally and revert changes when they do not work.

Setting Up a Build Machine

The two supported options for a build machine are Linux and OSX. Although developing Android applications from Windows is possible, no support for building Android itself on Windows exists.

Android is definitely most comfortable on Linux. A plurality of the work done on the Android system is done on Linux platforms. The tools, the support community, and even the code itself all originate and are most thoroughly used and tested in the Linux environment. Developers with Linux development platforms and comfortable using Linux systems are on the best maintained trail.

Many developers prefer to work on OSX. Fortunately, most versions of most of the Android code can be built from OSX. Linux kernels, custom drivers, and native Linux services can also frequently be built on OSX.

Choosing OSX as a build platform, however, is a charged decision. Developers who depend on OSX for building their products can expect to spend a significant amount of time porting and debugging tools. The ability to do an OSX native build can certainly be an important time-saver for an engineer developing on an OSX machine—when it works. The distinction between *expecting* a native OSX build to work most of the time and *depending* on having them work all the time may seem subtle. It can become very clear, though, when a deadline looms and the OSX native C compiler refuses to compile the most recent source.

Perhaps surprisingly, virtual machines can be realistic alternatives. They are the only way to do builds on a Windows system. Of course, builds definitely run slowly on a virtual machine. With a little forethought, though, the possibility exists that full builds may be necessary only rarely. Depending on the size of the incremental build, a virtual machine may be viable.

Note

Unfortunately, at least at the time of this writing, one of the most appealing possibilities, a shared folder, visible from both an OSX host and a Linux guest, does not work using either recent versions of VirtualBox or VMWare Fusion for virtualization. A flaw in the mapping between guest and host file permissions prevents the build from completing successfully.

Complete, easily followed directions for setting up the build machine are available on the AOSP source website at https://source.android.com/setup/build/initializing.

When building with OSX, creating a separate, case-sensitive volume to hold the source code is especially important. The volume can be a mountable disk image file or a physical external drive but it must, unlike the normal OSX file system, be case sensitive.

The next step is downloading the source.

Downloading the Code

The process of downloading the Android source tree is also well documented at the source website. The full source is fairly large (around 100 GB) and nearly twice that much space will be necessary for a complete build. Both the download and build processes can be quite lengthy and take hours, even on a fairly powerful machine with a good network connection.

The code is structured as a forest of `git` repository trees and maintained with a tool called `repo`. As described in the documentation, downloading the source consists of

1. Obtaining the `repo` tool

2. Obtaining the `repo` **manifest**

3. Using `repo` to download the `git` repositories named in the manifest

Repo

Repo is an interesting and powerful tool. It is a Python program that uses git to provide functionality similar to that provided by git submodules. Repo, however, was around well before submodules.

The following discussion assumes a good working knowledge of git. Several excellent resources for developers that are new to git are available, including Jon Loeliger and Matthew McCullough's excellent *Version Control with Git* (Loeliger, 2012) and the complete and readable documentation at GitHub (https://help.github.com).

Repo manages an interesting two-layered versioning system. The following command line initializes a directory as a Repo workspace:

```
repo init -u https://android.googlesource.com/platform/manifest \
        -m default.xml
```

Running this command in a directory creates a new top-level subdirectory named `.repo`. That directory contains, among other things, the manifest repository—a git repository identified in the initialization command by the argument of the `-u` option. The manifest repository is cloned into the `.repo` directory and named `manifests`.

The manifest repo may contain all kinds of things, but it must contain one or more manifest files. The manifest file that is named as the argument of the `-m` command line option (or the file named default.xml, if no −m option is specified) is soft-linked or included from the top level of the .repo directory as manifest.xml. The manifest.xml file controls the structure of the rest of the repository. Figure 2.1 illustrates the structure of the repo workspace.

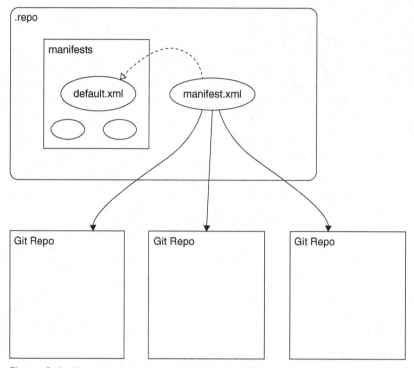

Figure 2.1   Repo Workspace

After the workspace is initialized, repo can download the actual source. This is done by issuing the sync command from the command line:

```
repo sync
```

In response to this command, the repo program parses manifest.xml, which is a list of git repositories. It clones each git repository into a location, also specified in the manifest. When the sync command completes, the working directory is an identical copy of every other workspace created with the same commands.

Caution!

Do not copy a repo workspace as you might a normal git repository. Repo workspaces make heavy use of soft links. A simple file copy will actually refer to the exact same workspace as the original.

Because the manifest itself is kept in a git repository, it may be versioned: It is a versioned list of names of versioned repositories. The manifest directory, in addition to having different manifests—say, one for each of several different customers—may also contain multiple versions of each of those manifests, each on a separate git branch. Repo's -b option allows the developer to check out the version of a manifest on a particular branch. That versioned manifest may, in turn, point to specific branches (or even commits) within each of the repositories that make up the workspace. A subsequent sync command will populate the workspace as specified by the branch version of the manifest.

A manifest is a fairly simple XML document. Listing 2.1 gives a partial example.

Listing 2.1   **Repo Manifest**

```xml
<?xml version="1.0" encoding="UTF-8"?>
<manifest>

  <remote  name="aosp"
           fetch=".." />
  <default revision="refs/tags/android-10.0.0_r33"
           remote="aosp"
           sync-j="4" />

  <project path="build/make" name="platform/build" groups="pdk" >
    <copyfile src="core/root.mk" dest="Makefile" />
    <linkfile src="CleanSpec.mk" dest="build/CleanSpec.mk" />
    <linkfile src="buildspec.mk.default" dest="build/buildspec.mk.default" />
    <linkfile src="core" dest="build/core" />
    <linkfile src="envsetup.sh" dest="build/envsetup.sh" />
    <linkfile src="target" dest="build/target" />
    <linkfile src="tools" dest="build/tools" />
  </project>
  <project path="build/blueprint" name="platform/build/blueprint"
  groups="pdk,tradefed" />
  <project path="build/kati" name="platform/build/kati" groups="pdk,tradefed" />

  <project path="build/blueprint"
           name="platform/build/blueprint"
           groups="pdk,tradefed" />

  <project path="build/soong" name="platform/build/soong" groups="pdk,tradefed" >
    <linkfile src="root.bp" dest="Android.bp" />
    <linkfile src="bootstrap.bash" dest="bootstrap.bash" />
  </project>
  <project path="abi/cpp" name="platform/abi/cpp" groups="pdk" />
  <project path="art" name="platform/art" groups="pdk" />
  <project path="bionic" name="platform/bionic" groups="pdk" />
...
</manifest>
```

The full syntax for the manifest file is specified in the documentation accompanying the repo source at https://gerrit.googlesource.com/git-repo/+/master/docs/manifest-format.md. Essentially, each `project` element in the XML identifies a git repository by its `name`, relative to some base URL, its `remote`; and where that repository should be placed in the local workspace, its `path`. The manifest in Listing 2.1, for instance, identifies a git repository named "platform/bionic", to be placed at the top level of the workspace in a directory named "bionic".

Deciphering the full URL for the "bionic" source git repository requires a bit more investigation. Because no explicit remote is specified for the bionic project, repo will use the default remote. The default remote for this manifest is specified up in the `default` element near the top of the manifest. The manifest in Listing 2.1 specifies the remote named "aosp" as the default. The "aosp" remote is defined in the element immediately above the default element. Normally a remote definition would include a name and a base URL. Instead, the "aosp" remote includes the somewhat cryptic "fetch" attribute "..", which has a special meaning. It indicates that the URL for this remote should be derived from the URL used to initialize the workspace (the argument to the –u option, the URL of the original manifest) by leaving off the last element. In this example, that URL was https://android.googlesource.com/platform/manifest. Removing the name of the manifest repository and the last path element leaves a base URL of https://android.googlesource.com/. Putting this all together, then, the URL for the "bionic" repository is https://android.googlesource.com/platform/bionic.

The ".." trick is essential for organizations that want to reduce network bandwidth usage by creating a local source mirror. Because the source for Android is very large and may take as much as an hour to download at WAN speeds, a distributed company with offices in Boston and Seattle, for example, might find that maintaining mirrors on each site's local network is preferable. The initialization-relative addressing made possible by repo's `fetch=".."` attribute makes it possible for the developers in the two offices to use identical manifests to download their workspaces from two different sources. The next section covers forking the tree and local mirrors in more detail.

Because each project in a manifest specifies its own source, creating a manifest that downloads code mostly from the canonical source and adds or replaces only things that must be customized for a particular development project is easy. It is unlikely, for instance, that customizing Android for a particular device will require modifications to the Android runtime (Dalvik or ART) or that it will require changes to one or more of the core Java libraries. Most projects' manifests can continue to refer to the canonical AOSP source for the runtime but their own repository for core libraries.

Repo is capable of several other excellent tricks. The `copyfile`, `linkfile`, and `include` elements all do just what their names suggest. The first two allow, for instance, placing files at the top level of the workspace (not otherwise possible, because the top-level directory is not a git repository). The `include` element allows multiple manifests to explicitly share common configuration (in fact, modern repo now "include"s the target manifest, instead of soft-linking it).

The `groups` attribute within the XML `project` element allows even further customization of a workspace by allowing the creation of coherent subsets of repositories. Consider, for instance, a codebase that is being developed for both Intel and ARM hardware architectures. Although integration testing must verify that all tests pass on both platforms, most developers will probably work only on one or the other. A developer working with the Intel platform might prefer not to download and build source related only to ARM architectures. Tagging `project` elements with groups makes it possible to do this.

Repo supports the Gerrit continuous integration tool used in the open source community and at Google to fold contributions back into AOSP. A typical repo workflow might look like this:

```
repo checkout working proj1 proj2 proj3
# normal edit/git commit cycle in project directories
repo upload --cbr proj1 proj2 proj3
# repeat edit/git commit to respond to code reviews
repo upload --cbr proj1 proj2 proj3
repo abandon working proj1 proj2 proj3
```

Here, the developer starts a new feature branch called "working" in three repositories: "proj1", "proj2", and "proj3". After doing some work using git, normally, to commit incremental updates and rebase, merge and squash as usual, the developer pushes the current state for all three of the working branches to Gerrit for review.

> **Note**
>
> `repo upload` is not atomic—it does not necessarily all succeed or all fail. Each of the three projects in the preceding example is a separate repository. It would be entirely possible that two of the three pushes succeed but that one fails, leaving the workspace in an inconsistent state.

As usual, the review/revise loop iterates until the new work is accepted and merged at the origin. After the merge is complete, the local branches can be abandoned.

Two final repo features may also be useful. One is the `forall` command. `Forall` executes a shell command in each of the named projects. For instance:

```
repo forall -c 'git reset --hard HEAD; git clean -xdf'
```

is one way of resetting all repositories to their initial state.

A second useful feature is repo support for local manifests. A local manifest—either `.repo/local_manifest.xml` (deprecated) or all of the files `.repo/local_manifests/*.xml`, in alphabetical order—are merged with the manifest in `manifest.xml` as part of the `sync` command. By using local manifests, developers can further customize their local workspace, adding definitions for remotes or for additional projects as appropriate.

Forking the Source

The first step to modifying Android for a new device is to create your project fork of the AOSP source. There are a number of ways of creating such a fork with repo and git. The choice of which approach to take is up to the development team and what makes sense for the organization. Not all of these options are a good fit for all organizations. This section outlines several approaches that a team might choose. In each case, a customized manifest specifies the projects that make up the platform. The details of the manifest changes are slightly different for each choice.

Android Version Selection

Before diving into the options for creating a fork of the Android sources, ensure that you select the correct version of Android. This is not as straightforward as one might think, partly because of variations in system on a chip (SoC) vendor support and the ever-changing landscape of Android's internals (as will be obvious in this book).

SoC vendor support for different Android versions presents a challenge for any project. Android is driven by mobile handset development, which has less than an 18-month lifecycle. This means that it is likely that the development for SoC chipsets used in new phones released today was started 18 months ago. It also means the chipsets have a support lifetime that is typically around 18 months after release. Traditionally, because Google has Android on roughly an annual release schedule, a given chipset is likely to receive vendor support for only one major OS version update after it is first released. At that point the SoC vendor moves its focus to its new "flagship" SoC.

This can present challenges when creating an IoT device that does not require the latest and greatest chipset features and performance, not to mention the hefty price point that comes with newer chipsets. Finding a chipset with the right price point, capabilities, and support for a version of Android appropriate for the product is a balancing act.

Further complicating version selection is Android's internal structure. Although Android's overall architecture has remained intact since its first release, it has had many enhancements to its internals over time. For the third-party app developer, these revisions are usually transparent. Exceptions exist, of course, such as the Android permission system overhaul that happened in the Android 6 (Marshmallow) release. The normally friction-free development environment does not apply when creating new products and working at the system level. Platform vendors are much more susceptible to Android's changing internals, which also factors in to the SoC vendor level of support over time.

One of the most disrupting changes for platform creators came with Android 8 (Oreo): project Treble. Project Treble completely changed the way that platforms/SoC expose hardware-related functions to the OS. The entire Hardware Abstraction Layer (HAL) was re-architected to allow vendors to upgrade to future versions of Android. All of these features come at the cost of increased complexity. The HAL is covered in more detail in Chapters 8 through 12, but it is worth an early word of caution.

In short, vendor integration prior to Android 8 was simpler from a HAL perspective. The vendor needed only to provide a kernel with the required hardware support, a set of shared libraries that followed a specific naming model, and a set of APIs at the C/C++ level. Starting with Android 8, the HAL forces a strict vendor interface that is exposed using Binder (Android's interprocess communication [IPC] mechanism). While this makes forward migration faster and easier, it complicates the platform developer's job when bringing up a new device.

Unfortunately, there is no one right answer when picking an Android version for use on a new platform. To benefit from fixes and enhancements made to future Android versions, going with Android 8 or newer is the way to go. Choosing such a recent release, however, can make the initial system bring-up process much more complicated, particularly if the device utilizes custom hardware or features not provided by the SoC vendor.

The choice of Android version also depends on whether the SoC vendor supports Android 8 or newer. If a product does not require regular updates or need to take advantage of new OS features, going with Android 7 (or even earlier) may be a good choice. Even if a product is released with an Android version prior to 8, updating units in the field via an over-the-air (OTA) update may still be possible. Of course, implementing a safe, secure OTA update mechanism is difficult, completely up to the platform vendor, and well outside the scope of this book.

Local Mirror

Although it is not strictly necessary, creating a local mirror of the Android source is almost certainly a good idea. Google maintains special repo manifest (*not* the manifest for AOSP source) to be used for creating a mirror. The process is documented in detail in the section "Using a local mirror" on the AOSP Downloading page (https://source.android.com/source/downloading).

Several reasons exist for using a local mirror. The chief reason is that local file copy or, at worst, local network transfer, is likely to be much faster than an Internet connection. Although the mirror takes a fair amount of space (around 150G) and takes more time to download than just the AOSP source, it all becomes worthwhile the first time it is necessary to check out the AOSP source at a new and different git tag or to download the source for some big component a second time.

> **Note**
>
> Understanding the file-system size requirements when building an AOSP derived tree or creating a local mirror are important. As noted previously, the local mirror size is around 150GB of disk space. This is the bare git repository size, not the size of an actual working tree used for development. Each instance of the AOSP tree that is initialized and synchronized will consume another 60+GB of space in its pristine state and close to double that size when fully built. There is also compiler cache, which consumes more space (but is configurable in size).
>
> The bottom line is that when using a local mirror on the same system that is being used for development, the total disk space needed is the size of the mirror plus the size of all the AOSP-based trees in use for development or building.

A second reason for creating a mirror is that doing so provides more control over the way the local fork of the source is updated. As described in the previous section, the repo tool maintains a manifest: a list of git repositories. The repo `sync` command clones each of the repositories listed in the manifest into the local workspace and then checks out the contents. As is usual practice with a git repository, the repo tool checks out the HEAD of a branch.

The whole point of a git branch, though, is that it is a moving target. The commit that is head of a given branch today is not the commit that was the head of that branch a week ago. For this reason, creating a local mirror is valuable because it makes local checkouts repeatable. The mirror is a static snapshot of the AOSP source. Unless the mirror itself is updated, two checkouts made weeks apart will result in identical source. Obviously, this is not the case if the checkouts are made directly from the Google source.

The Acme device manifest uses the *tag* android-10.0.0_r33 of AOSP. Note this is different than using one of the similarly named Android release *branches*, like android10-mainline-release. The HEAD of a branch may change between two repo syncs. Using tags or pinning specific commits mitigates this problem: Tags generally do not move. In fact, Google and SoC vendors often provide a manifest for Android on a particular SoC or development kit in exactly this way.

When using a local mirror, you have two different approaches: a local file-system copy (which is described on the AOSP Downloading page), or a local git server setup, a mirror of the Google-hosted repositories. The local filesystem mirror is a great approach for single developers but does not easily allow multiple developer contributions. This is where the local git server mirror is a better choice.

A local git server mirror, however, comes with the added overhead of setting up a hosted, accessible git server. Although there are plenty of resources available online for this, it may be more of a burden than some teams are willing to incur.

It is also worth noting that we definitely do not recommend using a single monolithic git repository. The AOSP source tree is made up of several hundred individual source code trees. Many of these are within the main Android sources whereas others come from existing open source projects. Putting all of these separate codebases into a monolithic repository would make it nearly impossible to stay in sync with either AOSP or third-party sources. Instead of pulling a single repository's git history into the local mirror, you would need to manually apply each patch to the appropriate directory within the tree.

Hosted Git Repositories

Another common alternative is the use of hosted git repositories, such as GitHub, Bitbucket, or GitLab. Many software development organizations are already using these services for their day-to-day work. Adopting them for an Android project allows teams to leverage the existing workflows and infrastructure with which they are already familiar. In addition, hosted repositories may already have IT support, provide useful continuous integration tools, and have refined controls for team member access.

There can be complications, though. Cloud-hosted repositories such as GitHub typically do not support the path-like, name-spaced layout used by AOSP. A common way around this issue is to replace the path separator (a slash) with an underscore. For example, the AOSP repository "platform/hardware/libhardware" becomes "platform_hardware_libhardware."

Additionally, hosted git services usually place a size limit on each repository. For most git repositories, this is not a problem. However, some repositories within the Android build tree exceed standard GitHub size limits (typically 2GB) and cannot be hosted with their full history. These include the frameworks/base and the Linux kernel repositories. The best approach to take when using a cloud-based service is to host only the repositories under active development. All other repositories should be pulled from Google or a local mirror.

Tree Snapshot

Another and somewhat more space-expensive way of providing this stability is simply to snapshot the entire AOSP source tree. That certainly is a very safe approach. If the space is available and the target version of the Android source to be used for the project is not sufficiently stable, it may also be the best. This is definitely not a recommended technique, though, especially when teams are developing the platform, because it removes the use of remote git repositories.

Repository Commit Pinning

As mentioned earlier in the "Local Mirror" section, one of the big advantages of a mirror is having a consistent "snapshot" of the AOSP tree at a point in time that does not change. When team members are setting up new machines, a continuous integration (CI) server, and so on, using the same source revisions to build the platform is critical. Local mirrors, though, are not always practical due to team size, IT infrastructure, or file system space constraints. The next best approach is specific commit pinning within the manifest file. In Listing 2.1, the remote property for the "aosp" specifies a revision attribute that points to a specific tag, `android-10.0.0_r33`. This means that all repositories fetched from the `aosp` remote will be checked out at this specific tag unless it is overridden at a given project's entry.

The same `revision` attribute, specifying a tag, branch, or even git commit ID can be used within a project tag to specify an individual repository within the manifest. For example, if a platform needed the Bionic C library implementation at commit `8c43445152e3372ea284b65845012fd` `fe7270f82`, it could specify that commit hash in its manifest as shown in Listing 2.2.

Listing 2.2   **Manifest Project Entry with Revision**

```
<project groups="default" name="platform/bionic" path="bionic"
revision="8c43445152e3372ea284b65845012fdfe7270f82"/>
```

Example: Local Mirror of Forked Repositories

This example uses the repo tool to replace only the individual portions of the AOSP code base that will be changed locally, in a more fine-grained and specific way. This partially forked concept can be used with a local mirror, third-party hosted git repositories, internally hosted git repositories, or a hybrid of these.

To use the repo tool to create partially forked source, first clone the AOSP manifest repo itself:

```
git clone https://android.googlesource.com/platform/manifest -b refs/tags/
android-10.0.0_r33
```

This manifest will become the manifest for the Acme project fork of Android source. It, and not the AOSP original, is the manifest that Acme developers will use to check out the Acme source code.

The new, local clone of the manifest directory contains the repo manifest file "default.xml" as shown in Listing 2.3.

Listing 2.3 **The AOSP Manifest File**

```
<?xml version="1.0" encoding="UTF-8"?>
<manifest>

  <remote   name="aosp"
            fetch=".."
            review="https://android-review.googlesource.com/" />
  <default revision="refs/tags/android-10.0.0_r33"
            remote="aosp"
            sync-j="4" />

  <project path="build/make" name="platform/build" groups="pdk" >
    <copyfile src="core/root.mk" dest="Makefile" />
    <linkfile src="CleanSpec.mk" dest="build/CleanSpec.mk" />
    <linkfile src="buildspec.mk.default" dest="build/buildspec.mk.default" />
    <linkfile src="core" dest="build/core" />
    <linkfile src="envsetup.sh" dest="build/envsetup.sh" />
    <linkfile src="target" dest="build/target" />
    <linkfile src="tools" dest="build/tools" />
  </project>
  <project
    path="build/blueprint"
    name="platform/build/blueprint"
    groups="pdk,tradefed" />
  <project path="build/kati" name="platform/build/kati" groups="pdk,tradefed" />
  <project path="build/soong" name="platform/build/soong" groups="pdk,tradefed" >
    <linkfile src="root.bp" dest="Android.bp" />
    <linkfile src="bootstrap.bash" dest="bootstrap.bash" />
  <project>

  <!-- … />

  </project
    path="device/linaro/hikey-kernel"
    name="device/linaro/hikey-kernel"
    groups="device,hikey,pdk"
    clone-depth="1" />
```

```
<!-- … />

<manifest>
```

Creating a clone of the source requires only a few small changes, as illustrated in Listing 2.4 after the comment, "Acme Projects."

Listing 2.4   **Manifest for a Forked AOSP Source**

```
<?xml version="1.0" encoding="UTF-8"?>
<manifest>

  <!-- Acme Remote -->
  <remote  name="acme"
           fetch="."
           revision="master" />
  <remote  name="aosp"
           fetch="https:/acme.net/acme/source" />
  <default revision="refs/tags/android-10.0.0_r33"
           remote="aosp"
           sync-j="4" />

  <!-- Acme Projects -->
  <project path="device/linaro/hikey"
           name="platform/device/linaro/hikey"
           remote="acme"
           revision="acme"
           groups="device,hikey,pkd" />
  <project path="device/acme/one/acme_one"
           name="platform/device/acme/one/acme_one" remote="acme" >
    <linkfile src="AndroidProducts.makefile"
              dest="device/acme/one/AndroidProducts.mk" />
    <linkfile src="acme_one.mk" dest="device/acme/one/acme_one.mk" />
  </project>
  <project path="device/acme/one/include"
           name="platform/device/acme/one/include"
           remote="acme" />
  <project path="device/acme/one/lib"
           name="platform/device/acme/one/lib"
           remote="acme" />
  <project path="device/acme/one/daemon"
           name="platform/device/acme/one/daemon"
           remote="acme" />
 <project path="device/acme/one/app/simple_daemon"
           name="platform/device/acme/one/app/simple_daemon"
           remote="acme" />
```

```
<project path="device/acme/one/hidl"
        name="platform/device/acme/one/hidl"
        remote="acme" />
<project path="vendor/acme/one/interfaces"
        name="platform/vendor/acme/one/interfaces"
        remote="acme" />

<!-- AOSP -->
<project path="build/make" name="platform/build" groups="pdk" >
  <copyfile src="core/root.mk" dest="Makefile" />
  <linkfile src="CleanSpec.mk" dest="build/CleanSpec.mk" />
  <linkfile src="buildspec.mk.default" dest="build/buildspec.mk.default" />
  <linkfile src="core" dest="build/core" />
  <linkfile src="envsetup.sh" dest="build/envsetup.sh" />
  <linkfile src="target" dest="build/target" />
  <linkfile src="tools" dest="build/tools" />
</project>
<project
  path="build/blueprint"
  name="platform/build/blueprint"
  groups="pdk,tradefed" />
<project path="build/kati" name="platform/build/kati" groups="pdk,tradefed" />
<project path="build/soong" name="platform/build/soong" groups="pdk,tradefed" >
  <linkfile src="root.bp" dest="Android.bp" />
  <linkfile src="bootstrap.bash" dest="bootstrap.bash" />
</project>

<!-- … />

<manifest>
```

First, the new manifest defines a new remote, `"acme"`, for the Acme project. The `"fetch"` attribute for the acme remote is `"."`, indicating that projects downloaded from this remote will have URLs that are the same as that used for the manifest file itself; that is, if the repo command used to initialize an Acme project workspace is:

```
repo init -u https:/acme.net/acme/source/manifest
```

The repo tool will search for the repository that contains the source for a project whose name attribute in the manifest has the value "zork" at the URL:

```
https:/acme.net/acme/source/zork
```

Next, note that the "review" attribute has been removed from the "aosp" remote. The process by which new code is submitted, reviewed, and committed, and the tools for doing so, are one more topic that is beyond the scope of this book. The repo tool does support a wide variety of commit processes and local customization. To find out more about this topic, look at the documentation for the repo tool's "repo-hooks" element at

`https://android.googlesource.com/platform/tools/repohooks/+/master/README.md`

The next modification to the manifest points the "aosp" remote explicitly at the local AOSP mirror. Instead of using the relative location ".." (a relative reference similar to the one now used by the "acme" remote), the AOSP source now comes absolutely from the mirror (located in this example at https:/acme.net/acme/aosp).

Finally, the new manifest contains the specifications for the several non-AOSP projects at paths like "device/linaro/hikey" and "vendor/acme/one/interfaces".

Kernel source and some pre-built binaries necessary to boot the HiKey960, the device used as the baseline for the Acme One device, are easily available.. Instructions for cloning them can be found in `device/linaro/hikey/hikey960/README`. Because it is very likely that you will need to modify the kernel source, you will probably also maintain forks of these repos, as well.

Nearly every Android-compatible device will require similar device-specific customization necessary to build a system image that will boot on the device. Finding, acquiring, and integrating the device-specific additions into the AOSP source code is an essential first step toward bringing up a device.

The directory structure for the server providing the source for the Acme project now looks something like Figure 2.2.

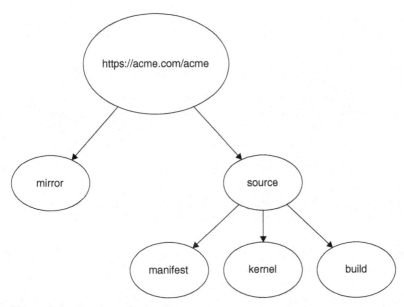

Figure 2.2   The Acme Source Tree

> **Note**
>
> You can find a manifest similar to the one shown in Figure 2.2 by using the following URL in the `repo init` command (discussed next): https://github.com/InsideAndroidOS/acme_platform_ manifest.git. This manifest contains references to repositories holding the code and changes for the Acme One platform covered throughout this book.

Time to build a workspace!

```
> cd workspace
> repo init -u https:/acme.net/acme/source/manifest
# output elided…
> repo sync
# lots of output elided…
```

The sync operation will certainly take a while; possibly several hours. It should, however, complete successfully. If it does not, carefully debug the manifest before proceeding.

Building an Image

The Android build system is large, complex, and not well documented. A full explanation of its history and usage is beyond the scope of this book. Future chapters address adding new pieces to the build relevant to the components being developed. Fortunately, for the moment, the goal is simply to get from code to a running Android.

An important part of the build system's complexity is the ability to customize it to produce images for the prodigious number of Android devices. The customization is accomplished by setting a number of shell variables using a tool called `lunch`.

> **Note**
>
> Distributions of the Android source code other than AOSP, as well as some versions of AOSP that have been extended with third-party code, may use variants of `lunch`, usually with cute names like `snackbar`, `brunch`, or some such thing. These alternatives all essentially accomplish the same task: assigning values to a set of shell environmental variables used to configure the build system.

The `lunch` tool is itself a shell script loaded by running another shell script `build/envsetup.sh`. Note that it is essential that the definitions provided by `envsetup.sh` are loaded into the *current* shell (using "." or "source"). Just running `envsetup.sh` from the command line accomplishes nothing at all.

```
> source build/envsetup.sh
including device/asus/fugu/vendorsetup.sh
including device/generic/car/car-arm64/vendorsetup.sh
including device/generic/car/car-armv7-a-neon/vendorsetup.sh
including device/generic/car/car-x86/vendorsetup.sh
including device/generic/car/car-x86_64/vendorsetup.sh
```

```
including device/generic/mini-emulator-arm64/vendorsetup.sh
including device/generic/mini-emulator-armv7-a-neon/vendorsetup.sh
including device/generic/mini-emulator-mips/vendorsetup.sh
including device/generic/mini-emulator-mips64/vendorsetup.sh
including device/generic/mini-emulator-x86/vendorsetup.sh
including device/generic/mini-emulator-x86_64/vendorsetup.sh
including device/generic/uml/vendorsetup.sh
including device/google/dragon/vendorsetup.sh
including device/google/marlin/vendorsetup.sh
including device/huawei/angler/vendorsetup.sh
including device/lge/bullhead/vendorsetup.sh
including device/linaro/hikey/vendorsetup.sh
including sdk/bash_completion/adb.bash
```

Now that all the tool definitions from the envsetup.sh script have been incorporated into the current running shell, they can be used from the command line. In this particular example, configuring the build system to build an image for the Acme project, based on HiKey960-like hardware, the appropriate lunch menu selection is "3": acme_one-userdebug.

```
> lunch

You're building on Linux

Lunch menu... pick a combo:
     1. acme_one-eng
     2. acme_one-user
     3. acme_one-userdebug
     4. aosp_arm-eng
     5. aosp_arm64-eng
     6. aosp_blueline-userdebug
     7. aosp_bonito-userdebug
     8. aosp_car_arm-userdebug
     9. aosp_car_arm64-userdebug
    10. aosp_car_x86-userdebug
    11. aosp_car_x86_64-userdebug
    12. aosp_cf_arm64_phone-userdebug
    13. aosp_cf_x86_64_phone-userdebug
    14. aosp_cf_x86_auto-userdebug
    15. aosp_cf_x86_phone-userdebug
    16. aosp_cf_x86_tv-userdebug
    17. aosp_coral-userdebug
    18. aosp_crosshatch-userdebug
    19. aosp_flame-userdebug
    20. aosp_marlin-userdebug
    21. aosp_sailfish-userdebug
    22. aosp_sargo-userdebug
    23. aosp_taimen-userdebug
    24. aosp_walleye-userdebug
```

```
25. aosp_walleye_test-userdebug
26. aosp_x86-eng
27. aosp_x86_64-eng
28. beagle_x15-userdebug
29. car_x86_64-userdebug
30. fuchsia_arm64-eng
31. fuchsia_x86_64-eng
32. hikey-userdebug
33. hikey64_only-userdebug
34. hikey960-userdebug
35. hikey960_tv-userdebug
36. hikey_tv-userdebug
37. m_e_arm-userdebug
38. mini_emulator_arm64-userdebug
39. mini_emulator_x86-userdebug
40. mini_emulator_x86_64-userdebug
41. poplar-eng
42. poplar-user
43. poplar-userdebug
44. qemu_trusty_arm64-userdebug
45. uml-userdebug

Which would you like? [aosp_arm-eng] 3

============================================
PLATFORM_VERSION_CODENAME=REL
PLATFORM_VERSION=10
TARGET_PRODUCT=acme_one
TARGET_BUILD_VARIANT=userdebug
TARGET_BUILD_TYPE=release
TARGET_ARCH=arm64
TARGET_ARCH_VARIANT=armv8-a
TARGET_CPU_VARIANT=cortex-a73
TARGET_2ND_ARCH=arm
TARGET_2ND_ARCH_VARIANT=armv8-a
TARGET_2ND_CPU_VARIANT=cortex-a73
HOST_ARCH=x86_64
HOST_2ND_ARCH=x86
HOST_OS=linux
HOST_OS_EXTRA=Linux-4.4.0-184-generic-x86_64-Ubuntu-16.04.6-LTS
HOST_CROSS_OS=windows
HOST_CROSS_ARCH=x86
HOST_CROSS_2ND_ARCH=x86_64
HOST_BUILD_TYPE=release
BUILD_ID=QQ2A.200405.005
OUT_DIR=out
============================================
```

The build system is now configured and ready to go.

The `make` command starts the build. It takes a wide variety of argument flags. For now, the important argument is `-j`, which tells it how many processes to run simultaneously. Common wisdom seems to suggest that a good choice for this number is two more than the number of available processors. Thus, on a build machine with an eight-core Intel processor, the build command might look like this:

```
> make -j10
# … pages and pages of output elided
```

Even on a very fast machine, the build is likely to take hours. The name of the configuration command, "lunch," is appropriate for much more than the process of choosing the target build device. Fortunately, the long build time is generally only for "clean" builds of the source. Iterative builds are usually considerably faster, often completing in just a few minutes.

With luck, the build will complete successfully. Unfortunately, hundreds of ways exist that it can go wrong. That is an important reason that getting something that builds reliably is such an important first step!

Many build failures involve incorrect or incompatible toolchains. This is especially common when trying to build on OSX. Another common cause of failure is that a particular device, although listed in the lunch menus, is simply not supported in the version of the Android source checked out in the workspace. It is absolutely not the case that every lunch option is tested on every git branch or at every git tag of the AOSP source.

No magic bullets exist for fixing a source that won't build. If the problem is something as small as a recognizable syntax error, something supported by some C++ compilers but not by others, simply patching the source may be possible. It is at least as likely, though, that a more effective strategy is finding (through the community or possibly even trial and error) some other version of the source or toolchain that does work.

Device Tools

When the build completes successfully, the directory `out/target/product` contains several file system images ready for installation on the target device. Installing the images on the device and then working with the running system requires two specialized tools: **fastboot** and **adb**. Getting familiar with them before proceeding makes sense.

The sources for both tools are part of AOSP. More conveniently, though, compiled versions are distributed as part of the Android SDK in the `platform-tools` folder. The Android SDK is available from the Android Developer Website (https://developer.android.com/studio/index.html) either as part of the Android SDK Developer Bundle (which includes Android Studio, the standard Android IDE) or separately as a zipped, stand-alone folder. Versions are available for each of the three most common development platforms: Linux, Mac, and Windows.

fastboot

`fastboot` is an overloaded term: It is both a boot mode for a device and the name of a tool used to communicate with a device when it is in fastboot mode. Incidentally, it is also the name of the protocol that the tool and device use to communicate when the device is in fastboot mode.

Booting an Android device into fastboot mode is very similar to booting a larger computer into its BIOS. In much the way one can boot a laptop computer into its BIOS by holding down a key-chord during boot, the most common way of booting an Android device into fastboot mode is to power cycle it while holding a specific set of buttons (frequently power and volume down). Instead of starting the normal bootloader, boot phase-2 instead loads and begins executing the fastboot program. (Figure 6.1 in Chapter 6 illustrates the boot process.)

> **Warning!**
>
> Bricking a device with fastboot is really, really easy to do!
>
> The fastboot program may have complete and unrestricted access to device memory. Overwriting not only the operating system and the backup recovery system but also the fastboot program itself may be possible. A device on which all phase-3 boot programs are garbage cannot be booted and cannot be repaired without physical access to device memory.

By default, the fastboot program communicates with a device over a USB connection. Perhaps surprisingly, when a device is booted into fastboot mode, it is likely to have a USB device identifier that is different from the one it presents after a normal boot. An operating system that controls access to naked devices (as `udev` does on Linux) may have to be configured to allow a fastboot connection, even if adb connections to the normally booted device work perfectly.

After the device is in fastboot mode and properly attached to a client, it will be visible to the fastboot program, invoked from the command line:

```
> fastboot devices
ZX1G324JBJ        fastboot
```

```
> fastboot getvar all
(bootloader) slot-count: not found
(bootloader) slot-suffixes: not found
(bootloader) slot-suffixes: not found
(bootloader) version: 0.5
(bootloader) version-bootloader: moto-apq8084-72.01
(bootloader) product: shamu
(bootloader) board: shamu
(bootloader) secure: yes
...
```

Until the `devices` command shows a device, no other commands will be useful. It is the indication that the tool has successfully established a connection to the device.

Fastboot supports a long list of commands, most of which have to do with flashing the device memory. As usual, the -h flag will cause fastboot to print a help message. You can discover additional commands not described in the help text by reading the fastboot source.

> **Note**
>
> As of late 2016, there is code in the fastboot tool to support TCP connections. For this to work, of course, the fastboot program on the device (as well as the client tool) must be recent and support TCP connections. TCP fastboot may be particularly valuable for small, proximity-charged devices that do not have a USB port. To use TCP fastboot, specify the IP address of the target device on the command line as follows:
>
> ```
> fastboot -s tcp:<ip/hostname>[:port] <command>
> ```

adb

Adb is probably the most important tool in the Android system developer's toolbox. It is the Swiss Army knife of Android and provides a variety of functions: file transfer, shell, application installation, and logging.

Adb communicates with the Android adb daemon, `adbd`, which is started early in the boot process of both the recovery and normal Android systems (but not fastboot). Like fastboot, the adb tool is most commonly used over a USB connection. Also, like fastboot, it supports TCP. Unlike fastboot, however, adb supports multiplexed communications. It can be used to follow a device's logging output in one window at the same time that another window is running an active shell.

A properly connected device should become visible to adb shortly after its boot screen appears. As with fastboot, use the `devices` command to verify that adb can connect to the device daemon process.

```
> adb devices
List of devices attached
ZX1G324JBJ      device
```

Depending on how the Android image running on a device was built, the `adbd` daemon may not start as root, and its value as an investigative tool will be severely limited. In such a case, if it is possible to run the daemon as root, the command `adb root` will do so. Note that, because of security restrictions, the daemon cannot be run as root on commercial or "user" builds.

```
> adb shell
shamu:/ $
> adb root
restarting adbd as root
> adb shell
shamu:/ #
```

> **Note**
>
> Although the tools described here will work for nearly any Android system, some development boards also support a UART console. With a little work—sometimes even a stock piece of additional hardware—it is likely that this console can be adapted to use USB and monitored from a computer using a serial console program such as `minicom` or `GNU screen`. The access to the startup logging available from such a console certainly makes it worth the effort.

Flashing the Device

Certainly the most convenient way of flashing a device is to remove its memory card and insert it into a card reader/writer attached to the build machine. On the build machine, all the standard partitioning and file system maintenance tools are available. In addition, a device that boots from removable memory is nearly impossible to brick: a huge advantage.

Many devices, even those that do not normally do so, are completely capable of booting from a memory card. Making this possible typically requires installing a custom bootloader. The custom bootloader, usually U-Boot, takes the place of the standard second-phase bootloader and boots from the removable memory card instead of from the on-board memory. Setting up a device so that it boots from removable memory is ideal.

The more common way of flashing images to a device, though, is by using fastboot. Again, the process of getting a device to fastboot mode is hardware dependent. On some devices, holding some combination of buttons immediately after powering on the device will cause it to enter fastboot mode. Some devices have DIP switches that in some configuration force the board into fastboot mode at boot. Nearly any device, if running, can be forced to reboot into fastboot mode with the command:

```
> adb reboot bootloader
```

When booting into fastboot, a device should power up and, after much less time than it takes for a full boot, should be visible from the flashboot program:

```
> fastboot devices
ZX1G324JBJ        fastboot
```

It will *not* be visible from adb.

What happens next depends on the version of Android to be flashed to the device. Those opaque binary blobs of proprietary software mentioned earlier in this chapter have always been a part of Android. They are the genesis of the **Hardware Abstraction Layer** (**HAL**) discussed in Chapters 8 and 10.

Prior to Android Oreo, standard practice was to drop the binary blobs into a device-specific section of the build tree along with the customized make files that knew where to find them. The blobs would then be incorporated into the installable image during the build process and installed as part of the image.

Clearly, however, that implies that each Android image is customized for a specific hardware platform. The Android Nougat image for a Nexus 5 device will almost certainly not work on even the fairly similar Nexus 5X. In addition to causing a proliferation of images, this necessary customization also gave carriers a way to drag their feet providing updates. It was not enough for Google to produce a new version of Android. In addition, each phone vendor had to produce a new image for each phone, incorporating all the changes.

With the advent of Android 8, Oreo, this changed. A Google project called Treble worked to standardize the Android image. Under Treble, proprietary binary blobs go into new file system partitions reserved exclusively for device- and carrier-specific binaries, where they are not affected by system updates. New releases of the Android system replace or rewrite partitions that belong exclusively to the Android system. The possibility exists that a single Android image will work for many devices. This is the way the Acme device is configured. Chapter 10 covers the updated HAL (HIDL) in more detail.

The change is important when flashing an Android version 8 or later to a device, because the Android that you flash will expect to find the proprietary shims in those new file system partitions. If they are not there, the device will fail to boot.

The code that installs the device binary shims should be part of the device-specific bundle downloaded to customize the basic AOSP source for the device. For the Acme device based on the HiKey960, the script `flash-all.sh` in the directory `device/linary/hikey/install/` does the trick. The initial flash for the new Acme device looks like this:

```
> cd device/linaro/hikey/installer/hikey960
> adb reboot bootloader
> fastboot devices
0483826824000000        fastboot
> chmod a+x flash-all
> ./flash-all.sh
android out dir:./../../../../..///out/target/product/hikey960
target reported max download size of 471859200 bytes
sending 'ptable' (196 KB)...
OKAY [  0.059s]
writing 'ptable'...
OKAY [  0.075s]
finished. total time: 0.134s
target reported max download size of 471859200 bytes
sending 'xloader' (151 KB)...
OKAY [  0.048s]
writing 'xloader'...
OKAY [  0.269s]
finished. total time: 0.317s
target reported max download size of 471859200 bytes
sending 'fastboot' (3346 KB)...
OKAY [  0.138s]
writing 'fastboot'...
OKAY [  0.074s]
finished. total time: 0.211s
target reported max download size of 471859200 bytes
sending 'nvme' (128 KB)...
```

```
OKAY [  0.045s]
writing 'nvme'...
OKAY [  0.087s]
finished. total time: 0.132s
target reported max download size of 471859200 bytes
sending 'fw_lpm3' (212 KB)...
OKAY [  0.047s]
writing 'fw_lpm3'...
OKAY [  0.054s]
finished. total time: 0.102s
target reported max download size of 471859200 bytes
sending 'trustfirmware' (145 KB)...
OKAY [  0.049s]
writing 'trustfirmware'...
OKAY [  0.053s]
finished. total time: 0.102s

# more uploads elided...

>
```

Running this initialization script again should not be necessary. Only a few changes could require it:

- The manufacturer discovers an important bug and offers an update.
- The Project Treble interface standards change, and a future Android is incompatible.

All that is left to do is to flash the newly built image:

```
> cd ../../../../..
> pwd
/home/acme/workspace
> fastboot flash boot out/target/product/hikey960/boot.img
target reported max download size of 471859200 bytes
sending 'boot' (9650 KB)...
OKAY [  0.345s]
writing 'boot'...
OKAY [  0.124s]
finished. total time: 0.468s
> fastboot flash dts out/target/product/hikey960/dt.img
target reported max download size of 471859200 bytes
sending 'dts' (14 KB)...
OKAY [  0.047s]
writing 'dts'...
OKAY [  0.048s]
finished. total time: 0.095s
```

```
> fastboot flash system out/target/product/hikey960/system.img
target reported max download size of 471859200 bytes
sending sparse 'system' 1/3 (445539 KB)...
OKAY [203.250s]
writing 'system' 1/3...
OKAY [ 10.197s]
sending sparse 'system' 2/3 (447504 KB)...
OKAY [198.764s]
writing 'system' 2/3...
OKAY [  8.254s]
sending sparse 'system' 3/3 (109822 KB)...
OKAY [ 46.770s]
writing 'system' 3/3...
OKAY [  1.566s]
finished. total time: 468.801s
> fastboot flash cache out/target/product/hikey960/cache.img
target reported max download size of 471859200 bytes
sending 'cache' (4280 KB)...
OKAY [  0.189s]
writing 'cache'...
OKAY [  0.154s]
finished. total time: 0.343s
> fastboot flash userdata out/target/product/hikey960/userdata.img
target reported max download size of 471859200 bytes
sending 'userdata' (147713 KB)...
OKAY [  4.627s]
writing 'userdata'...
OKAY [  5.587s]
finished. total time: 10.214s
>
```

You should now be able to boot your board!

Summary

This chapter introduced the Acme project, an example of customizing Android for specific hardware. The project consists of a build system, managed source, and a device based on well-supported hardware, the HiKey960. It described a couple of strategies for organizing source and the basic tools necessary to build and install the source on a device.

It is very likely that the process of creating a real project for a real device will not be as simple as the process described in this chapter. It might easily take days, even weeks, to get a board to boot at all. It might take many more weeks to find source that reliably and repeatably produces a running Android. It might even take several days to find a build machine that can be configured with a toolchain that will consistently build a flashable image without error.

Unfortunately, like the unhappy families in Tolstoy's *Anna Karenina*, each of the problems encountered on each individual project will be more or less unique to that project. Google and the community of people who have used similar hardware are the key resources. Finding the two other people in the world who corrupt their NTS+ file systems every time they run a build, the person who has figured out how to set the video resolution for the LCD panel you are using, or the one who has discovered the proper GNU Screen setting for your board's UART can be incredibly time consuming. It is, however, usually quite a bit faster than trying to solve each of those esoteric problems yourself.

Despite the warning, this chapter provides a powerful framework. It presents a path that will lead from chaos to the solid ground from which it is possible to move forward boldly and with predictable, measurable progress. If your project is forced from the described path at various points, the best course of action is to address the specific, limited problem and to get back on the path.

After you can repeatably build a working Android from a duplicable code base, you are out of the zone where dragons be. The rest is just engineering.

3

Getting Started

This chapter is an overview that provides context for the rest of the book. It will present three different, high-level views of the Android system. It is divided into two parts, a conceptual section followed by a practical section.

The conceptual half of the chapter explores Android, metaphorically, from the side. This section models Android as a geologist might, as a stack of strata. Each layer in the model has its own significance, and each supports the layer above it. The exploration will reveal most of the major components of the Android system as well as several key architectural structures.

The second half of the chapter—the practical half—explores the AOSP source. It addresses acquiring the code, its organization, its customization, and some of the tools used to maintain it.

Putting Android in Its Place

You have almost certainly seen one of the many illustrations of Android as a layer cake before. Figure 3.1 is another version.

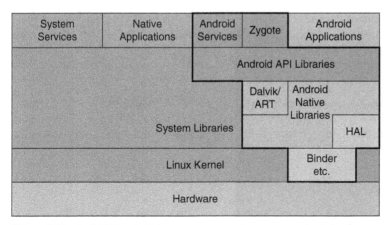

Figure 3.1   Android Layer Cake

Figure 3.1 shows the Android system in its context. The left half of the figure could be a generic Linux distribution such as Ubuntu or Mint. The right half illustrates the components specific to Android.

In the model, the system is divided into four major layers, each based on the one underneath it. Starting at the bottom, they are:

- **Hardware:** This is the physical device; a piece of metal you can hold in your hand.

- **Linux Kernel:** The kernel is software that creates the process and memory environments in which all applications run. As noted in Chapter 1, Android uses the very popular Linux kernel.

- **System Libraries:** System libraries are software libraries, frequently supplied as opaque binaries by third-party providers that implement services used by multiple applications.

- **Applications and System Services:** Applications use the environment provided by the lower layers to do work useful to the user. A set of special, long-running applications, called system services or sometimes "daemons," perform periodic tasks and manage system state.

In this model, most Android developers work predominantly in the block labeled "Android Applications" at the top right of the figure. They develop the applications that run in the Android environment. These developers spend their time learning and using the environment provided by the surrounding Android system.

The rest of this book is about customizing Android itself to adapt it to new hardware. Its focus is the shaded areas outlined with the bold border, most of which is in the System Services layer of Figure 3.1. Before launching into the discussion of the Android-specific components, though, reviewing the rest of the environment in which those components run will be useful.

Hardware

In this model, the bottom of the stack is the hardware. The hardware is the motivation: some device with cool new features. It is the part that you, the reader, bring to the party. The purpose of the entire software stack above the hardware is to enable the creation of applications that provide a human user with appropriate and intuitive control of some new, innovative hardware features.

Designing and bringing up hardware are dark arts that are well outside the scope of this book. Roger Ye's book, *Embedded Programming with Android* (Ye, 2016), part of the Android Deep Dive Series, is an excellent introduction to "bare-metal" programming and the process of bringing up a device from scratch.

The Linux Kernel

As noted in Chapter 1, Android's kernel is a variant of the Linux kernel. Linux is wildly popular, especially in embedded devices because it is open source and fairly easy to adapt to new hardware. Chapter 4 discusses it again in more detail.

The kernel is the Android system's primary porting layer. The process of porting Android to a new device consists in large part of getting an Android variant of the Linux kernel running on the target device and then pulling the rest of the Android stack over on top of it.

Although a kernel is a key part of Android, building a kernel is not normally part of building an Android system. Instead, the Android build tools treat the kernel as a black box: a pre-built, third-party binary. As Chapter 4 will illustrate, it is a device developer's responsibility to assemble the working kernel and to provide it for inclusion into the device-installable file system image that the Android build system creates.

You might be surprised to hear that the kernel is Android's primary porting layer. Much of Android programming is done in the Java programming language, whose motto was "write once, run anywhere." For Android, however, Java source code is compiled into instructions for Dalvik and ART, not instructions for the Java Virtual Machine (JVM). The purpose of the Android VM is to make applications portable across Android devices. Unlike the JVM, multi-platform and OS portability was not a goal at all in the design of Android's virtual machine.

System Libraries

There are common capabilities and functions that are used by multiple applications. Some of these capabilities—cryptography, video and audio rendering, a web browser—are large and complex. Implementing them as libraries that can be used by multiple applications makes sense.

Most system libraries are included in the Android system, as is the kernel, as third-party, black box binaries. They are essential to Android but are neither built nor maintained as part of the Android source tree.

This is an important area of customization for the developer of a new device. If software already exists—and that definitely includes software written in a language other than Java—that can be used as part of the interface to a new device, it can be included as part of this layer.

Enterprises that already have extensive investments in software may be, quite understandably, reluctant to abandon that investment simply to move to the Android platform. Including the proprietary code as a system library and then plumbing it into the Android framework with Java bindings may preserve the investment at a reasonable cost.

One of the system libraries that is part of a standard Android system and that deserves particular attention is **Bionic**. Bionic is Android's equivalent of the standard C library.

Most applications do not request kernel services directly. Instead, they use a standard library, the C library, to request them. The standard C library interface was specified originally as part of the ANSI C standard and subsequently accepted by ISO. The widely established POSIX C library standard is an incremental superset.

The C library standards are expressed as C header files (.h) against which applications are compiled. These header files define symbols that allow a compiler to emit code for macros, constants, variables, and functions in the application source code. Building an application requires only the header files. The actual implementations of the C library are not included in the compiled application.

Instead, at run time, a **linker** binds the compiled application dynamically to the implementation of the C library that is present on the system on which the application is running. Because the API definitions against which the application was compiled are (with luck!) identical to those actually implemented by the host system library, everything works. Usually, this just means that the C library is compiled using the exact same header files that the library clients use when they are compiled. A given piece of code can be binary compatible across multiple, similar platforms, as long as all the platforms have C libraries that implement the exact same API.

Bionic is Android's version of the standard C library. As part of Android's ongoing battle for frugality, it has been pruned relentlessly and is dramatically smaller than its BSD ancestors. It is so small, in fact, that it does not meet even the ANSI standard, let alone the ubiquitous POSIX standard. Applications that run perfectly well on other platforms may not run at all on Android, because Bionic does not support the functionality they require.

The implication that Bionic has its roots in BSD may come as a surprise. Most operating systems based on a Linux kernel use a version of the GNU C library, glibc. Instead, Bionic is derived from the BSD UNIX, libc. There are several reasons for this but the most obvious is that libc is licensed under the BSD license and is thus free of the constraints that its LGPL licensing imposes on glibc. One of the goals in Android's design was to eliminate any possible impediment to its acceptance. That goal absolutely implies removing any possible licensing constraints.

Many existing applications, libraries, and utilities may be used on Android as long as they are recompiled against the Android platform. Obviously, some limits exist because of the extent of the pruning in Bionic. For example, existing code that uses System V IPC or certain functions in the kernel concurrency feature, pthreads, cannot be built or run on Android. Additionally, as this chapter will make clearer, the Android software stack is fundamentally different than a typical Linux stack, which sometimes makes the use of existing Linux programs difficult or impossible.

Augmenting an Android system by adding one of the standard C-library implementations is entirely feasible. This simple and very common augmentation makes it possible to run many standard Unix applications and libraries on an Android system.

Applications

System services are those special applications, typically with minimal user interfaces, that maintain various subsystems: indexing files for search, locating and connecting to Wi-Fi networks, mounting and unmounting removable media, and so on. One special system service, init, is the first application run on system startup. It is responsible for much of the system startup process, including bringing up the other system services. It is discussed in more detail in Chapter 6.

The Android system service environment is not the same as that on typical Linux systems. On a Linux system, running the command:

```
ps -ef
```

produces a list of currently running applications. On one of these systems, running this command will typically result in tens of lines of output describing many processes. Even if the system has just been finished booting and is not yet running many user applications, there are still likely to be quite a few applications running. These are the system services: the long running "daemons."

Comparing the list of system services for a generic Linux system with a similar list from an Android system is instructive. Although the 30 to 40 system services that run as part of most common Linux distributions are fairly similar, the overlap with those running on an Android system is relatively small. The Android system has unfamiliar system services such as `installd`, `rild`, `surfaceflinger`, and `vold` instead of more common services such as `udevd` and `syslogd`. Although Chapter 6 addresses some of these daemons in a bit more detail, in-depth discussion of the differences between the daemons in the Android universe and those in the standard Linux universe are not the focus of this book. Linux daemons are well documented elsewhere. Although slightly dated, Karim Yaghmour's excellent book *Embedded Android* (Yaghmour, 2013) is a fantastic resource for work in this area.

The Android Framework

Figure 3.1 illustrates some of the Android-specific components of an Android system and their positions within the broader model of a working Linux system. The right side of the figure shows the Android framework in relation to the larger OS. Android has components that operate within each of the layers of the system model. From the bottom up, the components of the Android system are

- **Binder and other kernel plug-ins:** Android requires several non-standard kernel capabilities to function. These extensions are implemented as standard kernel extension modules. Chief among these extensions is **Binder**. Binder is an Interprocess Communications service and is, perhaps, the heart of Android.

- **HAL:** The Hardware Abstraction Layer (**HAL**) is a system library that supports binary compatibility for the Android system across multiple hardware/driver platforms. The HAL, actually a group of libraries, serves as the interface between Android and certain generic types of hardware devices. Like the C library, the HAL is, essentially, a set of header (.h) files that define an API for each of several common categories of hardware. The HAL abstracts an interface between the underlying hardware and Android almost exactly as the C library abstracts the interface to the kernel and other common functionality. The HAL has evolved over Android's lifetime. Newer versions of Android combine a library and a daemon/service to push the abstraction even farther. Most HAL code is written in C or C++ and compiled to device native binaries. Chapters 8 and 10 cover this in greater detail.

- **Dalvik, ART, and the Native Libraries:** These are the special system libraries that comprise the virtual machine and runtime environment in which Android applications execute. ART (and Dalvik, which it replaced) are Android's analog of the Java virtual machine and the libraries it provides. Both the runtime and many of the libraries that support it are written in C/C++ and compiled to native code for the device. Above this layer, however, nearly all source code is written in Java and compiled to virtual instructions. Chapter 7 discusses ART and Dalvik.

- **Android API Libraries:** These are system libraries written in Java, compiled to **dex** virtual machine code, and translated to near-machine code (.oat files) during installation. They are bound to Android applications at runtime, almost exactly as the C Library is bound to native applications. The code they contain, though, cannot be executed without the help of the virtual machine and its runtime environment. These libraries are the APIs to Android services.

- **Android Services:** The Android analog of a system service, these privileged Android applications written in Java provide essential Android functionality. The **Zygote** service, especially, plays a key role in an Android system. Zygote is covered in Chapter 6. The Android service model is covered in the next section and seen again in Chapters 10 and 11 as part of the binderized HAL.

- **Android Applications:** These applications are developed for Android, compiled against the Android API, and run within the runtime environment. Building an Android application is unlike developing applications either for other varieties of Linux or for other mobile platforms. Many other resources are available to a developer building an application. Application building is discussed only peripherally in this book.

The Android Service Model

A second, side-on view of the Android system gives a more functional perspective. Shown in Figure 3.2, it illustrates the basic structure of Android's service model.

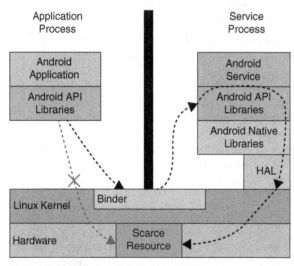

Figure 3.2   The Android System Model

This diagram is key. It illustrates two applications in two separate processes, one on the right and one on the left. The application in the process on the left side of the diagram needs access to the scarce resource at the bottom of the diagram. The arrow from the application to the scarce resource represents its request.

In the diagram the scarce resource is shown as hardware because it often is. Examples of scarce hardware resources might include a phone's screen, status lights, or a buzzer. Allowing all applications unrestricted access to these things wouldn't make sense. At best, applications would have to coordinate access among themselves. At worst, a malicious application could make a device unusable by seizing one or more of the essential resources and refusing to release them.

Hardware resources, of course, are not the only things that can be scarce or that need protection. A list of accounts or a database of acquaintances might require similar protection. Android uses the same mechanism to protect non-hardware resources.

In Figure 3.2, the arrow illustrating the application's intended request for the scarce resource is marked with an "X." The "X" indicates that application is blocked by the system from making the request directly.

The portal through which an application interacts with hardware—its driver—is almost certainly catalogued as a file in the /dev directory. Recall that as the creator of the file system abstraction, the kernel is able to represent nearly anything as a file. The driver is a special kind of file but still a file. To interact with the resource directly, the application must open the driver file and read and write from it.

Like all files in the Linux file system, the driver file is catalogued with permissions. These permissions determine which processes the kernel will allow to open the file.

Listing 3.1 shows excerpts from the listing of the contents of the /dev directory from a typical Android device. Most of these files are drivers for one device or another. In most cases, the file's permissions (the first column) limit access to the file's owner (second column) or owning group (third column). Only a couple of the files in this example allow unrestricted access (crw-rw-rw). The others are accessible only by processes with specific UIDs.

Listing 3.1 **Files in /dev**

```
crw------- root     root      233,   0 1970-07-29 16:48 adsprpc-smd
crw-rw-r-- system   radio      10,  56 1970-07-29 16:48 alarm
...
crw-rw---- system   audio      10,  40 1970-07-29 16:48 audio_slimslave
crw-rw---- nfc      nfc        10,  70 1970-07-29 16:48 bcm2079x-i2c
crw-rw-rw- root     root       10,  62 1970-07-29 16:48 binder

crw-r----- radio    radio     230,   0 1970-07-29 16:48 hsicctl0
crw-r----- radio    radio     230,   1 1970-07-29 16:48 hsicctl1
crw-r----- radio    radio     230,  10 1970-07-29 16:48 hsicctl10
...
cr--r----- root     system     10, 183 1970-07-29 16:48 hw_random
```

```
crw-------  root      root       89,   0 1970-07-29 16:48 i2c-0
...
crw-rw----  system    camera    239,   0 1970-07-29 16:48 jpeg0
...
crw-rw----  system    camera    251,   0 1970-07-29 16:48 media0
...
crw-rw----  root      mtp        10,  43 1970-07-29 16:48 mtp_usb
...
crw-rw----  radio     vpn       108,   0 1970-07-29 16:48 ppp
...
crw-rw----  system    drmrpc    244,   0 1970-07-29 16:48 qseecom
crw-------  root      root       10,  92 1970-07-29 16:48 ramdump_adsp
...
crw-------  root      root      232,   3 1970-07-29 16:48 smd3
crw-------  root      root      232,  36 1970-07-29 16:48 smd36
crw-rw----  system    system    232,   4 1970-07-29 16:48 smd4
crw-rw----  system    system    232,   5 1970-07-29 16:48 smd5
crw-rw----  system    system    232,   6 1970-07-29 16:48 smd6
crw-rw----  bluetooth bluetooth 232,   7 1970-07-29 16:48 smd7
crw-------  root      root      232,   8 1970-07-29 16:48 smd8
crw-r-----  radio     radio     231,  25 1970-07-29 16:48 smd_cxm_qmi

crw-rw----  bluetooth net_bt_stack 248,   0 2017-01-22 12:16 ttyHS0
crw-------  media     media     248,   3 2017-01-22 12:16 ttyHS3
crw-------  root      root      247,   0 1970-07-29 16:48 ttyHSL0
crw-rw----  system    vpn        10, 200 1970-07-29 16:48 tun
crw-rw----  system    net_bt_stack  10, 239 1970-07-29 16:48 uhid
...
crw-rw-rw-  root      root        1,   9 1970-07-29 16:48 urandom
crw-rw----  root      usb        10,  41 1970-07-29 16:48 usb_accessory
```

When Linux was first developed in the 1990s, it was designed for computers that were shared by many users. At that time, security in an operating system meant, exactly, protecting users of the same computer from each other. Although attacks from across a network were not unknown, it was far more likely that one of the users of a system would compromise another's resources on a single system than it was that an attack would originate externally. Over years of use, the ability of the Linux system to protect individual user accounts from one another has been tested, retested, and tested again. It is quite secure.

The permissions system is what prevents the request for the scarce resource shown in Figure 3.2 from succeeding. The application's process is not running with the user and group IDs that protect the resource and, therefore, the application does not have read or write permission on the driver. It does not have any way to obtain direct access to the resource.

Starting with KitKat, Android included an adaptation of SE Linux that further enhanced access controls. The original discretionary access control (DAC) model of permissions was not enough to prevent a system from being compromised. For example, using only DAC, a highly privileged system service (such as init), if compromised, might allow unfettered access to the system. SE Linux for Android introduced mandatory access control (MAC). It allows each running process to be further constrained from a security standpoint. All applications, including system processes, are assigned SE context that is enforced by the kernel. This limits the damage any one process can do, if compromised.

As Chapter 5 will demonstrate, writing and extending SE policies is a non-trivial task. Unless absolutely necessary, not altering the SE policies that are provided in the AOSP tree is best because they are CDD/CTS compliant. This is particularly important if the device is to be certified as an Android device.

The series of unblocked arrows in Figure 3.2 show how Android applications actually do get access to scarce resources when they need them. Instead of requesting the access directly, they use an interprocess communication (**IPC**) mechanism, Binder, to make a request to a system service. Normally, the IPC request is completely hidden from the caller because it is wrapped in in the Android API libraries. The client app sees only a call to a local method.

When the client app wants to obtain access to a scarce resource, it simply calls one of the methods in the Android API. The method call actually initiates an IPC conversation with Android service applications in one or more remote processes. These service processes, unlike the client, have the necessary security privileges that *do* permit them to access the scarce resource. The service can coordinate the requests as appropriate and manage access and control client use of the resource. Services provide fine-grained control over application access to the scarce resources they manage by declaring permissions. A *permission* is nothing more than a unique string that is recognized by the Android system. Android strictly manages permissions: Applications that want to use them must declare their intentions in their manifests and must get explicit approval from the application user before the permissions are granted. When an application requests access to a scarce resource from a service, the service can provide access in the firm knowledge that the application is acting on behalf of an informed user.

This mechanism, access to resources through a proxy service, is the key to hardware access in Android.

Exploring the Source

The last of this chapter's high-level views of Android is, as promised, much more practical. It's time to look at the AOSP code-base.

The primary source for Android code is the Android Open Source Project (AOSP) site at https://source.android.com/. Android system developers should be familiar with this site whether it is the source of the code for their project or not. Android originates here, and documentation and update information are available here before being available anywhere else.

In particular, the Overview section of the AOSP website contains important information about source branching and tagging strategies and the legal constraints on the use of the Android name, logos, and so on. Anyone working with Android code should read this documentation and be, at the least, generally familiar with it.

Other Sources

Several other sources for forks of the AOSP code exist, each with its own advantages and disadvantages. Among these forks, perhaps the best known are AOKP and MIUI. Sadly, one of the most important forks, CyanogenMod, has disappeared from the scene. The support community has rebranded it as LineageOS, and it may return to viability in the future.

What's in the Box?

The remaining sections of this chapter assume that the developer/build machine has been set up as described in Chapter 2. Let's take a quick walk through the source, just to get the lay of the land. Listing 3.2 shows the top-level directory structure.

Listing 3.2 **Source Top Level**

```
lrwxr-xr-x    1 aosp  staff      19 Oct 13 09:26 Android.bp
-r--r--r--    1 aosp  staff      92 Oct 13 09:26 Makefile
drwxr-xr-x   35 aosp  staff    1564 Oct 13 09:26 art
drwxr-xr-x   14 aosp  staff     816 Oct 13 09:26 bionic
drwxr-xr-x    3 aosp  staff     102 Oct 13 09:26 bootable
lrwxr-xr-x    1 aosp  staff      26 Oct 13 09:26 bootstrap.bash
drwxr-xr-x    5 aosp  staff     374 Oct 13 09:26 build
drwxr-xr-x    3 aosp  staff     102 Oct 13 09:26 compatibility
drwxr-xr-x   12 aosp  staff     748 Oct 13 09:26 cts
drwxr-xr-x    8 aosp  staff     476 Oct 13 09:26 dalvik
drwxr-xr-x    5 aosp  staff     170 Oct 13 09:26 developers
drwxr-xr-x   20 aosp  staff     748 Oct 13 09:26 development
drwxr-xr-x   10 aosp  staff     340 Oct 13 09:27 device
drwxr-xr-x  310 aosp  staff   10540 Oct 13 09:30 external
drwxr-xr-x   15 aosp  staff     510 Oct 13 09:31 frameworks
drwxr-xr-x   12 aosp  staff     408 Oct 13 09:31 hardware
drwxr-xr-x    5 aosp  staff     170 Oct 13 09:31 kernel
drwxr-xr-x   20 aosp  staff    1258 Oct 13 09:31 libcore
drwxr-xr-x    8 aosp  staff     680 Oct 13 09:31 libnativehelper
drwxr-xr-x    9 aosp  staff     306 Oct 13 09:32 packages
drwxr-xr-x    6 aosp  staff     272 Oct 13 09:32 pdk
drwxr-xr-x   10 aosp  staff     374 Oct 13 09:32 platform_testing
drwxr-xr-x   30 aosp  staff    1020 Oct 13 09:36 prebuilts
drwxr-xr-x   24 aosp  staff    1054 Oct 13 09:36 sdk
drwxr-xr-x   37 aosp  staff    1258 Oct 13 09:36 system
drwxr-xr-x   10 aosp  staff     340 Oct 13 09:36 test
drwxr-xr-x    4 aosp  staff     136 Oct 13 09:36 toolchain
drwxr-xr-x   21 aosp  staff     714 Oct 13 09:37 tools
```

Android.bp

The build system for Android is in transition. Up through the Marshmallow release, Android used an extension of GNU make as the underlying build system. The system used build files named Android.mk dispersed throughout the build tree, selected using a configuration describing the particular device being built. The process resulted in a large in-memory makefile to do the build. While powerful, this approach had limitations and never scaled well, especially noticeable as the Android source tree grew in size.

Nougat introduced a new build system, Soong, which is inspired by Bazel and uses a Go syntax. With Soong, the Android.mk files are replaced with Android.bp (blue print) files. As announced in late 2020, Google will be further transitioning the build system to Bazel in the near future.

Makefile

Makefile is the top-level makefile used in the legacy GNU make build system. It is copied here from the build directory when repo sync is executed.

art

The art directory contains the code for the Android Runtime (ART), an ahead-of-time compiled runtime that replaces the original Android virtual machine, Dalvik.

bionic

The bionic directory contains the code for the Android Standard-C-like library, Bionic. The earlier section of this chapter, "System Libraries," describes Bionic.

bootable

The bootable directory contains the source for the recovery executable. Recovery is used to apply OTA updates, write new firmware, and perform a factory data wipe.

bootstrap.bash

The bootstrap.bash script is part of the new build system, Soong.

build

The build directory contains the both the old and the new build systems. In particular, it contains the shell script envsetup.sh, used to configure the build environment. In addition to setting up required environment variables, this script introduces helper aliases and shell functions, such as lunch, which are used to configure and execute the build, as discussed in detail in Chapter 2.

cts

The cts directory contains the Android **Compatibility Test Suite** tests. Passing these tests is the minimum requirement for certification as an Android device.

dalvik

The `dalvik` directory contains the source for Android's original VM, Dalvik.

developers

The `developers` directory contains three different repositories of mostly legacy example code. The example Gradle plug-ins may be of interest.

development

The `development` directory contains odds and ends that may be useful to developers. It contains things such as tools for editing Android source using one of the popular IDEs, Eclipse or IntelliJ; more example code; developer debug applications; configurations for checkstyle, the emulator; and other tools.

device

`device` is an extremely important directory for a device developer. The Android source and build system are designed with the intention that all device-specific code—device-specific configuration of the build system, toolchain customizations, kernel selection, and even specialized versions of applications—go here. Although most device developers will find that very constraining, it is a smart strategy to keep as much device-specific code as possible in this directory. Only broader, more generic cross-platform changes should be made outside of the device-specific directory. Much of the work in the rest of this book will happen in this directory.

external

`external` contains all the buildable packages that are used, but not maintained, as part of Android. It contains things like `bouncycastle`, the Android cryptography library; `expat`, an XML parser; `junit`, a standard testing framework; and so on. All of these things are essential components of a running Android system but are obtained from external providers. Placing the code for these components in this directory makes the dependency explicit and makes Android less susceptible to versioning issues.

frameworks

The `frameworks` directory is the heart of Android. The public Android API is located here, in the directory `frameworks/base/core/java`. Core system services such as the `ActivityManagerService` and `PackageManagerService` are in `frameworks/base/services/core/java`. Input event management and sensors code can be found under `frameworks/base/native`. You can usually find native implementation code next to `java` directories in sibling `jni` directories and static resources in directories named `res`.

hardware

The `hardware` directory contains the HAL. This is the abstraction layer code for common devices: Wi-Fi, Bluetooth, and baseband radios; sensors; cameras; and so on. Although this directory contains shim code for many common devices, it is the `device` directory that contains customizations for a specific board and any one-off hardware on that board.

libcore

The most interesting things that live in the `libcore` directory are the sources for the Apache Harmony base implementations of the Java API. For example, the file

`libcore/ojluni/src/main/java/java/lang/Class.java`

is the source for Android's implementation of the Java type `Class`.

libnativehelper

As the name implies, the `libnativehelper` directory contains native helper functions. It is sort of a "commons" directory for HAL code that leverages Java Native Interface (JNI) to bridge the gap between the runtime code and backing native code.

packages

The `packages` directory contains applications that will be included as part of the system. The directory `packages/apps`, for instance, contains the standard DeskClock, Phone, and Camera apps that are pre-installed (and not uninstallable) on a typical Android device.

pdk

The `pdk` directory contains the platform development toolkit (PDK). It is given to **original device manufacturers** (ODMs) so that they can develop HAL and other specialization software for their devices. The PDK is a subset of the full Android source, so this directory doesn't contain much that is useful as part of the Android source tree.

platform-testing

The `platform-testing` directory contains odds and ends of tools for testing device functionality.

prebuilts

The large `prebuilts` directory is very similar to the `external` directory, except that the things that it contains are not built as part of the system build process. For instance, it contains the binaries for the `clang` and `gcc`, C compilers; the Python and Go language SDKs; and the kernel for the QEMU-based Android emulator.

sdk

`sdk`, a mostly historical directory, contains source for some of the Android development tools as they were just before Android Studio was introduced. Since Android Studio, the SDK tools have their own, partially overlapping, `repo`-maintained build tree (see http://tools.android.com/build). Most of the code here is obsolete.

system

Another very important directory, `system` contains the native daemons, system libraries, and data essential to an Android system. In here are the sources for `vold`, the SE Linux policies, and the system trusted certificates. These are the parts of the Android system that are illustrated in the top-left of Figure 3.1 and discussed in Chapter 7.

toolchain

The `toolchain` directory contains a set of automated tests that can be executed to gather benchmarking data. Building and running these tests require patching the source tree.

tools

The `tools` directory contains a number of helper tools, such as ones to ease the creation of Android AVDs and to analyze `atrace` data captures.

out

The `out` directory is not part of the build environment maintained by `repo`. It is, however, the default scratchpad for the build system. None of the previously mentioned directories should be affected in any way by a system build. From the build's point of view, they are all read only. Restoring a build environment to its pristine state should always be possible by simply deleting this directory. All intermediates as well as the final build artifacts are put here.

Summary

This chapter has been a very high-level tour of the Android system. It inspects Android from three very broad points of view: as a series of layers of abstraction, starting at the hardware and ending with user applications; as a client-server architecture in which servers regulate access to scarce resources; and as a build environment, with source and tools for generating the running system.

Subsequent chapters walk up the stack illustrated in Figure 3.1, illustrating the relation between the source code and the running system and demonstrating at each layer how to customize behavior.

4

The Kernel

As mentioned previously, the Android system uses a Linux kernel. The Linux kernel is a very large and extremely complex piece of software. Some developers spend their entire careers understanding and modifying it. It is the subject of many books, including the excellent *Building Embedded Linux Systems, 2nd ed.* (Yaghmour, 2008) and *Linux Device Drivers, 3rd ed.* (Corbet, 2005). This chapter is not, of course, a substitute for any of those books—or for a few years of experience.

Bringing up a kernel for a brand new device—setting up a build environment, choosing the correct compilation flags, and getting all the necessary drivers debugged and working—is a dark art that is likely to require a significant investment of time. A developer with specific kernel porting experience is likely to be able to accomplish the task in a fraction of the time required by even a very talented and motivated novice.

The Linux kernel is incorporated into an Android system as an essential but completely opaque binary. It is—at least from the point of view of the Android build system—just a dependency. There are, however, several very specific modifications, **kernel modules**, that are unique to the Android system. Those features are the central topic of this chapter.

The Linux Kernel

The kernel creates the virtual environment in which applications live. As discussed in Chapter 1, many kinds of kernels exist and create many kinds of environments. Linux is a member of the family of kernels that provide two broad environmental features to client applications: a virtual execution space and a file system. Other members of this class (chosen fairly arbitrarily) are the Windows NT Kernel, Dartmouth DTSS, and Digital Equipment Corporation's RSTS/E.

The astute reader will notice that two of these three kernels, Dartmouth DTSS and Digital Equipment Corporation's RSTS/E, are not exactly household words today. That is because within its family of operating systems, UNIX-like systems are by far the dominant genus. In particular, the Linux species has pretty much won the evolutionary battle, especially in the embedded system niche.

In addition to managing a virtual environment, the Linux kernel is also Android's porting layer. The process of porting Android to a new device is, for the most part, porting Linux to that device and then pulling the rest of the Android stack over on top of it. The Android virtual machines, Dalvik and ART, discussed in Chapter 6 and responsible for executing the virtual machine code into which Java language programs for the Android system are compiled, although analogs of the JVM, have very little to do with portability.

Kernel Process Management

Most modern computing hardware has, at its center, a small number (probably more than one but probably less than ten) of processing units (also called **cores** or sometimes **processors**). These are the components of a device that execute machine instructions.

A piece of computing hardware is capable of running a number of simultaneous processes more or less equal to the number of processors that it has. Simplistically, each core starts executing a stream of instructions when the power to the chip is turned on and stops when the power is turned off.

The other essential ingredient for a von Neumann architecture computer is memory. Modern hardware typically has several different kinds of memory, each of which is a different balance between cost and speed: registers, several levels of cache, and on-board and external RAM (**random-access memory**).

In an ideal, theoretical machine, each core has identical capabilities and identical access to all the memory. In practice, there are exceptions. Registers and, perhaps, some kinds of cache may be available only to a specific, associated core. Most memory, though, is globally accessible to all the processors. In the hardware environment, it is completely unremarkable for a value written by one CPU to be overwritten by another.

> ### Note
>
> Not all hardware is ideal. In an attempt to get the most bang for the buck, some hardware has specialized cores that have differing capabilities: more cores for common tasks, fewer for less common. One example of unequal core capability is hardware popular for many Android devices, which is capable of adjusting the clock speeds independently for each core. On such hardware, tasks of lesser importance may be assigned to slower processors.

The first job of the kernel is to create a virtual execution environment on top of the hardware. This virtual environment is very different from the hardware environment described earlier. In it, a nearly infinite number of processes appear to run simultaneously. Each process appears to use one or more virtual CPUs to execute instructions and to have its own, private address space in which the memory *cannot* be accessed from other processes. In this virtual environment, the CPUs are ideal and identical, and it would be very surprising if one process could overwrite a memory that belonged to another. This is the environment with which most application developers are familiar.

> **Note**
>
> Within this book, a **thread of execution**, or simply **thread**, is a sequence of instructions executed one at a time in order by a single, possibly virtual CPU, or **processor**. A **process** is one or more threads of execution with a single, private address space not shared with any other process.
>
> An **application** is a collection of code with a single purpose. Frequently, but not always, an application runs as a single process.

Kernel Memory Management

Managing memory is the second major task of a kernel. Hardware memory can roughly be divided into two categories: **random-access** and **block-structured**. Information can be stored into or retrieved from random access memory, RAM, exactly as its name suggests, simply by addressing the specific cell of the memory that is of interest. When the CPU requires the value that it stored at address 3730, it requests the value at address 3730 explicitly as part of executing an instruction. Access to address 3730 is completely independent of access to addresses 3731 or 3729.

In an ideal computer, all memory would probably be random access. In actuality, because random-access memory is expensive, most computer systems also have block-structured memory. Block structured memory is usually cheaper, bigger, and, most likely, slower to access than random access memory. Think of a disk drive or its modern equivalent, a solid-state drive (SSD).

Whereas a processor can directly access random access memory by address, accessing block-structured memory is considerably more complicated. Typically, a process that needs data that is stored in block-structured memory must first reserve a contiguous piece of random-access memory. Next, it must communicate to the block-structured memory device that contains the information that it needs, the addresses of both the block of memory in which it is interested, and the location and size of the RAM it has reserved.

This initiates a data transfer. The block-structured memory device copies the contents of the requested block from its internal store to the RAM. When the transfer is complete, it notifies the processor. The requested block of memory is now available as RAM.

> **Note**
>
> The differentiation between the two different types of memory is not arbitrary. Of course, it is true that both types of memory are block structured and addressable: The only real distinction is in the size of the block and the amount of time that it takes to move one of them across a device's data paths. As usual, though, size matters—a lot. If the number of bits in a block is less than or equal to the number of bits that can be transported simultaneously through the device (the device word size), the memory is considered random access. If the number of bits in the memory block requires that the block be transferred sequentially, word by word, the device is considered block structured.

Block-structured memory is used in two very important ways. The first is as a way of creating the virtual memory spaces in which applications run.

When an application process is not actively using some part of its memory (it is waiting; perhaps for user input or for a certain amount of time to elapse) the kernel, using a process that is exactly the reverse of that just described, can free the memory for other use. The kernel marks a section of the application's RAM as unavailable and requests that a block-structured device store it.

After the transfer is complete (the contents of the RAM have been "swapped" to block storage), the RAM can be reallocated for use by other processes and other purposes. Of course, when the paused application once again needs access to the piece of its address space that has been swapped to disk, the kernel must, once more, reverse the process. It reallocates memory for the stored data, reads it from the block storage device, and replaces the contents exactly as they were the last time the application looked. This is **virtual memory**, one of the main tools necessary to allow the sum of the memory used by all the applications running on a device to be much greater than the amount of hardware RAM that is installed in the device.

At the time Android was designed, the block-structured memory devices on most computers were *hard drives*: spinning magnetic disks with moveable read-write heads. Hard drives are fairly fragile and running them requires amounts of power that are out of the question for a battery-powered device.

Mobile devices, in contrast, even then used solid-state memory, similar in many respects to the memory ubiquitous in modern laptops: SSDs. The big difference between solid-state memory then and now is that, in 2002, solid-state memory devices deteriorated significantly with each write operation. At that time, a bit on a disc drive might be good for millions of read/write cycles, whereas a bit on a flash card might fail after only tens of thousands of cycles.

The implication is that, although storing data persistently was possible, the operating system had to be quite parsimonious in its use. In particular, trying to use flash memory as virtual memory swap space, in addition to being slow, would severely limit the life of the device.

Starting with Android 4.4 (KitKat), Android included a kernel module, `zram`, to provide swap capability. `zram` targets devices with very little memory: as low as 512MB of RAM. It provides a compressed memory space used to swap out process pages, just as they are swapped to nonvolatile block storage. This may seem counterintuitive: The kernel carves out a bit of RAM to use as swap space for application memory pages. The zram module, though, compresses pages as they are stored using a fast compress/decompress algorithm: LZ4 or LZO. Because it uses RAM as a virtualized swap space, zram is fast and efficient. zram notwithstanding, lack of virtual memory is second only to power as the most important constraint in the design of the Android system.

The kernel's second memory management trick is the catalog tree. Moving blocks of stored information in and out of RAM is nifty, but it doesn't go very far toward the nearly universally accepted abstraction for long-term memory, a tree of folders (catalogs) containing both other folders and sequentially accessible files. The kernel has one or more components, called **file systems,** which manage different varieties of block-structured memory hardware and use different strategies to create the tree-of-files abstraction.

An important thing to remember about the file tree is that the kernel creates it out of thin air. A block-structured memory device has not even the faint whiff of a tree structure about it. It is just a big, flat array of bits. If a kernel can make block-storage look like a tree-structured file system, it can make nearly anything else look like a file just as easily. This capability comes up again in Chapter 5, when we discuss Android's security and again in Chapters 8 and 10 in the discussion of Android's hardware abstraction layer.

The Android Kernel

Although the Android system is based on the Linux kernel, it is not the case that any Linux kernel will support Android. The Android system requires several very special kernel features. At least two of these features have been the source of extended and sometimes acrimonious discussion in the Linux community. These features can be a major hurdle in porting Android to a new device: finding a kernel that supports both the target hardware and Android at the same time.

Like most kernels, Linux implements a plug-in system that allows it to be customized for various hardware and software requirements. These plug-ins are either **kernel modules** or **device drivers**. The kernel software components that manage a mouse, a keyboard, speakers, and network communication are all examples of device drivers.

Device drivers have two roles. First, a driver may manage a specific piece of hardware. The driver may be programmed with the device protocol nearly at the level of controlling voltages and pulse timing.

Usually, the driver is also the public interface to the hardware. The driver is the definition of the hardware API. Drivers usually expose, for application use, either a random-access or a block-structured virtual interface that abstracts the details of a hardware device away from the rest of the system: no other code need be aware of it. An application that wants to use a given hardware mechanism will do so by connecting with that mechanism's device driver and interacting with it according to the driver's interface.

Android adds an additional layer of abstraction between user space Android framework processes and the hardware, called the **Hardware Abstraction Layer** (HAL). This additional layer of abstraction allows Android to use a single API for several different kernel drivers that provide access to similar types of devices, despite the fact that each is controlled by its own driver and that each of the drivers defines it its own, unique API.

Device drivers execute as part of the kernel. A driver can do anything any other part of the kernel can do, from scribbling in the memory of any application to changing what instructions it executes. An error in the driver frequently manifests as a "kernel panic" and is likely to bring down the entire system. Because of this, by convention, device drivers are as small and simple as they can possibly be.

In their seminal book, *Linux Device Drivers*, authors Corbet et al. admonish:

> ... it emphasizes that the role of a device driver is providing *mechanism*, not *policy*. The distinction between mechanism and policy is one of the best ideas behind the Unix design. Most programming problems can indeed be split into two parts: "what capabilities are to be provided" (the mechanism) and "how those capabilities can be used" (the policy). If the two issues are addressed by different parts of the program, or even by different programs altogether, the software package is much easier to develop and to adapt to particular needs. (Corbet, Rubini, and Kroah-Hartman, 2005)

This is probably the reason that the Linux community has been so reluctant to accept the device drivers required by Android, in particular Binder and wakelocks.

For quite a while, the Linux kernel used in Android systems was a complete fork of the Linux kernel. Android kernels could not be downloaded from the canonical Linux website, kernel.org. Instead, they were hosted on Google websites. The ensuing debates between the two communities, Linux and Android, were unpleasant and prolonged.

> **Note**
>
> As an example of the conflict, wakelocks and the debate surrounding them are discussed in detail by Rafael J. Wysocki in his *Linux Weekly News* article, "An alternative to suspend blockers" (Wysocki, 2010) and the articles it references at https://lwn.net/Articles/416690/.

Although it might be optimistic to say that the rift has been healed, a certain pragmatism has prevailed. Android has accomplished what no other Linux distribution has accomplished: making Linux ubiquitous. By orders of magnitude, most devices using Linux today are Android devices. Android is popular, and the Linux community has proved itself mature enough to assimilate the popularity. Downloading an Android Linux from kernel.org is now possible.

Android Kernel Features

Building an accurate catalog of the differences between a generic Linux kernel and a kernel necessary to run an Android device is difficult. Several people have attempted it over the years, and a small but useful body of literature on the topic exists (mostly rooted at http://elinux.org).

Because the Android kernels are stored in git, creating the patch set necessary to create the Android kernel from the vanilla kernel on which it is based is a relatively straightforward process. However, at last check, the exercise creates something just under 300 patches with a combined size of around 4 megabytes. What do all these patches do? The following subsections, while not exhaustive, describe most of the important features specific to Android kernels.

Wakelocks

Source	Now part of the standard Linux kernel

One of the special features required by Android is the **wakelock**. Wakelocks or **suspend-blockers** are a form of opportunistic power control.

By default, most Linux devices are running. Although it may seem obvious to point that out, it is important because at the time that Android was developed, most Linux devices were also attached to practically infinite supplies of power.

On a mobile device, the most important resource by far is the battery. At the time that Android was in its early development, running a standard Linux on a mobile device meant battery life that was measured in minutes, not in days. One of the first hurdles the original Android team had to leap was dramatically reducing the battery drain. An important step in this direction was reversing the default wake state. Like the dormouse from *Alice in Wonderland*, the Linux kernel on an Android device prefers to be asleep.

Obviously, although being asleep is great for battery life, it isn't much good for getting work done. Enter wakelocks.

A wakelock is a simple binary flag. The kernel is constantly trying to go to sleep. If any wakelocks are set, however, they prevent it from doing so. Application programs seize wakelocks and become responsible for keeping the kernel (and, by extension, the hardware) awake until they complete whatever useful work they are doing. A responsible application, when it is done with useful work, releases any wakelocks it holds. If no other applications are holding wakelocks, the kernel immediately puts the device to sleep.

The original implementation of wakelocks from the Google/Android team contained a serious race condition (described in detail in the article cited in the earlier Note). Because of this race condition, the possibility existed for the kernel to fail to notice an application's request for a wakelock if the request happened while the kernel was already in the process of powering down the device. A device could sleep despite an application's attempt to keep it awake.

In 2010, as part of healing the fork between the Android and the standard Linux kernels, Arve Hjønnevåg rewrote the original Google/Android patches, renamed them, "Suspend Blockers," and resubmitted them. They were accepted into the mainline kernel source. Subsequently, Android wakelocks were rewritten. They are now based on standard Linux suspend blockers.

In addition, Android introduced two additional power management tools in version 6.0 (Marshmallow): Doze and App Standby. When a device enters Doze mode, it may continue to operate but not at full power. The mode imposes some severe restrictions on apps, including limits on network access, Wi-Fi scanning, and other power-hungry operations. Because a device only enters Doze mode when the user is not actively interacting with it, the system assumes that applications do not have any valid reason for holding a wakelock and completely ignores them.

Binder

Google Source	Several locations, most commonly /drivers/staging/android/binder.c
Canonical Source	/drivers/android/binder.c
Exposed as	/dev/binder

Binder is an interprocess communication system based on shared memory that, as introduced in Chapter 3, is at the very heart of Android. It turns up again in Chapter 10, in the context of Binderized HAL (Project Treble). Binder's central role in the Android environment becomes apparent with a reconsideration of wakelocks and the way Android handles memory pressure.

As described in the previous section, the wakelock system places the responsibility for allowing a device to sleep with the user application. It takes only a moment's consideration to realize that that situation is simply too dangerous to permit. Clearly, a malicious application could stage the equivalent of a denial-of-service attack against a device on which it is installed, draining the battery by keeping the device awake. It is at least as likely, though, that an ignorant or incompetently programmed application might seize a wakelock and then crash before releasing it. Unless the system has some way of cleaning up after the crashed application, the wakelock it seized will keep the device awake until its battery dies.

To protect itself from this kind of problem, Android uses the architecture described earlier in the book in Figure 3.2, the Android System Model. The scarce resources, in this case, wakelocks, are not directly available to user applications. Instead, they are controlled by a system service. Specifically, wakelocks are controlled by the PowerManager. User applications cannot directly seize wakelocks. The Android system security model prevents normal applications from interacting with them directly. Only system services, in this case, PowerManagerService and its process, are granted the necessary permission. Instead, applications use the interprocess communications system, Binder, to ask the system service to seize a wakelock on their behalf.

Another situation that requires similar treatment is that of low memory, described in more detail in the following section. Android does not have the near-infinite memory space available to it that desktop Linux systems do. Instead, it must ruthlessly control available RAM and will kill processes to reclaim memory for use by another, more important process. Like the DoS example mentioned earlier, this could result in a process being killed while holding resources or IPC connections to other processes without being given a chance to release those resources.

Most interprocess communications systems are peer-to-peer and are, themselves, applications. Common IPC systems, whether System V IPC centered implementations of the D-Bus protocol, or based on some other architecture, are just applications. Though frequently special system-level applications, they support communications architectures in which all participants are equivalent. In these systems, distinguishing between a client that doesn't happen to be talking at the moment and one that cannot talk and will never talk again (for example, it has crashed) can be quite difficult.

Recall that the kernel is the thing that creates processes. It is the absolute authority on which processes exist and which have terminated. Because it is part of the kernel, Binder has immediate access to this information. Binder can tell, without a shadow of a doubt, whether one of the ends of an interprocess conversation is simply occupied elsewhere or whether it will never respond again. It can supply that information to other clients.

This is the solution to the wakelock and low memory killer problems. A system service controls wakelocks. Client applications do not have sufficient permission to seize their own wakelocks. Instead, they use Binder IPC to request that the system service (which does have permission) hold a wakelock on their behalf. The system service, in return, registers with Binder for notification of the death of the client app. Now the system service can guarantee that the wakelock will be released, either because the client app explicitly releases it or because it is eventually terminated. Processes using Binder to communicate with each other can register for notification about a peer process's death. This allows any application to manage resources that are no longer required because a peer ceased to exist.

Binder started life as part of BeOS, the would-be replacement for Apple's Classic Macintosh OS. Apple had other ideas. It offered a scant $125 million for BeOS. BeOS, for better or worse, rejected the offer. Instead, Apple ended up buying NeXTSTEP (along with Steve Jobs) for $429 million. BeOS (and the rights to Binder) were eventually sold to Palm, Inc., where Binder became the basis for their Cobalt OS. Around the time of the demise of Palm, a version of Binder called OpenBinder was released as open source under the Mozilla Public License Version 1.1.

Android's version of Binder, while clearly related, is none of these. It was reimplemented from scratch near the start of the Android project and added to Google's fork of the kernel tree in early 2009. Over time, it became available from kernel.org (www.kernel.org/) but was relegated to a special "staging" area (drivers/staging/android). Late in 2014—again, with much debate about its security and stability—it was moved into the "real" part of the kernel (drivers/android). There has been discussion (though little progress) toward writing a binder-compatible library that uses the stable, supported Linux kbus mechanism. At the moment, Android absolutely depends on Binder, and other Linux systems are warned to use it at their peril.

Low Memory Killer

Google Source	`drivers/staging/android/lowmemorykiller.c`
Canonical Source	`drivers/staging/android/lowmemorykiller.c`
Daemon Source	`system/core/lmkd`
Exposed as	Originally `/proc/<pid>/oom_adj`, now `/proc/<pid>/oom_score_adj`

As noted earlier, the early Android systems had to be careful about their use of persistent memory. Flash memory at the time simply could not support swapping and virtual memory. The Linux kernels for Android devices are configured with little (zram) or no swap space.

This presents a conundrum. The device is practically guaranteed to run out of memory! If the user of a mobile device keeps starting new applications, in the manner to which they have become accustomed with their other computer devices, eventually memory is filled and the system cannot start another. This almost never happens on, for instance, a laptop, because older applications are swapped to the nearly limitless virtual memory space. Without virtual memory, though, a device runs out of memory fairly quickly.

Given this constraint, only a couple of possible choices exist. Users would never tolerate a device on which an incoming call (which causes the phone application to run) generated an out-of-memory condition and forced the user to select an application to terminate, before allowing her to answer the call. The plausible alternatives are either that there is a limit on the number of applications that can be running at any given time so that there is always sufficient memory to run an important app or that the operating system can terminate any application to recover the memory that the application is using.

Most mobile operating systems chose the former path—limiting the number of applications that the OS allows a user to run. Users of most mobile OSs were limited to a small number of simultaneously running applications (usually one). A few designated special applications—maybe a camera, a music player, or the phone—were immune from the constraint. Most applications, though, had to be run one at a time.

However, Android from the very start allowed users to start as many applications as they liked. It is just that Android reserved the right kill those applications, any time *it* liked! This is, perhaps, the hardest thing for new Android developers to understand. On most computers, terminating an application abruptly (Unix signal kill -9) is a very rare occurrence. On Android, it is the most common way for an application to end.

All Linux kernels have an out-of-memory killer. If some process on a server in a rack somewhere misbehaves and runs out of memory, it is much preferable that the operator be able to connect to the device remotely, perhaps conduct some simple analysis, and then do a soft reboot, rather than having to walk into the data center, locate the crippled machine, and turn it off and on again. If the machine is out of memory, though, it is possible that no memory is left in which to start the remote connection application.

The Linux out-of-memory killer addresses this situation. When the kernel finds that it is dangerously low on memory, it will kill some processes to start others based on a priority table. Android, which, as described earlier, is constantly in a dangerous low memory situation, simply extends this facility.

The Android OOM-Killer is dynamic and based on two tables. The first table is static, is constructed at startup, and creates several priority groups for applications. For each of the priority groups, it establishes the memory threshold at which applications of that priority may be killed. On the original Android systems this table always identified 31 priorities, numbered from –16 to 15.

On a device with 192MB of RAM, for instance, the table specified that applications with priority 15 should be killed if there were less than 8192 4k pages of free memory. On the other hand, applications with priority 0 could be killed only if there were fewer than 2048 pages of free memory.

The second table assigns each process a priority dynamically, depending on how important it is to the user at the moment. Android's Activity Manager Service manages this second table.

Starting with Android 4.4 (KitKat), the low memory killer was moved out of the kernel and into user space as the low memory killer daemon (**lmkd**). This daemon is accessed via the Activity Manager Service over named socket, when it is available. When the daemon is not present in the system, Activity Manager Service reverts to the kernel low memory killer. The daemon leverages existing Linux kernel *vmpressure* events to perform the same operations as the kernel driver. The daemon, however, is more extensible and can be configured by OEMs. As of Android 9 and kernel 4.12, the kernel low memory killer (but not its behavior) has been completely removed from Android.

Shared Memory: Ashmem

Google Source	Originally `mm/ashmem.c`, now `drivers/staging/android/ashmem.c`
Canonical Source	`drivers/staging/android/ashmem.c`
Exposed as	`/dev/ashmem`

Binder works, as noted earlier, by mapping a single block of physical memory into the virtual memory spaces of one or more applications. Any write by any of the applications sharing the memory block will be visible in all the other applications. Interprocess communication is very efficient when no copies are necessary; the recipient sees the exact bits that the sender wrote. Ashmem makes this possible.

The Android team found the existing Linux shared memory system "shmem" insufficient for their needs and introduced a variant "ashmem." Ashmem, according to its documentation is, "a new shared memory allocator, similar to POSIX SHM but with different behavior and sporting a simpler file-based API." Its distinctive feature appears to be the ability to shed memory under pressure. Ashmem-allocated memory is reference counted and depends on Binder for sharing the reference to the ashmem-allocated memory between processes.

PMEM and Ion: Shared Memory

Google Source	Pmem was `drivers/misc/pmem.c`
	Ion was `drivers/gpu/ion/*` but is now `drivers/staging/android/ion/*`
Canonical Source	`drivers/staging/android/ion/*`
Exposed as	`/dev/ion`

Android needs other ways of sharing memory across processes. The most obvious of these needs comes from drawing on the screen.

One of the remarkable things about Android at the time of its first releases was its commitment to OpenGL. From the very start, the Android system included as standard components both 2D (Skia) and 3D graphics libraries. The latter library was a software implementation of the OpenGL API, providing OpenGL ES 2 compatibility. Because Android included this library as part of the system, it guaranteed that an application that used the OpenGL API would run on any Android device, whether the device itself supported OpenGL or not.

To operate efficiently, both the 2D and 3D drawing libraries require that the client be able to write to the memory that represents the pixels on the screen. Early versions of Android reserved the physical memory and mapped it into each process as it took control of the screen. Rendering, then, simply meant writing bits into the screen's physical memory.

The kernel module that allowed this mapping of specific regions of physical memory in early Android was called pmem. Pmem is very similar to its cousin ashmem, except that where ashmem allows the sharing of blocks of *virtual* memory, pmem allocates and shares blocks of contiguous *physical* memory.

For a time, Skia was removed from Android and the entire rendering chain depended on compiling small graphics programs run by a GPU. Google has reversed direction on this, however. Starting with Android 9, Skia has resurfaced and has a GL backend. The Android system also needs a way to reserve and share blocks of physical memory to handle the camera.

Modern Androids use Ion, pmem's successor, to manage pools of shared physical memory.

Logger

Google Source	`drivers/staging/android/logger.c` (obsolete)
Canonical Source	No longer used
Daemon Source	`System/core/logd`
Exposed as	See Table 4.1

As another consequence of having to be careful about its use of persistent memory, Android cannot write its system logs, as they normally are, to files. Spewing kilobytes per minute to a flash memory–based file system—even if the files were carefully managed to prevent filling the limited space on a mobile device—would wear out the flash memory very quickly.

Android addressed this problem by writing its logs to a circular buffer in the kernel: Logs do not go to files. If the drawbacks of this idea are not immediately obvious, they will become obvious during attempts to diagnose an unmonitored system crash. When an Android system reboots, its memory is reinitialized and all logs are lost.

The Android kernel logger supports four separate log buffers, shown in Table 4.1.

Table 4.1 **Android Logs**

Location	Use
/dev/log/main	Application logs. Where messages from the android.util.Log class go.
/dev/log/system	System logs. Where messages from the hidden android.util.Slog class and the native liblog library go.
/dev/log/events	Binary log of system events: garbage collections, ActivityManager state, and so on
/dev/log/radio	Logs from the baseband processor

Note that although these logs are catalogued in the file system, they are *not* files. This is an example of the kernel's ability to make anything, including a circular buffer in its own memory, look like a file.

As with the low memory killer support, logging functionality has also been moved into user space with the daemon **logd**. The daemon allows OEMs to adjust log buffer size instead of forcing a fixed size circular buffer size as the kernel driver did. The daemon also supports an additional buffer type: a crash buffer. The crash buffer provides a single place for process crashes, which usually include stack backtraces and register information and is not intermixed with the main logcat output. Unlike the kernel logger interface, logd exposes a named socket for processes to read and write logs. The details of this, however, are abstracted away in the Android logging APIs.

Alarms

Google Source	Originally drivers/rtc/alarm.c, now drivers/staging/android/alarm-dev.c, replaced by POSIX alarm timers, kernel/time/alarmtimer.c
Canonical Source	kernel/time/alarmtimer.c
Exposed as	/dev/alarm (Android Alarm Driver)
	timerfd_create and /dev/rtc*

Android depends on the ability to wake itself up at a pre-scheduled time. Even when in their lowest power modes, nearly all mobile chipsets include a clock capable of sending an interrupt signal that causes the rest of the chip to power up. Android supports this capability with the alarm driver, which allows applications to request that the kernel schedule a wakeup call at a specific time. This, in combination with a wakelock, allows an application to schedule itself at a time at which the system is otherwise asleep.

Android initially used a custom driver to supply this alarm and wake functionality. That driver was developed outside of the Linux kernel community and did not adhere to the best practices followed by the kernel team. It was never accepted into the tree. In 2011, John Stultz of Linaro introduced a POSIX alarm driver into the Linux kernel. This driver eventually replaced the

Android alarm driver in the kernel and in 2016 became the officially supported alarm support for Android.

Paranoid Networking

Google Source	`net/ipv4/af_inet.c`, `net/ipv6/af_inet6.c`, `drivers/net/tun.c`, `security/commoncap.c`
Canonical Source	`net/ipv4/af_inet.c`, `net/ipv6/af_inet6.c`, `drivers/net/tun.c`, `security/commoncap.c`
Exposed as	N/A

On most operating systems, networking, if it is available at all, is provided to all applications as a general service. The designers of Android thought it important that users be able to control access to the network.

There are several reasons for this. Perhaps the most important is that use of the network may, depending on your carrier, cost money. If something costs money, the user ought to be able to control it. Another possible reason is that a user may want control over what information leaves her device. She may be willing to give an application access to her list of contacts or to the network, but never both.

Paranoid networking, unlike the previous Android-specific kernel features, is not a separate driver. Instead, Android implements network access control with a very simple bit of code in the IP v4 network driver, switched by the compile time flag, CONFIG_ANDROID_PARANOID_ NETWORK. This code simply checks the group ID (gid) of the application making the network request. Unless the application belongs to the process group AID_INET, the request is denied.

On an Android system, each new application is assigned its own unique user ID when it is installed. At the same time, it may be assigned to one or more process groups. If the application requests access to the network, it is assigned to the AID_INET group and will thus be able to use the network.

Android's security features and its use of group and user IDs are the subject of the next chapter.

Other Custom Drivers

These are just the largest, most easily categorized features. In those four megabytes of patches there are, clearly, many other customizations. Among these smaller changes are specializations for the USB subsystem, the Bluetooth subsystem, and a RAM console that stores kernel panic information across reboots, in /proc/last_kmsg.

Building a Kernel

Fortunately, starting from scratch is not usually necessary. Most hardware manufacturers recognize the barrier that kernel development represents for potential customers. Most SoC vendors supply pre-built kernels—probably even Android compatible kernels—along with their chips. Nearly any vendor for external hardware (sensors, touchscreens, network interfaces, and so on) will provide, at the very least, a template Linux driver. Also, unless the target hardware is bleeding edge, it is very likely that a community effort addresses it.

> ### Note
>
> As mentioned in the introduction, the complexities of getting a kernel running on any specific piece of hardware can be quite daunting. This chapter is *not* a recipe for building a kernel for your device. In fact, even if you follow the process step-by-step for building a kernel for one of the hardware devices discussed in this chapter, you may not end up with a working system! Tiny changes in versions, both in hardware and in the software, may break things in ways that are quite mysterious and difficult to diagnose. Although we absolutely guarantee that we were able to build a working system, as described, with our copy of the source and our hardware, there is no way to guarantee that the same steps, even followed carefully, will work for you and yours.

The Build System

As noted in Chapter 2, the best way to build a Linux kernel is on a machine running Linux. As with building the AOSP source, building the kernel takes significant compute power. Investing in a build machine with fast processors and plenty of memory may be worthwhile.

Also, as noted in Chapter 2, a virtual machine running a Linux distribution on a normal development host machine is a plausible second choice. Attempting to build a kernel, native, on a non-Linux machine may work in specific cases but is not generally a workable solution.

The examples here use a standard installation of Ubuntu 16.04 running either on bare metal or in a VirtualBox.

Downloading the Source

The choice of source is probably the most important decision. Obviously, a kernel that is known to work for a given chipset, even if it will require significant modification, is the best choice. Time spent in research, even significant time, can easily be a very worthwhile trade-off against frustration and bring-up time. Probably the best starting point is the chipset manufacturer and any attached support community.

Many board manufacturers supply not only custom kernels but extensive systems for customizing the AOSP build. They include the various board configuration files necessary to appropriately customize AOSP to run on the board. Many of them also integrate the kernel build into the AOSP build system.

Although these third-party systems definitely can work, several of them ride roughshod over the standard AOSP tools: git, make, and so on. Different SoC manufacturers support Android with different levels of tools usage, and some are better than others. Regardless, where it is possible to do so, try to keep the patches that these systems install on their own git branch. At the very least, this will make cherry-picking patches from the AOSP source much easier to do.

> **Opinion**
>
> Google stopped building the kernel as part of the source in 2009 and made it, instead, an external binary dependency. The AOSP build is plenty complex already. Build the kernel separately. Drop it into the Android build when it changes.
>
> Automating the process of moving the kernel after it is built to a canonical location in the AOSP source is entirely reasonable. Trying to make the AOSP source build depend, in the sense of make, on the kernel build, exponentially increases the complexity of the build system. You have been warned!

This example builds a 4.9.176 kernel for the HiKey-960 board, used throughout this book as the Acme project. At the time of this writing, the AOSP pages include instructions for downloading and building the kernel for this board at https://source.android.com/setup/build/devices. However, in the interest of completeness, a walkthrough of acquiring the sources and building them follows.

Begin by setting up the AOSP tree, acquired in Chapter 2, to build for the HiKey-960:

```
$ source build/envsetup.sh
$ lunch hikey960-userdebug
```

Next, clone the kernel git repository into this tree, creating a new subdirectory, hikey-linaro. Immediately change into this directory.

```
$ git clone https://android.googlesource.com/kernel/hikey-linaro
$ cd hikey-linaro
```

This is the kernel source directory. Unlike kernel source trees provided by some vendors, this tree contains the git history for the HiKey kernel. Before attempting to build, the tree needs to be checked out to the correct release branch, android-hikey-linaro-4.9:

```
$ git checkout -b android-hikey-linaro-4.9 origin/android-hikey-linaro-4.9
```

The kernel build depends on a couple of environment variables. The first is clear enough:

```
$ export ARCH=arm64
```

The HiKey-960 is based on a Cortex A73/A53 ARM processor in a big.LITTLE architecture. The target architecture is arm64.

The next variable setting is significantly more mysterious:

```
$ export CROSS_COMPILE=aarch64-linux-android-
```

Do not make the mistake of thinking that this is a directory path or a specific file! This is a string that is prefixed onto the names of the major tools that the build process uses when building the kernel. If you look in the directory, ../prebuilts/gcc/linux-x86//aarch64/aarch64-linux-android-4.9/bin/, you will find common tools—ar, cpp, gcc, ld, and so on—all with prefixes added to their names. The value of the variable must exactly be the prefix!

To make sure that the build directory is in a pristine state, clean it:

```
$ make distclean
```

The distclean target does not remove the config file (discussed in a moment). To do that, so that you start completely fresh, also type:

```
$ make mrproper
```

The first step in building a kernel is configuring the build. "Configuring" sets the values of a couple hundred compile time variables that determine which drivers and which other features are included in the new kernel.

If the target device is already running, often the config file that was used to build it can be found in the directory /proc/config.gz. Simply download it, expand it, put it in the kernel directory, and rename it .config.

The Hi-Key960 kernel source contains a basic config file for the board. Use make to copy it into place:

```
$ make hikey960_defconfig
  HOSTCC   scripts/basic/fixdep
  HOSTCC   scripts/kconfig/conf.o
  SHIPPED scripts/kconfig/zconf.tab.c
  SHIPPED scripts/kconfig/zconf.lex.c
  SHIPPED scripts/kconfig/zconf.hash.c
  HOSTCC   scripts/kconfig/zconf.tab.o
  HOSTLD   scripts/kconfig/conf
#
# configuration written to .config
#
```

To make any further customizations, just edit the .config file. Alternatively, the kernel build system includes a simple menu-driven system for editing the config. Invoke it, again using make:

```
$ make menuconfig
```

menuconfig requires the ncurses libraries. If the build system does not have them installed, you will need to use the apt-get package management tool on Ubuntu to install them before invoking it.

Finally, build the kernel. It will take about 15 minutes on a bare-metal machine with a quad core i7 processor, 16GB of RAM, and SSD storage.

```
make -j4

scripts/kconfig/conf  --silentoldconfig Kconfig
  CHK     include/config/kernel.release
  WRAP    arch/arm64/include/generated/asm/bugs.h
  WRAP    arch/arm64/include/generated/asm/clkdev.h
  WRAP    arch/arm64/include/generated/asm/cputime.h
  WRAP    arch/arm64/include/generated/asm/delay.h
```

```
WRAP    arch/arm64/include/generated/asm/div64.h
WRAP    arch/arm64/include/generated/asm/dma.h
WRAP    arch/arm64/include/generated/asm/dma-contiguous.h
WRAP    arch/arm64/include/generated/asm/early_ioremap.h
CHK     include/generated/uapi/linux/version.h
WRAP    arch/arm64/include/generated/asm/emergency-restart.h
UPD     include/generated/uapi/linux/version.h
. . .
```

As previously mentioned, kernel builds and flashing for each SoC and/or board are unique and are not something this book can discuss in general. In the case of the HiKey-960, though, now that the kernel has been built, we'll need to create a new boot image that contains it. To do this, first copy the device tree information and the newly created kernel image into the HiKey-960 device tree, and then rebuild the boot image.

```
$ cp arch/arm64/boot/dts/hisilicon/hi3660-hikey960.tdb ../device/linaro/hikey-
kernel/hi3660-hikey960.tdb-4.9
$ cp arch/arm64/boot/Image.gz-tdb ../device/linaro/hikey-kernel/Image.gz-dtb-
hikey960-4.9
$ cd ..
$ m bootimage -j 24
```

Summary

This section introduced the Linux kernel as modified for Android. It describes the major features unique to the Android version of the kernel: Binder, the low-memory killer, wakelocks, and several others.

In addition, it demonstrated building a kernel for an Android system. Although not a recipe for building a kernel for every Android system, it is a starting point and, perhaps, provides a few hints that will make the process less distressing.

5

Platform Security

Securing an embedded platform is extremely challenging, especially with a large system such as Android. Android's security infrastructure permeates up through the entire software stack. Security encompasses numerous technologies and concepts. From encrypting data with the latest cryptographic techniques to ensuring that data in one application is not accessible by another, the system needs to be constructed so it can readily support the various facets of platform security.

Android's security stack starts with the kernel and is built up from there. It leverages readily available technologies, using common Linux concepts with a twist, and finishes out with some Android specifics. This chapter examines how Android's security stack is constructed and which pieces are often customized for new devices.

Types of Security

A platform like Android must be concerned with numerous types of security. When most people think of security and computing systems, they think of what cryptographic technique or protocol is in use. But there is more to security than just taking one set of bits and encrypting it into another set of bits. As with the layers of software in the stack, you must consider multiple facets of security:

- **Chipset:** How does the system on a chip (SoC) know it is executing the right thing?
- **Operational:** How does the system know this operation is allowed?
- **User:** How do the app and system secure their data and operations?
- **Customization:** How can apps or the system extend what is available?

Android addresses each of these facets with varying levels of complexity and completeness. An original equipment manufacturer (OEM) must understand not only how security is handled within the platform so it can be used effectively, but also how to avoid introducing security holes by inadvertently misusing the system.

Verified Boot

Starting with Android 7, verified boot is required for all Android devices. Android's support for verified boot is derived from the secure boot techniques used in ChromeOS. It is a combination of secure boot-chain support embedded in the silicon as well as the dm-verity feature of the Linux kernel. Verified boot is used to ensure the system is only executing a trusted kernel and a trusted Android system. It is worth reiterating that although verified boot is required for all Android devices running Android 7 or newer, not all AOSP-based devices will be "Android" devices.

Typically, the chipset uses public cryptography techniques to ensure that the boot-chain is secure. The chipset has a set of public keys (certificates) in one-time write storage on the device (that is, burned in). Just like the way X.509 certificates are used to secure TLS/SSL connections, there is a trusted "root" within the chip's ROM along with one or more intermediate signing certificates. The OEM is responsible for creating its own set of keys/certificates, getting them signed by the silicon vendor (or another trust present in the ROM), and ultimately "burning" the OEM public certificate into the one-time write area of the chipset. A final one-time write operation permanently sets the secure boot operation, commonly referred to as "blowing the fuse" in the device. Depending on the chipset, this may be done when the OEM keys/certificates are written or as a separate operation. This enables the device's secure boot mode and requires signed firmware/images to be present for it to execute the boot loader and start the Linux kernel.

When the fuse has been blown in the chipset and the OEM's certificate is present, the ROM boots the lowest level bootloader (trusted) and verifies the next bootloader in the chain. Most chipsets' secure boot functionality verifies the validity up through the "application bootloader" (for example, what loads the kernel and ultimately Android). From this point, it is up to the OEM to provide the necessary support to verify that any kernel it loads is valid and trusted. This is where it gets interesting for the OEM. Each silicon vendor may provide different application bootloaders to use, such as uboot or a custom bootloader. It is up to the OEM to either enable the silicon vendor's support for secure boot or extend the provided bootloader to properly provide this support.

After the application bootloader has validated the Linux kernel using a crypto signature, the kernel is loaded and control transferred to it with details about the Android system image (and possibly vendor and oem images) and secure hash metadata that corresponds to it. Starting with Android 8, a reference implementation of Android verified boot is provided as part of AOSP. You can enable this support to build secure images by adding a line to the platform makefile (for example, acme_one.mk), as shown in Listing 5.1.

Listing 5.1 **Makefile Change to Enable Android Verified Boot**

```
BOARD_AVB_ENABLE := true
```

This causes the build system to create a metadata image, vbmeta.img, for the target that includes hash data for the boot image and hash tree details for the system image and sets up the command line boot arguments for the kernel to use dm-verity for the system image. Other images, such as the vendor image used for vendor-provided binderized HALs, are also supported. The default implementation uses SHA-256 with an RSA 4096 bit key from external/avb/test/data in the AOSP tree. This *must* be overridden by the OEM and a custom key provided. The algorithm and key content can be specified using two additional platform makefile variables, as shown in Listing 5.2.

Listing 5.2   **Makefile Change to Specify AVB Signing Key**

```
BOARD_AVB_ALGORITHM := SHA512_RSA4096
BOARD_AVB_KEY_PATH := /path/to/rsa_key_4096bits.pem
```

The public portion of the provided key must be available for the bootloader to use to verify the image(s). The reference implementation includes the tools necessary to extract this data into the correct format. Additionally, the reference implementation includes a C library, libavb, which can be integrated into application bootloaders to provide the required support for verified boot.

After the boot image is validated, the kernel is loaded and instructed via its command line arguments to use dm-verity to ensure certain images are secure. The kernel's dm-verity support uses the secure hash data for validating the system image at runtime. Each block of the file system is cryptographically hashed as part of a hash tree, up to a root hash. The root hash is what gets signed by the OEM at build time. At runtime, the kernel's dm-verity driver computes the secure hash for a block of the file system any time it is read, up to the root hash in the tree. Although this sounds like it would hurt performance, the computation does not really add significant overhead on top of the I/O wait times needed to read the data from storage. The hash result is then compared to the signed hash in the metadata. If they differ, the file system has been tampered with or corrupted. In this case, the kernel will return an I/O error from the low-level file system driver, causing failures higher in the stack. This means that dm-verity can only be used to verify read-only file systems or ones that should not change for a given build of Android for the device! The file systems that fall into this category for Android are system, system_ext, product, vendor, and odm images.

For more information about verified boot, dm-verity, and Android verified boot, see these pages from the AOSP project:

https://source.android.com/security/verifiedboot

https://source.android.com/security/verifiedboot/avb

https://source.android.com/security/verifiedboot/dm-verity

Operational Security

Complex operating systems, such as Android, are constantly performing operations by applications or other types of processes. These operations may be simply executing the internal code of an application or performing some action based on the request of the application. In either case, the system manages what operations are allowed and enforces the necessary restrictions. Android leverages several different mechanisms to ensure operational security: process sandboxing, SE Linux for Android, and Android-defined permissions. Each of these plays an important role with platform security. However, this is all made possible because of the distinct layers of the software stack and the underlying Linux kernel.

Android Software Layers

Recall from Chapter 3 the concept of the Android software stack as a "layer cake," shown again in Figure 5.1. At the bottom of this stack is the Linux kernel. Not only does the kernel control the underlying hardware and all processes running in the system, but it also provides the base of the security architecture.

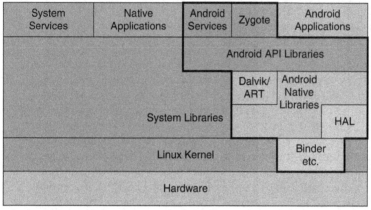

Figure 5.1   Android Software Layers (reprise of Figure 3.1)

The Linux kernel is the primary security boundary within the system. The kernel is in complete control of the underlying hardware, process scheduling, memory management, and SE enforcement. The runtime used to execute application code (ART or Dalvik) provides no additional security. That detail surprises most Android app developers but is crucial for understanding how the system uses and enforces security. All user space processes, whether they are third-party applications (APKs) or daemons running native code, are subject to the same exact security boundaries. In other words, just because code is written in C/C++ or compiled using the NDK does not mean it can bypass system security. By default, each process in the system is "sandboxed" into its own little world.

The Process Sandbox

Just like other Linux-based systems, Android loads and executes applications within their own process. Each process has its own distinct memory space, providing isolation from other processes in memory. Further, each process is given a section of the file system which, by default, only it can access. Other areas of the file system are generally off limits. Processes really cannot interact with much outside of their own memory and file system space. As discussed in Chapter 3 in the "Android Service Model" section, application processes cannot keep the device awake, access kernel device handles, and so on. Thus, the application is sandboxed. On the surface, this sounds like a solid approach. However, even this is not enough. Some subtle details are at work to keep the various components in the system isolated. Figure 5.2 illustrates how processes, by default, are not only restricted from accessing scarce resources but also cannot directly interact with each other due to sandboxing and their Linux user ID.

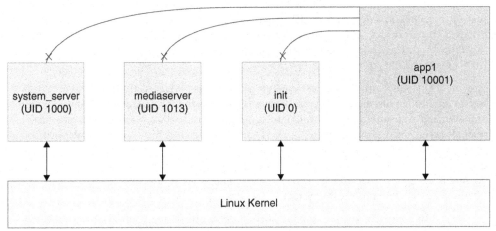

Figure 5.2   Android Process Sandbox

The traditional Linux UID concept (and GID) is turned on its head in Android. Rather than a UID representing a specific person using the system, each *application* in Android is assigned a UID when it is installed. When the running Android system is using multiple user profiles, each app is assigned unique UIDs for the app plus the specific user.

Note

With the introduction of multiple user profiles in Android 4 (Ice Cream Sandwich), UID/GID assignment utilizes an "encoding" to bind together the application portion of the UID and the user profile for which the application belongs. The general form is

```
user_app_uid = 100000 x user_profile_id + app_uid
```

where `app_uid` is the same for all instances of a given app and third-party app assigned values starting with `10000`, and `user_profile_id` is `0` for the first user (owner) then `10, 11, 12,` and so on after that. When viewed via the `ps` command, an app process assigned `app_uid` `10022` will be shown as `u0_a22` for the first user, `u1_a22` for the second user, `u2_a22` for the third user, and so on, and the actual encodings of each would be `10022`, `1010022`, and `1110022`, respectively.

System processes (for example, daemons/services) get similar treatment: They are assigned special UIDs at build time. The UID and GID assignment ensures the running processes stay isolated from each other. Without this concept, each process would effectively be able to change and manipulate things from other processes as they do on some other embedded real-time operating systems.

The base UID/GID definitions in Android are defined within the AOSP tree at `system/core/include/private/android_filesystem_config.h` rather than in `/etc/passwd` and `/etc/group` as they would be on a traditional Linux system. Applications are assigned a UID when they are installed on a device. The UID assignment does not change for as long as the app is installed on that device. After the app is removed, though, the UID is free and can be assigned to another app. The Android framework tracks installed app packages and their assigned UID/GID via the file `/data/system/packages.xml`.

The use of UID/GID with the process sandbox provides very coarse-grained control of the system, also called discretionary access control (DAC). Originally, Android used only this technique for app and system process isolation, as discussed in Chapter 3 with respect to scarce resource access. As Android grew in popularity and expanded its features, DAC was no longer adequate to protect the apps from each other and the system from itself. For example, a compromised version of the system server process could potentially damage the entire system because it holds superuser privileges. Using DAC alone, there is no way to impose a consistent, system-wide policy to protect the system.

An alternative approach, known as mandatory access control (MAC), mitigates this problem. MAC allows all processes, even system processes running as the superuser, to be contained. Use of MAC allows a consistent, system-wide policy to be established in the system. Processes are not only sandboxed in memory and via file system access but further restricted from performing other fine-grained operations in the system.

Returning to our example of a compromised system server process, with MAC even a process with superuser permissions can be restricted so that it is not allowed to fork another process, access specific device files, and so on. MAC support was first added in Android 4 via SE Linux for Android. With MAC, all packages, executables, devices, and so on are assigned contexts or labels that are then granted permission to do things based on policy, which is defined at system build time.

SE Linux for Android

Security Enhanced Linux, or SE Linux, was created by RedHat and the NSA. It was first released in 2000. SE Linux is a combination of Linux kernel changes along with user space tools to manage and control SE operations.

Just like traditional DAC support in Linux, MAC enforcement is handled by the Linux kernel. SE Linux refines the way security is handled by the OS, making it much finer grained and capable of restricting process functionality beyond the simple "owner-oriented" mechanisms used by traditional DAC. When enabled, the kernel is given a set of policies and what to do when a policy is violated.

The two different operating modes for the kernel with SE enabled are permissive and enforcing. With permissive mode, the kernel emits audit logs when policy violations occur, but does not stop the operation from continuing. Enforcing mode, on the other hand, both logs the violation and stops the operation from continuing.

Adding SE Linux to Android helped the platform to meet several goals for securing the OS:

- Prevent privilege escalation, even for system apps/executables, which would allow a process to access resources for which it would normally not have access

- Prevent data leakage between processes

- Prevent security bypass techniques

SE is not a replacement for traditional DAC. Instead, the Linux kernel still has DAC controls in place, and SE simply builds upon it. This takes the Android process sandbox to a whole new level. The kernel is responsible for enforcing the SE policies. The kernel is loaded with the SE policies at startup from the `initram` file system (read only). SE operates in a "default deny" mode. This means that unless a policy (rule) is defined that allows an operation, the operation will be denied.

This shift from DAC to MAC is not a lightweight change. Policy definition is everything in SE. If the policy is wrong and processes are not constructed in a way to handle failures, the system can come to a very abrupt halt. Similarly, bad policy might inadvertently allow operations that could compromise the system or an app.

For this reason, SE was rolled out slowly: first added in Android 4.2 (Jelly Bean) in permissive mode, then refined and placed in full enforcing mode in Android 5 (Lollipop). Taking a step back to look at a complete, Linux-based system architecture, the ideal architecture would be constructed to have decentralized, least privilege, separation of concerns, and corresponding SE policy along with it. Because of this, the SE policies and system structure continue to evolve to better contain critical operations. Chapter 10 builds on this idea in its discussion of the binderized HAL, which, as of Android 8, allows for vastly improved separation and constraint of OEM and vendor components.

SE Policy Definition

SE policy definitions can be extremely granular. Essentially, anything that is known to the kernel can be protected using a policy. From device files to sockets and shared memory areas, it can all be protected. With this functionality comes a large increase in complexity. Fortunately, SE for Android simplifies this slightly compared to desktop or server Linux.

With pure SE Linux, policies are made up of several fundamental building blocks: users, roles, types, labels, and multi-level security (MLS) levels. Adding to the complexity, types can be called "domains" and labels can be called "contexts." The number of terms becomes dizzying very quickly. Briefly, the key terms and their definitions are as follow:

- **Users:** SE-defined users, which are not the same as the Linux user. The SE user does not change during a session (as a Linux user can change using `su` or `sudo`.) It is worth noting, however, that in many configurations, there is a 1:1 mapping of SE user to Linux user.

- **Roles:** A grouping of users.
- **Types:** A means of determining access to something.
- **Domains:** Process types can be referred to as domains.
- **Labels:** A combination of user, role, type, and MLS level. A label can also be referred to as a "context." For example, on Android the device files /dev/tty* are given the label tty_device via the following label definition:

  ```
  /dev/tty[0-9]*    u:object_r:tty_device:s0
  ```

The preceding concepts are still rather vague, but it is clear that SE policies are both powerful and complicated. Because of Android's nature, some of the complexity of SE Linux is reduced; in practice, Android does not use the concepts of users, roles, or MLS levels in their full generality. Instead, there is only a single user, a single role, and a single MLS level used across all policies. The user is always u, the role is always object_r, and the MLS level is always s0.

Whew! Android's approach to SE, using only a portion of all the available features, makes this a lot easier to digest! Unfortunately, although this makes it a bit easier to grasp SE for Android, there are still a lot of details in the policies.

So what exactly are SE policies? SE policies are a collection of "type enforcement" files that are compiled into a build for a device. These files have a .te suffix and are provided as part of AOSP and by OEMs/vendors. Policy rules can be built up as well as overridden. Rules have one of the following keywords:

- **allow:** A domain is allowed to use an SE type/object type with permissions.
- **neverallow:** A domain is never allowed to use an SE type/object type with permissions.
- **dontaudit:** Violations of rules for this domain are not logged/audited.

Think of SE policies as rules: Rules that can say something like, "Allow/deny this domain when using this type based on these permissions." The snippet from the Android SE policy for the init process, shown in Listing 5.3, will make this breakdown understandable.

Listing 5.3 **A Snippet of init.te**

```
allow init tty_device:chr_file rw_file_perms
```

This rule states that the init domain (a process) is allowed to operate on something with the label tty_device, a character special file, using the permissions defined as rw_file_perms. Conceptually, this is relatively straightforward.

In practice, some details here still may not be obvious when crafting new policies: what/where are chr_file and rw_file_perms defined? Beyond the .te files used to define policies, several other special files define different objects, contexts, and macros for use in the SE policy files.

The type `chr_file` is defined in a file called `access_vectors`, which establishes which kernel-defined objects, entities, or operations make up this type. Similarly, `rw_file_perms` is defined in `global_macros` as a combination of read and write file operations exposed by the kernel.

> ### Note
> The location of the AOSP files depends on the version of AOSP in use. Prior to Android 8, these files are in `external/sepolicy` within the AOSP tree. Starting with Android 8, the files are in `system/sepolicy` within the AOSP tree. These policies are CDD compliant for the specific version of Android to which they belong. OEMs and vendors should ensure that any changes or customizations do not result in CDD violations!

The standard SE policies cover functionality defined by AOSP, protecting the system as well as processes from each other. However, what about when OEMs have customizations? Just like anything else in AOSP, the provided components could be modified, but an OEM should not. Modifying the AOSP-provided SE policy files is an almost sure way for the device to fail to be CDD compliant. Even if an OEM is not seeking to have the device labeled as Android, modifying the base SE policies potentially opens security holes in the end device. Instead, OEMs who need to add to or revise SE policy should place SE policy additions or customizations beneath the board-specific area and leverage special build variables. For example, the HiKey devices contain some customizations to SE policies and can be found at `device/linaro/hikey/sepolicy` in the AOSP tree setup discussed in Chapter 2.

The Acme One platform built up throughout this book will need some SE policy additions, covered in later chapters. If you used the Acme repo manifest from GitHub (refer to Chapter 2), some SE policy files used in later chapters are present in `device/acme/acme_one/sepolicy` in the build tree.

Two different build variables are available for vendors to use to pull in new SE policies or revisions. The first, `BOARD_SEPOLICY_DIRS`, specifies a directory to add to the SE policies when building the platform. The contents of this directory will extend or override other policies. Only `.te` files will be pulled from this directory when you're compiling the policies for the target.

The second variable, `BOARD_SEPOLICY_UNION`, defines files that should be combined with existing files from AOSP of the same name. This is how an OEM can create new type labels or extend existing type labels for a new executable or device file. Any file(s) called out here must have the same name as files from the AOSP tree, such as `file_contexts`. For example, if the OEM, such as Acme used throughout this book, adds a new daemon to monitor a device feature, called `monitord`, there would need to be a policy file defined as well as an addition to `file_contexts` so the executable is assigned the correct label. The net result would be two additional files in the `device/acme/one/acme_one/sepolicy` directory: `monitord.te` and `file_contexts`. In the board-level makefile, `acme_one.mk`, two additional lines will be added, as shown in Listing 5.4.

Listing 5.4 **Example SE Policy Changes**

```
BOARD_SEPOLICY_DIRS += \
    device/acme/one/sepolicy

BOARD_SEPOLICY_UNION += \
    file_contexts
```

Chapters 6, "System Startup: Installing and Booting the System," and 12, "Clients for a Custom Binderized HAL," demonstrate adding custom SE policies.

Android Permissions

As described in the previous section, Android's permissions system builds on top of the MAC and process sandbox systems to provide even more granular control. The permissions system, while powerful, can also be confusing for both developers and end users. Permissions are used to control access to apps, features, and even specific API calls. Unfortunately, this complexity can sometimes be subtle and depends on good documentation to understand when, where, and how permissions are used.

Permissions are defined to be one of four protection "levels":

- **normal:** Protects features that do not expose hardware, device specifics, user private data, and so on

- **dangerous:** Protects features that could expose hardware, device specifics, user private data, and so on

- **signature:** Can only be used (granted) by packages signed with the same certificate

- **signatureOrSystem:** Just like signature, but can also be used by system apps

The permissions themselves are implementation defined and identified simply by the name of the permission.

You read that correctly: The permissions are just strings that have implementation specific meaning. In certain cases permissions are defined by Android that are also tied to specific SE context or GID, but this is more the exception than the rule. Furthermore, there is no central authority or required form for the permission names. This creates a potential for naming conflicts which are largely resolved by the system on a first come, first serve basis. As a best practice, when new permissions are being defined, they should be namespaced to minimize the potential for collisions. For example, instead of creating a new permission, "PROXIMITY_ACCESS", it would be better to use "com.acme.permission.PROXIMITY_ACCESS".

Enforcing permissions boils down to two different approaches: automatic enforcement and manual enforcement. Both approaches are needed for Android to provide the different types of protection.

Automatic Permission Enforcement

The AOSP framework provides automatic enforcement of permissions when they are used to protect app components: `Activity`, `Service`, `BroadcastReceiver`, and `ContentProvider` (via URI). Apps, including system apps, that need to protect their components via a permission can do so using the app's manifest or in some cases at runtime.

Permissions may be specified for a given component via the appropriate tag in the app's manifest. For example, to protect a `BroadcastReceiver` so that only apps holding the permission `com.example.permission.USE_FEATURE` may send it an `Intent`, the manifest entry would look similar to what is shown in Listing 5.5.

Listing 5.5   **Example Permission for a BroadcastReceiver**

```
<receiver android:name=".FeatureReceiver"
        android:permission="com.example.permission.USE_FEATURE">
    <intent-filter>
        <action android:name="com.example.action.FEATURE">
    </intent-filter>
</receiver>
```

If the sender of the `Intent` does not hold the required permission, the call will fail with a `SecurityException`. The same concept can be applied to `<activity>`, `<service>`, and `<provider>` elements.

Note, however, that some features are available only for specific component types:

- **Service:** The permission is used to protect starting as well as binding to the specific service.

- **ContentProvider:** Separate `readPermission` and `writePermission` attributes can be used to specify separate permissions for read and write. Additionally, `grantUriPermission` attribute and `<grant-uri-permission>` subelement can be used to grant temporary access to apps based on a URI served by the provider.

Also, if the `<application>` tag within the manifest has a `permission` attribute set, that permission is a fallback for access to *any* of the components within the application!

The framework-provided enforcement is relatively coarse grained. The Android-provided Settings application again provides a working example of this. The Settings activity for requesting access to Bluetooth is protected by the permission `"android.permission.BLUETOOTH"`. So any application that wants to enable Bluetooth or make the device discoverable (which it must do by running the Setting app) must have this permission. If it does not, its call to `startActivity()` will fail.

Manual Permission Enforcement

Automatic permission enforcement is great for protecting an entire feature or component implementing a feature. However, it is a broad level of protection. What if a specific API within a feature set needs to be protected, but not the feature as a whole? For example, ConnectivityManager does not require a permission to call isDefaultNetworkActive(), but it does require the android.permission.ACCESS_NETWORK_STATE permission in order to access the APIs that provide specific details about a network (such as getNetworkCapabilities()). How does this actually work?

These types of APIs are generally accessed via Binder-based calls (for example, AIDL-defined interfaces). In fact, Android's various "manager" classes, which are retrieved via Context.get-SystemService(), are just wrapper APIs around binder proxies. System services and binder and Android's service model were covered in Chapter 3. The API implementations manually check and enforce the permission requirements.

The approaches used by different implementations can vary, but permissions checks are typically performed very early in the API implementation. The check must be done on the service side; otherwise, there is no way to enforce it! The framework's Context object, part of the backing service's process, provides the APIs used to manually verify that the caller has the necessary permission.

Two types of calls are available: check and enforce. The difference between the two is that the "check" calls simply return PackageManager.PERMISSION_GRANTED or PackageManager.PERMISSION_DENIED as appropriate. The "enforce" calls, on the other hand, automatically throw SecurityException if the caller does not hold the required permission.

These APIs are called on the service side by code that is aware of the context of the calling application. The service side "knows" the calling application's process ID (PID) and user ID (UID), and the framework can use this information to check whether or not the caller has been granted the required permission. This illustrates another reason the Binder subsystem is backed by a kernel module: the kernel provides details about the calling process's context and resources.

Revisiting the ConnectivityManager.getNetworkCapabilities() API, the backing service implementation for Android 10 is in frameworks/base/services/core/java/com/android/server/ConnectivityService.java. Listing 5.6 shows the relevant code.

Listing 5.6   **ConnectivityManager Manual Check for Permissions**

```
@Override
public NetworkCapabilities getNetworkCapabilities(Network network) {
    enforceAccessPermission();
    return getNetworkCapabilitiesInternal(
        getNetworkAgentInfoForNetwork(network));
}

...
```

```
private void enforceAccessPermission() {
    mContext.enforceCallingOrSelfPermission(
        android.Manifest.permission.ACCESS_NETWORK_STATE,
        "ConnectivityService");
}
}
```

File Systems

The final piece of the "operational level" security is the file system. A portion of this has been discussed briefly in the application sandbox and SE Linux for Android sections. However, more details are important for an OEM to understand.

Just like other Linux-based systems, the file system layout in Android is a hierarchical tree that has one or more backing physical devices and some virtual devices mounted at locations in the tree. What level of access is available to these mount points is dependent on the backing media and the SE policies of the platform.

You can find additional information on Android's storage mechanisms, file systems, and partitions in these two AOSP locations:

https://source.android.com/devices/storage

https://source.android.com/devices/bootloader/partitions

The remainder of this section enumerates the key file systems and how security affects them.

Mount Point: /

This (/) is the root of the file system and is a Linux initial RAM disk. This image is part of the boot.img image file for the target. It contains startup scripts, SE policies, configuration files, property files, and so on. This file system is read-only, both in the way it is mounted and because it is an initial RAM disk. The contents cannot be modified at runtime.

Mount Point: /system

Typically, this file system is backed by eMMC, NAND, or some other type of non-volatile storage. Depending on the storage media, it might be formatted ext4, jffs, yaffs2, and so on. On most modern Android builds, it is ext4. Its contents are exactly the system.img file after a successful build. This is where the core Android services, framework, libraries, daemons, and native binaries are stored. It is mounted as a read-only file system, which is critical from a security standpoint. See the previous section, "Verified Boot," for more information.

Note

Non-production builds can often include the su command, which can be used to gain elevated access and then remount the /system partition as read-write. This can be helpful during an initial system bring up or debugging. However, it *should never* be possible on a production build. Rewriting the /system partition on a release build is a huge security hole!

Mount Point: `/data`

The `/data` file system is also typically backed by eMMC or some other non-volatile storage. Also like `/system`, most modern Android systems utilize the ext4 format for this file system. It is mounted read-write and contains data for both the platform as well as apps. Although it is mounted read-write, write access is strictly controlled by permissions and SE policy. The image from the build that is used for this file system is the `userdata.img` file.

App data is located at `/data/data/<package name>`. This is the file system portion of the application sandbox, outlined earlier in this chapter. When an app wants to create a database, shared preferences, or even a regular file, this is where its app private storage is located. This is protected by file system permissions based on the application's assigned UID/GID. This also means that it is possible for apps to "share" files from this private space by setting file system–level permissions (though this is generally not recommended).

The Android framework also uses portions of the `/data` file system for its own purposes. Application installs, granted permissions for packages, new permissions, package native libraries, and optimized DEX/OAT binaries are some examples of what the framework stores here. Just like the app private areas, these files are protected by file system–level permissions as well as SE policy so the contents are kept from prying eyes.

Mount Point: `/sdcard`

Prehistoric Android phones included a SD/MMC slot used for additional storage or removable content, such as pictures or video. This is because back in the 2008 timeframe, NAND or other flash devices were relatively expensive per MB of storage but SD cards were not. Plus, in the days of NAND flash, the typical Linux file systems (such as ext4) were not good about spreading data throughout the device, or "wear leveling," that was necessary to prevent the SSDs of the time from failing.

Although most devices in the market today do not have separate SD/MMC card slots, the system retains a symbolic link at the root file system, `/sdcard`. Depending on the hardware, this can point to a real SD card device (which is mounted elsewhere) or to emulated "external storage."

Perhaps even more confusing is the concept of "primary" versus "secondary" external storage. Secondary external storage devices are just like primary, with the exception that some of the permissions handling is different. On both types of external devices, apps can read and write to their own private namespace without any additional permissions. This is handled by synthesized permissions provided by the kernel and a user space file system (FUSE) daemon.

Apps can read other areas of external storage by holding the Android permission READ_ EXTERNAL_STORAGE. However, the WRITE_EXTERNAL_STORAGE permission only gives apps the ability to write to non-package private areas of primary external storage. Any secondary external storage device(s) can only be written by system apps or processes.

When emulated external storage is used, the device is typically eMMC soldered on to the board and treated like an SD card. When no separate device exists for "external storage," it is layered on top of the `/data` file system, effectively sharing the same storage space. The intent of this storage media is for larger files. Refer to the AOSP storage documentation for examples of external storage configurations:

https://source.android.com/devices/storage/config-example

Mount Points: `/product`, `/odm`, and `/vendor`

Android 8 introduced the concept of the `/vendor` image containing any vendor-specific proprietary binaries for a platform. This is typically where board or SoC-specific customizations, such as a HAL or custom daemon, are located.

Starting with Android 9, manufacturers can use `product` file systems so that a single system image can be used with different `product` images to support different software SKUs. With this support in place, different Android software loads can be built for a single device using the same core Android OS with only the manufacturer-supplied software differing for the various products.

Android 10 introduced the concept of original design manufacturers (ODMs) file systems. These allow ODMs to further customize SoC or board-specific changes while having a common `/vendor` area. The concept is similar to the `/product` file system, except this is used to differentiate multiple hardware SKUs rather than software SKUs.

These mount points are treated like `/system` from a security perspective: They are read-only mount points that are typically secured using `dm-verity` to ensure they are not manipulated after being flashed to the device.

Mount Points: `/sys`, `/dev`, and `/proc`

The Linux kernel can expose different types of virtual file systems to user space: These can be mounted like file systems–backed storage devices. As described in Chapter 4, the kernel creates the file system out of thin air: It can put anything it wants into it.

These three mount points expose kernel internals, devices interfaces, and kernel runtime information. In Android, the content of these areas is generally locked down for access only by system or privileged processes. It is easy to understand why: Exposing kernel internals or direct calling access can cause a number of security problems.

The AOSP framework's SE policies allow for certain interfaces to be accessed by end apps (such as the binder interfaces), but by and large, most apps/processes cannot access these areas. In fact, the CDD specifically limits access, and there are CTS/VTS tests to verify this. Any OEM creating a new device with new kernel interfaces needs to be especially careful not to allow unfettered access to custom kernel objects and interfaces!

Miscellaneous Mount Points

Several other mount points and partitions can exist in a running Android system. For example, the `/cache` mount point is a read-write area that can be used by the system and applications to store temporary data. Files and directories here are scoped per application, utilizing a similar file system sandbox per application as used in the `/data` partition. Depending on the manufacturer, other mount points may exist as well. As a general rule to keep with CDD compliance, any mount point added to the system should be treated read-only or have special SE policies defined to strictly limit access. For example, some manufacturers include a /firmware partition that contains firmware binaries for hardware on the board. This type of partition should be read-only and also protected with strict SE policy so only the OEM/vendor-provided binaries and/or the kernel can use the contents.

User Protections

Android is first and foremost a mobile phone operating system. Although it has been shipped on numerous tablets and IoT devices, at its heart it was made to power a mobile phone. With phones and tablets, users really do carry their lives with them. From contacts and email to video players and social media apps, people have become accustomed to carrying their life's details on a device that can be lost or stolen. Protecting this information is critical.

Android has supported a variety of user identification mechanisms beyond simple passwords or drawing sequences. Face unlock capability was first introduced in API 14 (Android 4.0, Ice Cream Sandwich). Since then, it has expanded to include fingerprint readers and other biometrics. For many IoT type devices, this functionality is likely to be less important. One feature that is used to protect the user and could be useful for IoT devices is the encrypted file system support.

Full disk encryption (FDE) was added to the platform as far back as API 11 (Android 3.0, Honeycomb). FDE was a great step in protections as it allowed users to protect data on the device until their credentials had been entered. One major drawback is that with FDE, the device can only perform some very basic operations until credentials are entered. No phone calls can be made (other than emergency), no alarms set, and so on. Starting with API 24 (Android 7.0, Nougat), file-based encryption (FBE) was added to the platform.

FBE is built on top of a feature called Direct Boot. With Direct Boot, devices have two different types of storage locations to manage device data before and after the user has entered credentials. The Credential Encrypted (CE) storage area is the default location for data storage. It is available only after the user has unlocked the device.

The Device Encrypted (DE) storage area is available during Direct Boot as well as after the user has entered credentials. Each area is protected using independent keys and encrypted data. Not only does this allow Android and some system apps to operate before the user has unlocked the device, but it also better separates user profiles because each is encrypted with a different key.

> **Note**
>
> Starting with Android 10, all new devices are *required* to support FBE. There are also certain limitations with FBE and adoptable storage, depending on the version of Android in use, if earlier than Android 10. See the AOSP documentation on file-based encryption for more details: https://source.android.com/security/encryption/file-based.

FBE and Direct Boot require several lower-level features to be supported in the platform: kernel support, keymaster support (using HAL 1.0 or 2.0), Trusted Execution Environment (TEE) to implement keymaster and keystore, and hardware root of trust and Verified Boot bound to keymaster initialization. Additionally, system apps that must work before the user unlocks the device must add support for new lifecycle events and APIs so CE protected areas are used appropriately.

You can find details about FDE, FBE, and Direct Boot on the AOSP and main Android developer websites:

https://source.android.com/security/encryption/full-disk

https://source.android.com/security/encryption/file-based

https://developer.android.com/training/articles/direct-boot

Customizing Permissions

Earlier, this chapter described the Android Permissions model and showed how the permissions are leveraged by the framework to protect features. Although Android defines a multitude of permissions within the SDK, those are not the only permissions that are present in a running system. Some third-party SDKs, including some of Google's SDKs for Android, define their own permissions, which may be used by apps. Both system-bundled applications and third-party applications can extend the system in this way.

Note

Defining new permissions is normally only necessary for system-level applications or apps that are part of a "suite" where there is a need to provide a level of protection when accessing certain features and components. It is important to remember that in most cases, Android permission protection for a package is a fairly low barrier for potential attackers to overcome if it is not defined and used correctly.

New Android permissions outside of the core framework are defined by individual packages for package-specific reasons. For system-bundled applications, the custom permissions are added to the system when the first boot optimizes and installs the APK on the platform. For apps installed by third parties or installed after first boot, the permissions are defined when the package is installed.

How is this done? Via the application's manifest, of course! The easiest way to understand custom permissions is to see an example in action.

Sample Custom Permission–Protected App

A simple example of using custom permissions requires both a "host" application, which defines the permissions, and a "consumer" app, which uses the permissions. The Acme One platform tree, set up in Chapter 2, contains both the host and client app. Rather than walk through creation of the build files, resources, and so on, this section and the next show only the files relevant to customizing permission usage.

The host sample app is in `device/acme/one/app/PermsSampleHost`. The app defines two new permissions, `com.acme.one.permission.GET_MIN_TGT_SDK` and `com.acme.one.permission.NOTIFY_MIN_TG_SDK`. These permissions are used to protect a `BroadcastReceiver` and specific broadcast `Intent` response so that only apps granted the permissions can request and receive the minimum target SDK supported by the Acme platform. The minimum target SDK supported by the platform is stored in a system property (`ro.build.version.min_supported_target_sdk`), but is not exposed via a public Android framework API. Although not incredibly useful to the consumer application, it provides a clear illustration of how custom permissions can be defined and used with a simple example.

> ### Note
>
> This contrived example of a custom permission protecting something within the platform also illustrates one of the dangers an OEM must bear in mind: accidentally exposing details to other apps, which is called a *side channel leak* or *feature leak*. OEMs need to carefully consider what platform private APIs or information is exposed via a custom API.

When Android permissions are defined, they can be grouped together for organization purposes. Surprisingly, permission cannot be granted or denied to groups as a whole. Permissions can only be controlled individually. In other words, permission groups are useful for end users to view permissions via the Settings application. Otherwise, though, they do not come into play. The manifest for the example host application defines a permission group and the two new permissions. The new permission group for these two permissions is optional and shown here for completeness.

Listing 5.7 shows the manifest file for the sample host application.

Listing 5.7   PermsSampleHost `AndroidManifest.xml`

```
<?xml version="1.0" encoding="utf-8"?>
<manifest xmlns:android=http://schemas.android.com/apk/res/android
    coreApp="true"
    package="com.acme.one.permssamplehost" >

    <permission-group android:name="com.acme.one.permission-group.TGT_INFO"
                android:description="@string/perm_group_tgt_info_descr"
                android:label="@string/perm_group_tgt_info_label" />

    <permission android:name="com.acme.one.permission.GET_MIN_TGT_SDK"
                android:description="@string/perm_get_min_tgt_sdk_descr"
                android:label="@string/perm_get_min_tgt_sdk_label"
                android:permissionGroup="com.acme.one.permission-group.TGT_INFO"
                android:protectionLevel="signature" />
```

```
<permission android:name="com.acme.one.permission.NOTIFY_MIN_TGT_SDK"
            android:description="@string/perm_notify_min_tgt_sdk_descr"
            android:label="@string/perm_notify_min_tgt_sdk_label"
            android:permissionGroup="com.acme.one.permission-group.TGT_INFO"
            android:protectionLevel="signature" />

<application android:label="@string/app_name"
             android:icon="@drawable/app_launcher_icon"
             android:supportsRtl="true"
             android:allowBackup="false" >

    <receiver android:name=".MinTargetReceiver"
              android:label="@string/min_tgt_receiver_name"
              android:permission="com.acme.one.permission.GET_MIN_TGT_SDK" >
        <intent-filter>
            <action android:name="com.acme.one.service.GET" />
        </intent-filter>
        <intent-filter>
            <action android:name="com.acme.one.service.NOTIFY" />
        </intent-filter>
    </service>
</application>
</manifest>
```

Note how the permissions are defined in the <permission> subelements of the <manifest> tag, and both are signature-level permissions. Similarly, both are part of a new permission group, defined via the <permission-group> tag. Be very careful when using the group that the permissionGroup attribute in the permission matches exactly with the name attribute of the permission group! It must be exact, and the specified group actually defined in the manifest (or elsewhere in the system), otherwise the new permissions will not be created!

The soong blueprint file (see Listing 5.8) calls out the app as product specific and utilizes platform APIs. This means that the app will be built against the internal framework libraries, not the one that is stripped for inclusion in the Android SDK. Because the app utilizes a hidden class to access the system properties, it must be built this way.

Listing 5.8 **PermsSampleHost Android.bp**

```
android_app {
    name: "PermsSampleHost",
    product_specific: true,
    certificate: "shared",
    srcs: [
        "app/src/**/*.java",
```

```
    ],
    resource_dirs: [
        "app/src/main/res",
    ],              .
    manifest: "app/src/main/AndroidManifest.xml"
}
```

The main source of the application is a BroadcastReceiver, which is started via an explicit Intent and responds accordingly.

The requesting application sends the Intent with one of two actions specified. The GET action requires an extra to be included with a Messenger that the receiver will use to send back the response as a Message. The NOTIFY action will send a response via broadcast Intent which can only be received by applications that hold the NOTIFY_MIN_TGT_SDK permission. The receiver code is contained in app/src/main/java/com/acme/one/permssamplehost/ MinTargetReceiver.java, and Listing 5.9 shows the key portions of it.

Listing 5.9   **PermsSampleHost MinTargetReceiver.java**

```
package com.acme.one.permssamplehost;

...

public class MinTargetReceiver extends BroadcastReceiver {
    private static final String TAG = "MinTargetReceiver";
    private static final String ACTION_GET = "com.acme.one.action.GET";
    private static final String ACTION_NOTIFY = "com.acme.one.action.NOTIFY";
    private static final String ACTION_NOTIFY_RESP =
            "com.acme.one.action.NOTIFY_RESP";
    private static final String EXTRA_MESSENGER =
            "com.acme.one.extra.EXTRA_MESSENGER";
    private static final String EXTRA_MIN_TGT_SDK =
            "com.acme.one.extra.EXTRA_MIN_TGT_SDK";
    private static final String PERMISSION_NOTIFY =
            "com.acme.one.permission.NOTIFY_MIN_TGT_SDK";
    private static final String SYSTEM_PROP_MIN_TGT_SDK =
            "ro.build.version.min_supported_target_sdk";
    private static final int MESSAGE_MIN_TGT_SDK = 1000;

    public int getMinTargetSdk() {
        return SystemProperties.getInt(SYSTEM_PROP_MIN_TGT_SDK, -1);
    }

    @Override
    public void onReceive(Context context, Intent intent) {
```

```java
        String action = intent.getAction();

        if (action == null) {
            Log.e(TAG, "No action provided");
        }

        if (TextUtils.equals(action, ACTION_GET)) {
            Messenger msgr = intent.getParcelableExtra(EXTRA_MESSENGER);
            if (msgr != null) {
                Message resp = Message.obtain();
                resp.what = MESSAGE_MIN_TGT_SDK;
                resp.arg1 = getMinTargetSdk();
                try {
                    msgr.send(resp);
                } catch (RemoteException e) {
                    // Ignore, client has died
                }
            } else {
                Log.e(TAG, "No Messenger provided for response");
            }
        } else if (TextUtils.equals(action, ACTION_NOTIFY)) {
            Intent respIntent = new Intent(ACTION_NOTIFY_RESP);
            respIntent.putExtra(EXTRA_MIN_TGT_SDK, getMinTargetSdk());
            sendBroadcast(respIntent, PERMISSION_NOTIFY);
        } else {
            Log.e(TAG, "Invalid action: " + action);
        }
    }
}
```

After it is built into the system image, you can launch the application by sending the appropriate `Intent`. Because the shell does not have the necessary permission granted, an attempt to run the app from the command line will fail, as shown in the logcat output:

```
$ am broadcast -a "com.acme.one.action.GET" \
-n "com.acme.one.permssamplehost/.MinTargetService"

W/BroadcastQueue( 2742): Permission Denial: broadcasting Intent
{ act=com.acme.one.action.GET flg=0x400010
cmp=com.acme.one.permssamplehost/.MinTargetReceiver } from null (pid=19015, uid=2000)
requires com.acme.one.permission.GET_MIN_TGT_SDK due to receiver
com.acme.one.permssamplehost/.MinTargetReceiver
```

Sample Custom Permission Client App

To complete the example of custom permissions, we'll need a client app that uses the permissions. This sample can be found in `device/acme/one/app/PermsSampleClient`. This app uses the permissions defined by the host app by declaring that it uses them in its manifest. When the app is installed on the platform, it will be granted the custom permissions as long as it was signed by the same certificate as the host. Listing 5.10 shows the manifest for the client app.

Listing 5.10   **PermsSampleClient** `AndroidManifest.xml`

```xml
<?xml version="1.0" encoding="utf-8"?>
<manifest xmlns:android=http://schemas.android.com/apk/res/android
    package="com.acme.one.permssampleclient" >

    <uses-permission android:name="com.acme.one.permission.GET_MIN_TGT_SDK" />
    <uses-permission android:name="com.acme.one.permission.NOTIFY_MIN_TGT_SDK" />

    <application
        android:label="@string/app_name"
        android:icon="@drawable/app_launcher_icon"
        android:supportsRtl="true"
        android:allowBackup="false">

        <activity android:name=".MainActivity">
            <intent-filter>
                <action android:name="android.intent.action.MAIN" />
                <category android:name="android.intent.category.LAUNCHER" />
            </intent-filter>
        </activity>
    </application>
</manifest>
```

It may not be obvious, but a potential race condition exists with custom permissions. What happens if the client app is installed but the host app is not? In this case the custom permissions are *not* granted to the consumer app, because they do not exist in the system at the time the consumer app is installed. This is true even if the host app is installed at a later point in time! The client app's permissions are not revisited just because the host app is installed.

Another interesting situation occurs when the host app is removed after its permissions have been granted to another app. In this case the custom permissions are wiped from the system's known permissions, but the client app retains the permissions being granted until it is removed or reinstalled!

> **Note**
> Android custom permissions work on a "first come, first defined" basis. If two app packages define the same exact permission, the first one to be installed is the one that defines it from the system's point of view. Remember, it's just a string associated with a package and signature! The exception to this is if the system (or system package) defines a permission. Since Android 4.4.3, the system ensures that system-defined permissions take precedence.

The client app has a painfully simple UI. It presents two buttons for retrieving the minimum target SDK, one using the "get" technique and the other using the "notify" technique. The text status area shows the result or a failure, if encountered. When the "get" button is tapped, an Intent is sent to the service and includes the `Messenger` where the response is to be sent. The `Messenger` is bound to a new `Handler` object that runs in the main thread of the app. When the "notify" button is tapped, the `Intent` is sent to the service, and the `BroadcastReceiver` is listening for the response. Listing 5.11 shows the key parts of the activity source file, written in Kotlin. You can find detailed information about Messenger and Message in the book Android Concurrency, published by Pearson, Inc.

Listing 5.11   **PermsSampleClient `MainActivity.kt`**

```kotlin
package com.acme.one.permssampleclient

...

class MainActivity : Activity(), Handler.Callback {
    companion object {
        private const val TAG = "MainActivity"
        private const val ACME_MIN_TGT_RXR_PKG = "com.acme.one.permssamplehost"
        private const val ACME_MIN_TGT_RXR =
            ACME_MIN_TGT_RXR_PKG + ".MinTargetReceiver"
        private const val MESSAGE_MIN_TGT_SDK = 1000
        private const val ACTION_GET = "com.acme.one.action.GET"
        private const val ACTION_NOTIFY = "com.acme.one.action.NOTIFY"
        private const val ACTION_NOTIFY_RESP = "com.acme.one.action.NOTIFY_RESP"
        private const val EXTRA_MESSENGER =
            com.acme.one.extra.EXTRA_MESSENGER"

        private const val EXTRA_MIN_TGT_SDK =
            com.acme.one.extra.EXTRA_MIN_TGT_SDK"
    }

    private lateinit var statusText: TextView
    private lateinit var getButton: Button
    private lateinit var notifyButton: Button
    private val handler = Handler(this)
    private val messenger = Messenger(handler)
    private var active = false

    private val respRxr = object : BroadcastReceiver() {
```

```kotlin
        override fun onReceive(context: Context, intent: Intent) {
            when (intent.action) {
                ACTION_NOTIFY_RESP -> {
                    val minTgtSdk = intent.getIntExtra(EXTRA_MIN_TGT_SDK, -1)
                    if (minTgtSdk != -1) {
                        handler.obtainMessage(MESSAGE_MIN_TGT_SDK, minTgtSdk, 0)
                            .sendToTarget()
                    } else {
                        Log.w(TAG, "[onReceive] no min target SDK provided")
                    }
                }
            }
        }

    }

    private fun createReceiverIntent(action: String): Intent {
        val intent = Intent(action)
        intent.component = ComponentName(ACME_MIN_TGT_RXR_PKG, ACME_MIN_TGT_RXR)
        return intent
    }

    override fun onCreate(savedInstanceState: Bundle?) {
        super.onCreate(savedInstanceState)
        ...

        getButton.setOnClickListener {
            val getIntent = createReceiverIntent(ACTION_GET)
            getIntent.putExtra(EXTRA_MESSENGER, messenger)
            statusText.setText(R.string.using_get)
            Log.d(TAG, "[GET] starting service")
            sendBroadcast(getIntent)
        }

        notifyButton.setOnClickListener {
            val notifyIntent = createReceiverIntent(ACTION_NOTIFY)
            statusText.setText(R.string.using_notify)
            Log.d(TAG, "[NOTIFY] starting service")
            sendBroadcast(notifyIntent)
        }

    }

    override fun onResume() {
        super.onResume()
        ...
```

```
        active = true
    }

    override fun onPause() {
        active = false
        ...
        super.onPause()
    }

    override fun handleMessage(msg: Message): Boolean {
        if (!active) {
            ...
            return true
        }

        when (msg.what) {
            MESSAGE_MIN_TGT_SDK -> {
                ...
                statusText.text = getString(R.string.min_tgt_sdk_fmt, msg.arg1)
            }

            else -> {
                Log.e(TAG, "[handleMessage] unknown message type: ${msg.what}")
            }
        }

        return true
    }
}
```

Note

Although the sample client app does use Kotlin, note that it does not use any androidx libraries or other third-party libraries. This is intentional, because the app is built as part of the AOSP platform, which does not use Gradle. This means "standard" libraries available in Android Studio via Maven repositories are not readily available with the built-in Android app package rules when building via soong. Integrating Gradle into the AOSP build is possible, but it is outside of the scope of this book.

The build files and other resources are not interesting for this sample. Running the app on the platform and touching the "get" button shows the output, and monitoring the logcat output shows the expected details:

```
D/MainActivity(20455): [GET] requesting min target SDK
D/MainActivity(20455): [handleMessage] received min target SDK: 23
```

Summary

Android utilizes numerous security features to keep the device, OS, and user data safe. This chapter looked at the basic security concerns of any computing environment:

- The device is running valid code.
- The operation being performed is allowed.
- The app or user data is safe.
- The security features can be extended and customized.

The chapter examined how Android verified boot works and how vendors enable or customize it. After Android is up and running, the process sandbox, SE policy and Android's permissions system work to keep apps isolated from each other and user data safe. This sandboxing in memory, file system, and via SE policy has morphed over Android's lifetime to better protect the system. Rounding out this chapter is a sample of how Android's permission system can be extended with custom permissions. Utilizing a custom permission can be particularly useful for OEMs or package creators where only certain packages should be able to use the functionality. Pre-bundled app packages from the OEM or a suite of packages from an app vendor signed with the same certificate are good examples of where this can be leveraged.

System Startup: Installing and Booting the System

The diagram of the Android system, shown in Chapter 3 in Figure 3.1, is more than simply allegorical. It is meant to show, from the bottom to the top, dependencies within the Android system. The kernel creates an environment for applications; system applications and libraries create an environment for the Android system; and so on up to the top of the chain: Android user applications. Clearly, if each layer depends on the one beneath it, the components that comprise any given layer must be initialized before those in the layer above. The process of initializing the successive layers takes place at system startup when a device is booted. This chapter describes that process.

The Boot Process

Booting a device is a complex and multi-phase process. It is likely to involve several programs that are, themselves, large and complex. To further complicate matters, the entire process takes place in an environment very close to the hardware: something that most developers never experience. Chapter 5 discussed the ways in which the boot process affects device security. Even if a project does not require creating or customizing it, having a general understanding of how the boot process works and how its internal phases relate to one another is useful.

Figure 6.1 outlines the phases of the boot process from power on through the initialization of the Android system.

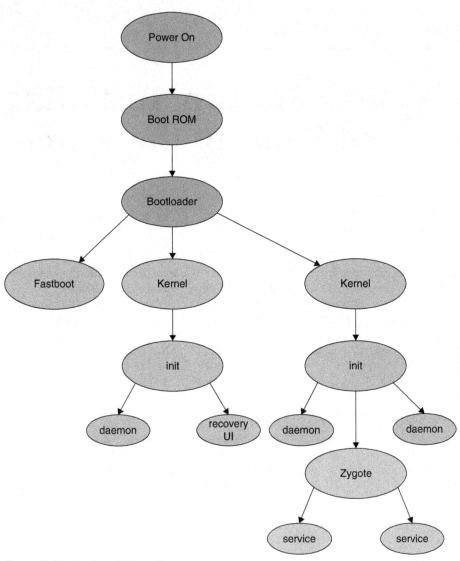

Figure 6.1   The Android Boot Process

More specifically, here are the steps that most Android devices take when booting:

1. Hardware Boot

    a. Power Stable

    b. Reset CPU

    c. Load and start Boot ROM (hardwired address)

2. Bootloader (Device dependent, usually proprietary)

   a. Power-on Self-Test (POST)

   b. Video boot

   c. External storage probe

   d. Device-specific hardware initialization

   e. Fastboot, system update, other features

   f. Cryptographic verification of kernel

   g. Load and start kernel

3. Kernel

   a. Phase 1

      i. Memory initialization

      ii. File system initialization

      iii. Network initialization

   b. Phase 2 (overwrites phase 1 code)

      i. User-space initialization

      ii. Load and start `init`

4. `init`

   a. Start system daemons

   b. Start Android

5. Android

   a. Start Zygote

   b. Android System Services

To examine these steps in full detail, in the next few sections we follow the abbreviated log of the boot of a HiKey960. Although, obviously, even minor changes in software and hardware will cause substantial changes in the boot log, key events are similar across machines. Reviewing an actual log is useful in the interests of specificity.

Bootloader

Functionally, the early phases of system boot are part of the hardware. The code implementing them is frequently stored in on-chip read-only memory (ROM). They are not something that can be changed easily, even in the unlikely circumstance that doing so would be desirable. For all practical purposes, both can be considered part of the device.

Listing 6.1 shows power-on through the initiation of the software bootloader.

Listing 6.1   **xloader Boot Log**

```
^@hikey960 boarid:5301 xloader use UART6
scsysstat_value[0].
clear reset source
last_keypoint0,reboot_type0
secdbg not DCU.
SecDbgVer exit

 xloader chipid is: 0x36600110, start at 470ms.
Build Date: Dec  6 2017, 15:31:59 [clock_init] ++
hikey960 [hikey960_clk_init]
hi3660 [clk_setup]
[clock_init] --
storage type is UFS
ufs retry: 6 count v_tx:0 v_rx:0
ufs set v_tx:0 v_rx:0
Hikey960[5301] no need avs_init.
ddr ft:0xf20332a3,mode:1 target:4
UceLdOk

<lines omitted…>

1244M
1866M
C2R,V0x00000015 e:193
C2R,V0x00000016 e:66
C0R,V0x00000017 e:66
C1R,V0x00000017 e:66
boot_c0 PROFILE 4
slave0 irq0:0x00000004
slave1 irq0:0x00000004
main:     ******** Fastboot for Kirin *****************
```

> **Note**
>
> Access to the boot log is essential for debugging the boot process. Clearly, the log will not be available through adb, a daemon process that is started relatively late in system startup. Although on most systems, retrieving most of the log produced by the most recent boot is possible via the dmesg command, the process is cumbersome and requires that the board successfully boot at least far enough to support a shell.
>
> The logs shown in this chapter were captured from a UART mezzanine board attached to the booting Hikey960. Such a board, or at least something similar, is an essential tool for bringing up a board and debugging the boot process.

When the device is powered on, the first thing that happens is that the power supply changes to a powered-up state. When the power supply senses that board power levels have stabilized in the new state, it sends a RESET signal to the CPU. This signal causes the CPU to load data from boot ROM and to start executing it.

The bootloader program is likely to execute in several stages. Typically, the first stage is a small program that performs some very low level and device-specific initialization tasks. Among these tasks on most devices is a power-up self-test (POST) that does basic sanity checks of the various hardware subsystems (memory, bus, and so on) to verify that they are working normally. If one of the POST tests fails, the entire boot process is usually aborted with some very minimal perceptible feedback: a pattern of sounds, flashing LEDs or, at most, a very simple error code on the console display.

If the POST passes, the bootloader loads additional code from a location specified in a canonical location on a canonical memory device. For Android, this is nearly always a special partition on the main flash card. The exact specifications and format of the special file depend on the device and the version of Android. Historically, Android devices were formatted using the **Master Boot Record** (MBR) standard. Newer devices are more likely to use a newer standard, the **GUID Partition Table** (GPT).

Regardless of the specifics of how the additional bootloader code is discovered, the process of executing it is very nearly still part of the hardware. The second stage of the bootloader, however, is the first code that a starting system executes that is not in read-only memory.

Because the later stages of the bootloader are mutable code, one of the tasks of the first stage of the bootloader is verifying the code for subsequent stages before it is executed. The bootloader computes a cryptographic signature for any code obtained from a writable device and compares the computed signature with one that is stored in the secure area of chipset memory. If the two do not match, the boot process fails, much as it would fail a POST.

Starting with code that is in read-only memory (and which, therefore, cannot be changed), each piece of code cryptographically verifies the next piece of code before executing it. This creates a chain of trust that guarantees that the running system has not been tampered with or altered. This trust is important to keep the user of a device safe from malware: viruses and trojans that might be hidden in the boot code. It also may be important to protect the device from its user. Applications such as digital rights management (DRM) and secure funds transfer may depend on code that has been verified and that is free from meddling.

The strategies used by various manufacturers for configuring the hardware and communicating with the bootloader vary widely. One common way of building a bootloader that is both flexible and extensible involves storing configuration parameters and code in hidden partitions on the device storage.

Examining the persistent storage for an actual device will usually reveal a handful of partitions that are never mounted as part of the Android file system. Recent revisions of Linux will list these partitions by name, even if they are never mounted, in the subdirectory of /dev, appropriately called, "by-name." For example, Listing 6.2 shows the partitions included on the HiKey960 used in most of these examples.

Listing 6.2   **Files in /dev**

```
adb shell 'ls -R /dev' | grep by-name
/dev/block/platform/soc/ff3b0000.ufs/by-name
adb shell ls -l /dev/block/platform/soc/ff3b0000.ufs/by-name
total 0
lrwxrwxrwx 1 root root  15 1970-01-01 00:00 boot -> /dev/block/sdd7
lrwxrwxrwx 1 root root  15 1970-01-01 00:00 cache -> /dev/block/sdd5
lrwxrwxrwx 1 root root  15 1970-01-01 00:00 dts -> /dev/block/sdd8
lrwxrwxrwx 1 root root 15 1970-01-01 00:01 fastboot -> /dev/block/sdd2
lrwxrwxrwx 1 root root 15 1970-01-01 00:01 fip -> /dev/block/sdd4
lrwxrwxrwx 1 root root  15 1970-01-01 00:00 frp -> /dev/block/sdc1
lrwxrwxrwx 1 root root  15 1970-01-01 00:00 fw_lpm3 -> /dev/block/sdd6
lrwxrwxrwx 1 root root 15 1970-01-01 00:01 nvme -> /dev/block/sdd3
lrwxrwxrwx 1 root root 16 1970-01-01 00:01 reserved -> /dev/block/sdd12
lrwxrwxrwx 1 root root  16 1970-01-01 00:00 system -> /dev/block/sdd10
lrwxrwxrwx 1 root root  15 1970-01-01 00:00 trustfirmware -> /dev/block/sdd9
lrwxrwxrwx 1 root root  16 1970-01-01 00:00 userdata -> /dev/block/sdd13
lrwxrwxrwx 1 root root  16 1970-01-01 00:00 vendor -> /dev/block/sdd11
lrwxrwxrwx 1 root root  15 1970-01-01 00:00 xloader_reserved1 -> /dev/block/sdd1
```

The boot, recovery, vendor, system, cache, and userdata partitions are all canonical Android partitions and will be discussed shortly. The remaining partitions, though, are likely to be part of the proprietary system boot process.

> **Note**
>
> The inquisitive can take an even more accurate and low-level approach to identifying the partitions on a device by reading the partition map itself. Where mountable partitions have names that end in numbers (for example, sdd7, sdd11), the raw device is usually cataloged in /dev without any partition number (for example, sdd). The HiKey960 used in these examples, for instance, has four separate block storage devices: /dev/block/sda, /dev/block/sdb, /dev/block/sdc, and /dev/block/sdd.
>
> Each of these devices is likely to have a partition map. To decode that map directly, simply dump the first several thousand bytes from the device. Presuming adb is running as root, for instance:
>
> ```
> adb pull /dev/block/sdd
> ```
>
> There is no need to pull the entire file, so press Ctrl+C after a few seconds. Having obtained the file header using a byte dump tool like od and a description of the appropriate partition table format (https://en.wikipedia.org/wiki/GUID_Partition_Table), completely identifying all the partitions is simply a matter of time.

Some bootloaders support *unlocking*. Unlocking a bootloader is bypassing the cryptographic verification of the bootloader code before it is executed. Doing this allows the execution of bootloaders other than the one whose signature can be verified by the boot ROM. It also breaks chain of assurance and means that subsequent layers in the OS stack that implicitly trust their environment are in danger.

Because they are so nearly part of the hardware, there will be no more detailed investigation into bootloaders here. Roger Ye's book, *Embedded Programming with Android* (Ye, 2016), part of the Android Deep Dive Series, is an excellent investigation of this part of the boot process. In addition, Jonathan Levin's much more casual self-published essays on Android Internals (http://newandroidbook.com) document some deep and useful research.

Most Android bootloaders, like their large-scale computer counterparts (Grub, LILO, Open Firmware, or the various BIOSs), as their last task identify and initiate a successor. After all, the bootloader's only real reason for existence is to prepare the device for the real operating system. Bootloaders typically support simple user interfaces that can be used, among other things, to choose that successor. Android devices usually support three choices: fastboot, recovery, and normal Android boot.

Fastboot

Fastboot is a very lightweight system that is usually part of the bootloader itself. Although part of the bootloader, it bears separate discussion because it has a UI, as described in Chapter 2. Its functionality typically is limited to flashing the persistent storage of the device.

A system is usually forced into fastboot mode using some kind of hardware flag: flipping a DIP-switch or holding some combination of buttons during system startup. The bootloader inspects the switches as part of initialization and determines whether it should run the fastboot program or not.

Listing 6.3 is the continuation of the log started in Listing 6.1. It shows the initialization of the fastboot program that is part of a normal (non-fastboot) startup.

Listing 6.3 **fastboot Log**

```
main:     ******** Fastboot for Kirin *****************
main:     ******** Build Date: Jun 14 2018, 17:48:58 **
main: ******** Fastboot start at 1836 ms **********

main: print soc_id computed in xloader phase, is below:
main: 00000000  main: 00000000  main: 00000000  main: 00000000  main:
main: 00000000  main: 00000000  main: 00000000  main: 00000000  main:
led_alwayson: can't get dtb operators
bbox: bbox_register_module_ops success.
bfm: : >>>>>enter bfm_init
bfm: : [disable_boot_fail_system] boot_fail_system state is 0
clock: PLL Stat
```

```
clock: PLL2 ctrl0=0x04909604,ctrl1=0x02000000
clock: PLL2 acpu en_stat:0x00000008, acpu gt_stat:0x00040000
clock: PLL2 final en_stat:0x00100000, final gt_stat:0x00020000
clock: PLL3 ctrl0=0x04904005,ctrl1=0x07000000
clock: PLL3 acpu en_stat:0x00000000, acpu gt_stat:0x00000000
clock: PLL3 final en_stat:0x00200000, final gt_stat:0x00040000
clock: clock init OK
ufs: ufs start on platform[36600110]ufs: ufs current mode: 0x00000011
ufs: ufs current gear: 0x00000003
ufs: ufs mphy reg 0x4A = 0x00000000
ufs: bUD0BaseOffset: 0x00000010, bUDConfigPLength: 0x00000010
ufs: UFS device manufacturerid = 0x000001ad
ufs: UFS device: H****
bfm: : >>>>>enter set_boot_stage

<lines omitted …>

usbloader: iddq is 0x0000000000000000
usbloader: hpm is 0x0000000000000000
usbloader: dieid is 0x0a048009d1170d0a977947122140ee1c06d65993
load_kernel: Hikey960: Enable all ip regulator
pmu_ip: Hikey960:switch from PPLL0 to PPLL3
pmu_ip: Hikey960:Enable ispfunc
pmu_ip: Hikey960:Enable clock-gating
pmu_ip: [regulator_power_all_enable] all IP regulator is power on!
load_kernel: set ISP_CORE_CTRL_S to unsec, val = 0x00000007
load_kernel: set ISP_SUB_CTRL_S to unsec, val = 0x0000000f
load_kernel:
```

Kernel

At this point, the bootloader is ready to load and run the kernel. Listing 6.4 is a continuation of the boot log started in Listing 6.1 and continued in Listing 6.3.

The complete log of the kernel boot contains a wealth of useful information. In reading the log, it is important to remember that with the kernel come multiple processes. The log is no longer a single path through ordered tasks. It is now the interleaved output of multiple processes that may be running simultaneously.

The listing is extremely abbreviated. Excellent documentation is available elsewhere that describes the kernel boot process. This log shows only a few highlights.

Note that this log was produced by booting the kernel built in Chapter 4.

Also note the initialization of a couple of the key Android components mentioned in Chapter 4, ion (hisi_ion at time 0.000000) and ashmen (at time 1.891833).

Finally, note that the log shows the command line with which the kernel was started. This command line is a key means of communicating configuration information to the kernel.

The bootloader finds the kernel in the device storage boot partition (shown in Listing 6.4), one of the canonical partitions on an Android system. Unlike the Linux systems common on larger machines, the storage partition that holds the kernel is not mounted in the Android file system. Although the bootloader (and, in fact, any other application with low-level access to the storage device) can read and probably even write to boot partition, the partition does not contain a file system, files, or catalogs and is never mounted in the Android file tree.

To maintain the chain of trust, the bootloader verifies the kernel code by computing its cryptographic signature and comparing it to the signature stored on the device (which was, in turn, verified when the hardware verified the bootloader).

Listing 6.4 **Kernel Boot Log**

```
load_kernel:

----boot time is 3442 ms----
load_kernel: boot_from_bl31: boot to trusted firmware. addr=0x00000000
[    0.000000] Booting Linux on physical CPU 0x0
[    0.000000] Initializing cgroup subsys cpuset
[    0.000000] Initializing cgroup subsys cpu
[    0.000000] Initializing cgroup subsys cpuacct
[    0.000000] Initializing cgroup subsys schedtune
[    0.000000] Linux version 4.4.59-02536-g679a543 (jstultz@buildbox) (gcc version
5.4.0 20160609 (Ubuntu/Linaro 5.4.0-6ubuntu1~16.04.4) ) #2507 SMP PREEMPT Wed Aug 9
09:52:10 PDT 2017
[    0.000000] Boot CPU: AArch64 Processor [410fd034]
[    0.000000] efi: Getting EFI parameters from FDT:
[    0.000000] efi: UEFI not found.
[    0.000000] Ion: base 0xbe200000, size is 0x1e00000, node name graphic, heap-name
    carveout_gralloc namesize 17, [99] [97] [114] [118]
[    0.000000] Ion: insert heap-name carveout_gralloc
[    0.000000] Reserved memory: initialized node graphic, compatible id hisi_ion
[    0.000000] Reserved memory: created CMA memory pool at 0x0000000016c00000, size
64 MiB
[    0.000000] Reserved memory: initialized node fastboot-cma-mem, compatible id
shared-dma-pool
[    0.000000] cma: Reserved 64 MiB at 0x00000000ba000000
[    0.000000] On node 0 totalpages: 785600
[    0.000000]    DMA zone: 12288 pages used for memmap
[    0.000000]    DMA zone: 0 pages reserved
[    0.000000]    DMA zone: 785600 pages, LIFO batch:31
[    0.000000] psci: probing for conduit method from DT.
[    0.000000] psci: PSCIv1.0 detected in firmware.
[    0.000000] psci: Using standard PSCI v0.2 function IDs
[    0.000000] psci: MIGRATE_INFO_TYPE not supported.
```

```
[    0.000000] PERCPU: Embedded 19 pages/cpu @ffffffc0be100000 s47256 r0 d30568 u77824
[    0.000000] pcpu-alloc: s47256 r0 d30568 u77824 alloc=19*4096
[    0.000000] pcpu-alloc: [0] 0 [0] 1 [0] 2 [0] 3 [0] 4 [0] 5 [0] 6 [0] 7
[    0.000000] Detected VIPT I-cache on CPU0
[    0.000000] CPU features: enabling workaround for ARM erratum 845719
[    0.000000] Built 1 zonelists in Zone order, mobility grouping on.  Total pages:
773312
[    0.000000] Kernel command line: androidboot.hardware=hikey960
androidboot.selinux=permissive firmware_class.path=/system/etc/firmware loglevel=15
buildvariant=userdebug androidboot.swtype=normal
fastboot_version=DailyBuild_201708091533_FASTBOOT setup_logctl=1 fastbootdmd=0
enter_recovery=0 androidboot.mode=normal low_volt_flag=1 boardid=0x000014b5
normal_reset_type=coldboot ddr_die=3072M@0M  efuse_status=2
androidboot.serialno=0123456789ABCDEF himntn=1111111111111101011111101001100010001
boot_slice=0x00019c31 reboot_reason=AP_S_COLDBOOT recovery_update=0 userlock=locked
bootlock=unlocked hw_bfm_enable=0 ddr_density=3 swiotlb=2 mdmreglogbase=0x00000000
mdmreglogsize=0x00000000 modem_socp_enable=0 androidboot.hardware=HiKey960
androidboot.veritymode=enforcing androidboot.verifiedbootstate=ORANGE
ufs_product_name=THGBF7G8K4LBATRC format_data=1 cpu_buck_reg=0x;;
androidboot.ddrsize=3 kce_status=1  console=ttyAMA6,115200

<lines omitted …>

[    1.891833] ashmem: initialized

<lines omitted …>

[    6.895248] usb 1-1.5: new high-speed USB device number 4 using xhci-hcd
[    6.902456] Freeing unused kernel memory: 1016K (ffffff800901b000 -
ffffff8009119000)
```

The File System

As part of initialization, the kernel mounts the Android file system. Listing 6.5 shows the root of that file system. Several of these partitions were introduced in Chapter 5.

Listing 6.5   **Android File System**

```
rootfs on / type rootfs (ro,seclabel,size=1444252k,nr_inodes=361063)
tmpfs on /dev type tmpfs (rw,seclabel,nosuid,relatime,mode=755)
devpts on /dev/pts type devpts (rw,seclabel,relatime,mode=600,ptmxmode=000)
proc on /proc type proc (rw,relatime)
sysfs on /sys type sysfs (rw,seclabel,relatime)
selinuxfs on /sys/fs/selinux type selinuxfs (rw,relatime)
none on /acct type cgroup (rw,relatime,cpuacct)
none on /dev/memcg type cgroup (rw,relatime,memory)
none on /dev/stune type cgroup (rw,relatime,schedtune)
tmpfs on /mnt type tmpfs (rw,seclabel,relatime,mode=755,gid=1000)
```

```
none on /config type configfs (rw,relatime)
none on /dev/cpuctl type cgroup (rw,relatime,cpu)
none on /dev/cpuset type cgroup
(rw,relatime,cpuset,noprefix,release_agent=/sbin/cpuset_release_agent)
pstore on /sys/fs/pstore type pstore (rw,seclabel,relatime)
/sys/kernel/debug on /sys/kernel/debug type debugfs (rw,seclabel,relatime,mode=755)
/dev/block/sdd10 on /system type ext4 (ro,seclabel,relatime,data=ordered)
/dev/block/sdd5 on /cache type ext4
(rw,seclabel,relatime,discard,noauto_da_alloc,data=ordered)
/dev/block/sdd13 on /data type ext4
(rw,seclabel,relatime,discard,noauto_da_alloc,data=ordered)
tmpfs on /storage type tmpfs (rw,seclabel,relatime,mode=755,gid=1000)
tracefs on /sys/kernel/debug/tracing type tracefs (rw,seclabel,relatime)
```

The key section of Listing 6.5 is the last five lines, which show the mount points for three of the six (five, before Android release 26) canonical Android partitions. These important partitions were introduced in Chapter 5, and again in Listing 6.2, where they appeared as named partitions found on the main block storage device. They are system, cache, and data.

- **system (/system):** This is the read-only part of the Android file system discussed in Chapter 5. It is sometimes called the ROM, although its contents are not sufficient to create a running Android system, and the ability to write to it is controlled only by software.

- **cache (/cache):** System cache. Originally, this partition kept such things as optimization data for Android's just-in-time Java compiler. It now holds a wider variety of ephemeral data. It is a separate partition so that it can be easily erased when, for instance, a system update renders it useless.

- **userdata (/data):** System managed writeable data. Also introduced in Chapter 5, this is where Android applications are stored and where the system stored the data that is private to a given application.

These partitions are essential and will be found on every Android device. In recent versions of Android, they are often mounted by name from the directory shown in Listing 6.2.

In addition, several other partitions appear frequently on Android devices. The boot partition has already been discussed as the location of the kernel. A few common partitions are

- **boot (unmounted):** As discussed earlier, this is the partition that contains the Linux kernel.

- **vendor (/vendor)** Android Oreo introduced Project Treble, Google's effort to separate the Android system binaries from the proprietary vendor binaries necessary to shim the hardware to the OS. Vendor proprietary code is now stored on the vendor partition, where it can be updated independently. This partition was also mentioned in Chapter 5.

- **recovery (unmounted):** Another partition that is never mounted or used by the Android system. It contains the operating and file systems for the recovery system, discussed later in this chapter. It is very similar to the boot partition but used for recovery mode.

- **persist (unmounted):** Many vendors and carriers have found it useful to store mutable information in a way that is not destroyed when the phone is reset. Those that are willing to be blatant about this "feature" may choose an obvious name for it. Others may choose a subtler name. This partition is usually accessed through a special driver and available only to privileged applications.

- **radio (unmounted):** This partition contains the operating and file systems for the cellular radio processor. Its contents are likely to be quite proprietary.

- **storage (/sdcard):** Most Android systems support relatively unprotected bulk storage. Originally, this was likely to be removable (Micro SD cards) and was mounted at /sdcard. When Android moved away from removable media and added support for multiple users, the mount point was changed. Soft links point /sdcard at the appropriate emulated file system.

- **product and odm (/product and /odm)** Introduced to the platform in Android versions 9 and 10, respectively, these partitions were described in Chapter 5. They provide additional flexibility, allowing a single hardware image to support multiple similar devices. Software for a specific device can be configured to read only the data and code that apply to it.

init

As the last step of the process of booting Linux, the kernel starts the init application. init is the first application to run in a completely normal application environment, so called *userspace*, with mapped virtual memory, a mounted file system, and no direct access to hardware. It is also the root of the process tree, process id 0, and the ancestor of every other process.

Listing 6.6 shows the last phase of device boot, again, edited heavily to save space.

Listing 6.6 **init Boot Log**

```
[    6.912976] init: init first stage started!
[    6.934559] init: Early mount skipped (missing/incompatible fstab in device tree)
[    6.942061] init: Loading SELinux policy
[    7.031172] random: init: uninitialized urandom read (40 bytes read, 45 bits of
entropy available)
[    7.032940] init: init second stage started!
[    7.036781] init: property_set("ro.boot.hardware", "HiKey960") failed: property
already set
[    7.041578] init: Running restorecon...
[    7.109305] init: waitpid failed: No child processes
[    7.109546] init: Couldn't load properties from /odm/default.prop: No such file or
directory
[    7.109604] init: Couldn't load properties from /vendor/default.prop: No such file
or directory
```

```
[    7.110252] init: Created socket '/dev/socket/property_service', mode 666, user 0,
group 0
[    7.110322] init: Parsing file /init.rc...
[    7.110559] init: Added '/init.environ.rc' to import list
[    7.110568] init: Added '/init.usb.rc' to import list
[    7.110584] init: Added '/init.hikey960.rc' to import list
[    7.110591] init: Added '/init.usb.configfs.rc' to import list
[    7.110601] init: Added '/init.zygote64_32.rc' to import list
[    7.111239] init: Parsing file /init.environ.rc...
[    7.111304] init: Parsing file /init.usb.rc...
[    7.111547] init: Parsing file /init.hikey960.rc...

<lines omitted …>

[    7.115910] init: processing action (wait_for_coldboot_done)
[    7.380541] init: Command 'wait_for_coldboot_done' action=wait_for_coldboot_done
returned 0 took 264.577ms.
[    7.380569] init: processing action (mix_hwrng_into_linux_rng)
[    7.380601] init: /dev/hw_random not found
[    7.380633] init: processing action (set_mmap_rnd_bits)
[    7.381191] init: processing action (set_kptr_restrict)
[    7.381366] init: processing action (keychord_init)
[    7.381384] init: processing action (console_init)
[    7.381424] init: processing action (init)

<lines omitted …>

[    8.197664] init: computing context for service 'hidl_memory'
[    8.197820] init: starting service 'hidl_memory'...
[    8.198948] init: computing context for service 'bluetooth-1-0'
[    8.199153] init: starting service 'bluetooth-1-0'...
[    8.199873] init: computing context for service 'configstore-hal-1-0'
[    8.200025] init: starting service 'configstore-hal-1-0'...
[    8.200707] init: computing context for service 'wifi_hal_legacy'
[    8.200852] init: starting service 'wifi_hal_legacy'...
[    8.201482] init: starting service 'healthd'...
[    8.202088] init: computing context for service 'lmkd'
[    8.202241] init: starting service 'lmkd'...
[    8.202976] init: computing context for service 'servicemanager'
[    8.203120] init: starting service 'servicemanager'...
[    8.203804] init: computing context for service 'surfaceflinger'
[    8.203935] init: starting service 'surfaceflinger'...

<lines omitted …>

[   11.087269] init: computing context for service 'bootanim'
[   11.087503] init: starting service 'bootanim'...
```

```
[   13.044371] init: processing action (sys.sysctl.extra_free_kbytes=*)
[   14.099973] init: computing context for service 'wpa_supplicant'
[   14.100518] init: starting service 'wpa_supplicant'...
[   14.102545] init: Created socket '/dev/socket/wpa_wlan0', mode 660, user 1010,
group 1010
[   15.089361] init: processing action (sys.boot_completed=1)
```

The listing highlights several important things. The first is that init runs in multiple phases. The first phase is initialization and configuration. In it, init examines the file system and sets up communications with the kernel. One of the key means of accomplishing this communication uses the /sys and /proc file systems.

As noted in Chapter 4, the file system, a hierarchical arrangement of files and directories of files, is largely an abstraction created by the kernel. Drivers in the kernel organize the raw, flat blocks presented by hardware storage devices into the familiar tree of directories and files.

Again, because the kernel creates the file system, more or less, out of thin air, no need exists for it to restrict the abstraction to block storage devices. In fact, the /proc storage system is, precisely, kernel memory cataloged as files. Applications with write permission on certain files in /proc can write directly to kernel memory. Although many programs can read the files in /proc, init is one of the few that can write to them. This is how it communicates with the kernel.

In its second stage, init reads and parses its configuration files, usually named "init.<something>.rc." The locations and contents of these files are described in some detail in a README file in the AOSP init source (https://android.googlesource.com/platform/system/core/+/master/init/README.md).

init starts a very limited number of Linux daemons and then the root process of the Android system, Zygote.

Recovery

As shown in Figure 6.1, many Android devices support an alternate boot path: Recovery Mode. Unlike fastboot, recovery mode boots a complete, if limited, operating system. It has a full network stack, can mount and unmount volumes, runs adb and a shell, and so on. Although it is a complete, if minimal, Linux, recovery mode does not start the Android container. It is similar to the "safe-mode" on larger systems.

Some devices have pre-installed, proprietary recovery systems. Obtaining the source for them will require contacting the board manufacturer. AOSP also contains code for a flashable recovery image in the bootable/recovery directory. To generate the flashable image file, recovery.img, use the make target the recoveryimage:

```
make -j9 recoveryimage
```

In addition, there have been other well-known recovery systems; among them ClockworkMod and Team Win Recovery Project (TWRP). Both are open source.

The source for the ClockworkMod recovery system is included in the source for Lineage OS, formerly CyanogenMod, in the `android_bootable_recovery-cm` repository. As of this writing, although the code continues to be available in the repositories of the old CyanogenMod organization, it does not appear to be maintained there. The version in the Lineage repositories (https://github.com/LineageOS) is maintained and up to date.

The source for TWRP is also on GitHub (https://github.com/TeamWin). It is in active development and has been ported to a wide variety of hardware platforms.

Building a Daemon

One of the biggest advantages of being a developer creating a custom Android for a new device is the ability to add Linux level daemons. All Android programs run in the Android container, rather like a web server, and are thus one layer of abstraction removed from the operating system and the hardware. An application installed in a typical Android system—regardless of whether it is written in Java, C, or even assembler—has very little control, even over when it starts and stops. It is a group of components that are created and destroyed as necessary by the container.

When building a custom Android, however, adding a new native daemon requires no more than writing the necessary code, probably C, and starting it from `init`.

The unique hardware feature in the Acme device is a proximity sensor.

Note

The Acme device is actually emulated with the same HiKey960 used in previous chapters and an attached Arduino Uno. The Arduino is configured as a capacitive proximity sensor as described on the Arduino website at https://playground.arduino.cc/Main/CapacitiveSensor.

The Arduino periodically reports proximity levels over its USB serial port using a simple binary protocol. The Android device, the HiKey960, sees the Arduino as a readable USB serial device. You can find the code for the project, along with all the rest of the code in this book, in the GitHub repo at https://github.com/InsideAndroidOS/.

The first approximation to porting the new hardware to Android will be a daemon that reads the proximity sensor and reports the values by logging them to the system log.

Creating the Acme Device

Chapter 2 outlined the process of customizing Android for a new device, the HiKey960. The process involved downloading some hardware-specific code, necessary for the HiKey device, and modifying the AOSP manifest to include it. The next step extends those modifications to create an entirely new device, the Acme One.

An Android device is defined by two directories in the source tree, one in .../device and one in .../vendor. The former is where most of the action is.

A device is represented in .../device as a two-level hierarchy. The first layer represents an organization, in this case Acme. The second represents the specific device; in our case, the One.

> **Note**
>
> Unless explicitly stated otherwise, all directory paths from this point on are relative to the root of the build directory, the directory from which the repo tool was run. They are specified without a leading "/" or "...".

In addition to creating a home for device code, you must register a new device in the build system. Prior to Android 7, registering the device was accomplished using a special script, vendorsetup.sh, which would be detected and included by the envsetup.sh script. The vendorsetup.sh script would call the special function, add_lunch_combo, to add device-specific options to the lunch menu. With the Soong build system, this is now accomplished via the AndroidProducts.mk makefile by setting the special variable, COMMON_LUNCH_CHOICES.

The AndroidProducts.mk file for a device is likely to register at least a couple of builds because a given device may be built in several different ways. The type of the build is encoded in the values set in the COMMON_LUNCH_CHOICES variable.

The variable's value must contain exactly one hyphen ("-"). The build system parses the variable values, separating each at the hyphen, before the hyphen, the name of the device to be built and after the hyphen, the build type. The name of the device can be anything descriptive. There are, though, exactly three build types:

- **eng:** eng builds are debugging builds. They include a variety of debugging tools that would be a waste of space except during development. adb runs as root by default on an eng build.

- **userdebug:** userdebug builds are similar to eng builds but have fewer debugging tools. They were originally intended for debugging on hardware with limited storage space. adb does not run as root by default on a userdebug build, but the su command works.

- **user:** user builds are production releases. All debugging software is stripped, adb is not run at all by default, and it cannot be run as root, if started.

Only one of these three words will work, after the hyphen, as the values of COMMON_LUNCH_CHOICES.

Listing 6.7 demonstrates creating a directory for the Acme One device and registering all three possible build types.

Listing 6.7 **Registering the Acme One Device**

```
mkdir -p device/acme/one
cat > device/acme/one/ AndroidProducts.mk
COMMON_LUNCH_CHOICES := \
        acme_one-eng \
        acme_one-userdebug \
        acme_one-user

PRODUCT_MAKEFILES := \
        $(LOCAL_DIR)/acme_one.mk
^D
```

The Acme One device is now registered. After you re-run setenv.sh, it is visible in the Lunch menu.

Listing 6.8 **Acme Lunch**

```
. build/envsetup.sh
including device/acme/one/vendorsetup.sh
including device/asus/fugu/vendorsetup.sh
...

> lunch

You're building on Linux

Lunch menu... pick a combo:
      1. acme_one-eng
      2. acme_one-user
      3. acme_one-userdebug
      4. aosp_arm-eng
      5. aosp_arm64-eng
      6. aosp_blueline-userdebug
      7. aosp_bonito-userdebug
...
      45. uml-userdebug
```

Choosing one of the Acme builds at this point will cause an error. Although the device has been registered, it has not yet been set up.

Repo Again

The new device is now registered with the build system. It is not yet, however, registered in the repo manifest. The new directories and their contents cannot yet be downloaded or managed using the repo tool (as can the rest of the source tree). Let's fix that.

Chapter 2 described the organization of a hypothetical git service for the Acme project, located at https:/acme.net/acme/source. It is time to add several new repositories to that service. (Note that this is the hypothetical project source. The code from this book can be found online at https://github.com/InsideAndroidOS/)

Figure 2.2 (in Chapter 2) showed the manifest for the first fork of the AOSP code. That fork did not actually create space for any Acme-specific code at all; it just made room for the non-AOSP code for the HiKey960 device and for the new kernel created in Chapter 4. Listing 6.9 shows the fragment of the new manifest with additional repos for Acme-specific code.

Listing 6.9   **The Acme One Manifest**

```
<!-- Acme Specific Projects -->

  <project path="device/acme/one/acme_one"
          name="platform_device_acme_one_acme_one" remote="acme" >
    <linkfile src="acme_one.mk" dest="device/acme/one/acme_one.mk" />
    <linkfile src="AndroidProducts.makefile"
              dest="device/acme/one/AndroidProducts.mk" />
  </project>
  <project path="device/acme/one/proximity"
          name="platform_device_acme_one_proximity"
          remote="acme" />
  <project path="device/acme/one/app/simple_daemon"
          name="platform_device_acme_one_app_simple_daemon"
          remote="acme" />
  <project path="vendor/acme/one/interfaces"
          name="platform_vendor_acme_one_interfaces"
          remote="acme" />
  <project path="device/linaro/hikey"
          name="platform_device_linaro_hikey"
          remote="acme"
          revision="acme"
          groups="device,hikey,pdk" />
```

The vendor repo contains the binderized HAL definition. It is used along with the HiKey960 vendor tree, which is populated by a setup script in the HiKey device tree. The Acme device still requires the non-AOSP device-specific vendor configuration. Perhaps surprisingly, even with the addition of the code for the new device, the manifest still forks the code for the HiKey device, on which it is based.

This is an unfortunate reality. Ideally, the Acme device would simply reference code in the HiKey device directory, on which it depends. Practically, because of idiosyncrasies in the build system, it is nearly inevitable that it will be necessary to modify the code for the device on which the Acme One is based—in this case, the HiKey960. Forking the dependency makes it possible to maintain control over updates. The Acme device will depend on the forked HiKey device and the stable, forked version of the HiKey code. This makes applying updates from the upstream authoritative source in a managed and predictable way possible.

The first repository in the Acme-specific section of the manifest is the first new one: platform_ device_acme_one_acme_one. This is the root of the Acme One device tree. A couple irritating constraints govern it.

The first is that it cannot be checked out as the actual root of the Acme device tree. Because of the way repo works, it cannot be device/acme/one. Instead, following the pattern set at the root of the AOSP tree, this repository gets checked out as device/acme/one/acme_one, and then the files from it that must be cataloged in device/acme/one are linked by the tool into the parent directory.

The second constraint is imposed by the build system, which looks for files with names that follow specific naming conventions. The files required at the root of the Acme One device tree must be at the root—and they may not be anywhere else. The files in the one base repository must have names that are sufficiently different from those that the build system recognizes so that they do not confuse it.

The other three new repositories are the implementation of the new daemon. Because the code that accesses the new hardware (the proximity sensor) will eventually be used not only in this daemon but also to plumb the new sensor into Android, it is implemented as a separate library. The library and the include file that describe its API comprise two of the three. The third is the implementation of the actual daemon.

Starting the Daemon

As described earlier in this chapter, starting the daemon code requires that a script be run by the init process during system startup. The script is straightforward in its content: It defines a "service" that points to the daemon binary and applies certain attributes to it. The Acme One proximity sensor daemon should not run until the system is fully up, all file systems have been mounted, and its startup requires no special action. Because it is so nearly generic, the service can be part of the main class: init will start it with all other services of this class during the main phase. The service will execute as the system user and within the system group. Listing 6.10 shows the content of the init script.

Listing 6.10 **Acme One Proximity Sensor init Script**   .

```
service acmesimpledaemon /vendor/bin/hw/acmesimpledaemon
    class main
    user system
```

```
group system
oneshot
```

Because the daemon is dependent on a specific USB device being plugged into the system, it is marked as a oneshot service. This means if the process exits, the init process will not attempt to restart it. Ideally, the daemon would be written so it would wait for the necessary device(s) or dependencies to be present before starting. Were it written that way, the oneshot property would be removed so that, if the daemon died or exited, init would automatically restart it. This simple example does not wait for the device to appear, so oneshot is necessary.

The script is located in the device/acme/one/app/simple_daemon directory, alongside the daemon source. The Soong blueprint file used to build the daemon also specifies the init script, as shown in Listing 6.11.

Listing 6.11   Acme One Proximity Sensor Daemon `Android.bp`

```
cc_binary {
    name: "acmesimpledaemon",
    relative_install_path: "hw",
    init_rc: ["vendor.acmesimpledaemon.acme.one.rc"],
    header_libs: [
        "libacmeproximityshim_headers",
        "liblog_headers",
    ],
    srcs: [
        "acme-simple-daemon.cpp"
    ],
    shared_libs: [
        "liblog",
        "libcutils",
    ],
    static_libs: [
        "libacmeproximityshim",
    ],
    vendor: true,
    proprietary: true,
}
```

The script in Listing 6.10 is processed by init, starting the daemon as part of the normal Acme One system startup. Unless the system SE policy information is updated to include details about the daemon, though, it will not run for very long! The daemon accesses the proximity sensor via USB serial device interface, which normal processes cannot access. Recall from Chapter 5 that the SE's default behavior is to deny permissions and access to everything. This includes executing a binary, loading special files, and so on. Because the daemon accesses a device, it requires an SE policy that permits file operations and access to USB serial interface device files.

Note

The simple daemon described here demonstrates how a custom daemon for a platform can be created and added to the platform, including access to device interface files. Not all custom platform daemons will require device access, but they will still require a customized SE policy. The device file in use here is /dev/ttyUSB0, but this could be anything exposed by the kernel. It is critical that any custom AOSP-based device limits a daemon's access to hardware interfaces for security purposes and also to pass CTS/VTS.

Even though the daemon executes as the system user/group, allowing it to have full access to everything in the system_app domain is dangerously insecure. The SE policy file for all Acme proximity daemons (more will be created in the HAL chapters), shown in Listing 6.12, defines a new application domain as well as an execution domain for the binary and grants for access to the components it needs to do its work.

Listing 6.12   **Acme One Proximity Sensor Daemon SE Policy**

```
init_daemon_domain(proximityd)

type proximityd, domain;
type proximityd_exec, vendor_file_type, exec_type, file_type;

allow proximityd serial_device:chr_file rw_file_perms;
```

A key detail in this SE policy file is the use of the init_daemon_domain macro. This sets up the proximityd domain as an init started daemon. What exactly does that mean? It means that it sets up the SE *process domain* as the domain to which the process initiated by proximityd_exec automatically transfers. Without this, the daemon would fail to start because the SE rules for init do not allow it to execute another binary unless the new process changes domains!

The SE file for the proximity daemon is located in device/acme/one/sepolicy/proximityd.te.

In addition to the proximityd domain and execution type, the SE policy file also contains an allow rule that grants the daemon access to serial devices for reading/writing. This is necessary to allow the daemon to access the proximity sensor (which, as mentioned earlier, is connected via USB serial device).

This is still not quite enough, though, because the default AOSP SE policies do not label the USB serial device interfaces as serial_device. Now that a SE domain and context have been defined, they need to be applied to the daemon binary; otherwise, it will not be available for execution by `init`. The two file context changes require adding two lines to the SE file context details for the platform. Recall this is accomplished using a union of the SE file, `file_contexts`. This file is located at `device/acme/one/sepolicy/file_contexts`, shown in Listing 6.13.

Listing 6.13 **Acme One SE Context Labels**

```
# Acme One Specific Changes
/dev/ttyUSB[0-9]*              u:object_r:serial_device:s0
/vendor/bin/hw/acmesimpledaemon    u:object_r:proximityd_exec:s0
```

With all of these SE policy changes and additions in place, the Acme One build for the HiKey960 starts `acmesimpledaemon` during system startup.

Summary

This chapter outlines the process of booting Linux in an Android system and describes creating a new, pure Linux daemon. It outlines the behavior of the root of the process tree, `init`, and demonstrates using `init` to start the daemon process. It also outlines the somewhat arduous task of configuring SE Linux to accommodate starting a new hardware-based daemon.

## 7

Android Startup: Dalvik and Zygote

Chapter 6 reviewed the process of booting the Linux system. This chapter investigates the startup of Android's subsystems.

The processes are quite analogous. Figure 2.1 depicted an Android system as a layer cake; each new layer depending on services provided by the underlying layer. The Linux kernel provides a "container," an environment that abstracts hardware into standard resources and facilities in which programs run.

Similarly, Android is a container. It provides abstract services to applications that run "inside" it. Thinking of the Linux kernel as a container is a useful exercise because Android is a container in exactly the sense usually reserved, for instance, for web servers. Android applications are not associated with the processes that power them in the way that most applications are.

A typical desktop application owns its process: It is application code that gets control when the application starts up. Although it may include code from third-party libraries, invoke code in memory shared with other applications, use services from other processes either local or through network connections, it is application code that is at the bottom of the call stack. The application code may temporarily delegate control elsewhere but it always gets it back. At the extreme, it is the application that makes the call that terminates its process.

This is not the case for Android applications. An Android application, even one that has been completely compiled to native code, is not in control of its process. Instead, exactly as is the case with many web service containers, it is the container that controls an Android application process. In Android, that container is a program called **Zygote**.

To start a new Android application, the Android system creates a new process (using the `clone` system call) that is a copy of the already-running Zygote. The new instance of Zygote loads the components for the target application and invokes them as appropriate. In contrast to the typical desktop application, then, Zygote may temporarily delegate control to the application, but it is *Zygote* that always gets control back.

Perhaps even more interesting, even Zygote does not get control over when an application stops. As described in Chapter 4, the most common way for an Android application to be terminated is that the operating system terminates it with a `kill -9` when it needs memory for other applications. Exactly as with a web server, the Android system creates a process for an application only when its services are required and terminates the process when its resources are required for some other application. Zygote will be discussed in detail in the second half of this chapter.

Another important service that Android provides is the interpreter. A single Android application can run on a wide variety of hardware platforms: Intel, multiple ARM architectures, and even (dramatically less common) MIPS. This feat is accomplished through the use of an **intermediate language (IL)**.

Intermediate languages, popularized by the Java language, are machine languages for virtual computers. The idea is that code written in a computer language such as Java, designed to be read and written by human beings, is compiled to the intermediate language. The intermediate language is a machine language for a virtual computer: hardware that probably doesn't actually exist. Running applications written in the intermediate language on a given real computer requires an application—a compiled binary that uses the native instructions of the target computer—that interprets successive instructions in the virtual machine language, translates each into one or more native instructions, and executes those native instructions. This program is called the interpreter or **virtual machine (VM)**.

Clearly, a virtual machine has a cost in efficiency. If it takes three native instructions to execute a single instruction from the intermediate language, and if that intermediate language instruction is not significantly more powerful than a single native instruction, then it will take three times as long to run a program that is compiled to the intermediate language (and then run in the virtual machine) as it would to run exactly the same program compiled to native instructions and run directly.

The benefit of a virtual machine, however, is portability. Instead of having multiple binary versions of an application—one for each target computer architecture—there is a single intermediate language "binary." It is only the virtual machine that interprets the intermediate language that must be built separately for each architecture. An intermediate language binary can be run on any architecture that has an implementation of the virtual machine.

Portability is essential to the Android model and, therefore, most Android code is compiled to an intermediate language, DEX, the IL used by the original Android virtual machine, Dalvik.

Dalvik

Dalvik, the DVM (Dalvik Virtual Machine), was the original virtual machine for Android. ART, the Android Runtime, succeeded it in Lollipop, API 21. Although Dalvik is gone, a brief discussion of its design will introduce its successor.

Though it may seem obvious, the most important thing to note about Dalvik is that it has almost nothing at all to do with Java. It is not a JVM. It isn't designed like a JVM, and it doesn't act like a JVM. It cannot execute Java bytecode, and the constraints that drove its architecture are very different from those that drove the design of the JVM.

Efficiency means a very different thing on a mobile device; especially the small, underpowered (both in CPU and battery) devices that were the targets for the original Android OS. On a rack-mounted machine, efficiency means 100 percent usage: memory full and CPU running at full speed. If the machine has spare cycles, using those cycles to pre-compute values that might be useful in the future makes sense. Even if those values have only a 30 percent chance of being used, computing them in advance will make the machine appear, on average, to run 30 percent faster.

For a mobile device, the situation is dramatically different. By far the most valuable resource on a mobile device is the battery. Parsimony with power was an essential goal in the design of Dalvik.

Note

I, Blake, experimented with Java and Linux on early smartphones. Even after making all the obvious optimizations, the batteries on the fairly typical devices with which I experimented lasted between 20 and 40 minutes under normal usage.

Another of the central goals in the design of Java's virtual machine was portability. It is a stack-based machine: Most op-codes operate on operands that have been pushed onto a system stack by previous operations. Although nearly all real hardware is register based, the JVM makes absolutely no assumptions about the host's architecture.

One artifact of Java's focus on portability is the API through which it interacts with the host operating system. All Java developers are familiar with the fairly elegant API (the various java.* packages) that their programs import and use and through which they interact with the Java runtime environment. A second API, the one through which the Java runtime environment interacts with the host operating system, is an abstraction that is much less familiar but at least as elegant. It is a clever and extensible API that makes porting Java to a new OS straightforward, if not quite trivial.

Portability was not even in the running as a goal for Dalvik. Although Dalvik has been ported to a few hardware architectures, most of those architectures are versions of ARM. In addition, Dalvik runs on only one operating system, Android/Linux. The abstractions that make it a relatively simple task to port Java to a new OS would be completely pointless for Dalvik and do not exist.

Because a register-based virtual architecture more closely matches the architectures of their target hardware, compilers that target a register-based VM may be able to do a better job of preparing their output so that it can be pre-optimized for the target hardware. This makes power consuming just-in-time (**JIT**) optimization—essential for a high-performance JVM—less important for the DVM. In fact, in the early versions of Android, Dalvik had no JIT optimizer at all.

This is the biggest difference between the Dalvik VM and the Java VM. To squeeze the last drop of performance out of the underpowered CPUs for which it was designed, Dalvik is register based, not stack based.

Although still a subject of debate, many academic studies (for example, [Davis, 2003]) seem to agree that a given program can be represented with fewer instructions in a register-based intermediate language than in a stack-based VM: The stack-based VM must move each operand onto its stack before it can use it. On the other hand, individual instructions in a register-based intermediate language are likely to be bigger (more bits) than their stack-based counterparts. In the register-based IL, each instruction must allocate bits used to specify the locations of each of its operands. In a stack-based language, however, the location of the operands is implicit: on the stack.

According to the research, these two opposing influences on the size of the IL binary do not balance out. The studies suggest that the representation of a program in a register-based IL, although it contains fewer instructions, is likely to be overall larger than the same program represented in a stack-based IL. To counteract this bloat, Dalvik has some clever tricks up its sleeve to reduce the size of its binaries.

The dex compiler translates Java .class files into .dex files. Unlike the Java compiler, however, which creates a separate .class file for each Java class, the dex compiler produces a single .dex file for an entire application. This provides the opportunity for its most important space-saving trick. The dex compiler tries very hard never to say the same thing twice.

DEX format is thoroughly documented on the Android Source website (https://source.android.com/devices/tech/dalvik/dex-format). Generally, it is structured as shown in Figure 7.1.

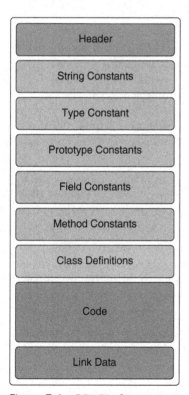

Figure 7.1   DEX File Structure

Dex structure has two key differences from the structure of Java's package for an application's bytecode, the Java Archive or .jar file.

The most significant difference is that, in a .jar file, the structure shown in Figure 7.1 is repeated for each class in the source code. Because the jar contains multiple files, there are several string constant pools, several code definition blocks, several method signature definition pools, and so on. The .dex file contains the entire program. There is only one of each of the blocks.

The global structure of the .dex file provides the first opportunity for optimization. In this format, every object is represented in the file exactly once. A reference to an object is simply its offset into the block in which the object is defined.

For instance, if two different classes each contain a method whose signature is View findViewById(int) (different classes may contain methods with exactly the same name), those two method definitions will be represented in the respective class definitions by offsets into the methods constants section for the definitions of the method. Those two definitions, though they point to different code, will contain references to exactly the same constants in the strings constants section that define the method name and to exactly the same constants in the types constants section, where the method signature is defined. This extensive use of references dramatically reduces the size of the .dex file.

As a further example, consider the definitions for two dissimilar methods:

```
void setWallpaper(android.graphics.Bitmap arg)
```

and

```
void setWallpaper(java.io.InputStream arg)
```

In a .dex file, these two definitions are nearly identical and take exactly the same amount of space. The only difference is that the reference to the type of the parameter in one (a reference to the type java.io.InputStream) is different than the reference to the type of the parameter in the other (a reference to the type android.graphics.Bitmap). There are two function prototype definitions, but each uses all but one element from the other: a considerable savings in space.

Dalvik, for all its good points, leaves significant room for improvement. The most important problem is that, because it is a virtual machine, it does the work of translating each intermediate language instruction every time an application is run. Similarly, a just-in-time optimizer, the state of the art for virtual machines, is a wasteful choice when power use is a crucial consideration.

The Dalvik JIT does store optimizer information across runs of a given application. Although effective, storing state information for just-in-time optimization is a bit of a kludge. There is nothing "just in time" about the stored information. If stored optimization is the goal, why not just build a system from the start that is organized around optimizing only once?

The Android engineers agree! That system is ART.

ART

ART, the Android Runtime, was introduced as an experimental runtime environment in Android KitKat, 4.4, API 19. It replaced Dalvik in Android Lollipop, 5.0, API 21.

The ART system uses the same intermediate language that Dalvik used: DEX. Most programs that were compiled before ART existed and that ran on Dalvik will run in the ART environment with no change. ART's strategy for optimizing and executing a program, however, is significantly different. Google coined the term **ahead-of-time** (**AOT**) optimization to distinguish it from Dalvik's JIT strategy.

"Ahead of time" means that an application, compiled to the DEX intermediate language, is translated to native code, only once, using a tool named dex2oat, at some point after its installation on a device. This strategy preserves the essential goal of an intermediate language: portability. Each Android device has installed as part of the operating system a version of dex2oat that, analogous to a virtual machine, targets its specific hardware platform. When a new application is installed, dex2oat translates the application intermediate language to a native binary. When the application is run, it is executing code that is native to its platform. No further translation is necessary, and no waste occurs due to repeated translations of the same instructions.

Actually, ART's strategy has evolved over time.

> **Note**
>
> To determine whether a system is using Dalvik or ART, find the value of the system property persist.sys.dalvik.vm.lib.1:
>
> ```
> > getprop persist.sys.dalvik.vm.lib.1
> ```
>
> On a system running Dalvik, the property will have the value libdvm.so. If it is using ART, the value will be libart.so.

ART Basics

The ART system does far more than simply compile code and run it in a garbage-collected environment. A closer description might be that it compiles, links, and even starts running the application, and then stores the running image.

The most common invocation of the compiler occurs when a new application is installed on the system. As part of the application installation process, the Android system runs dex2oat, over the DEX code, newly downloaded and installed in the applications directory /data/app/<application package name>. The verified, optimized native code is stored in the directory /data/dalvik-cache as data@<application package name>-<n>.apk@classes.dex. Despite the .dex suffix, the file is an OAT file.

The format of the OAT file is complex and not well documented. Although at the time of this writing it appears that the format is still in flux, some things are stable. The file is an ELF file, a standard format for Unix binaries. It contains both the compiled native code and also the entire pre-compilation DEX format "source." Figure 7.2 is a rough outline of the OAT file format. (The format is described in the file $AOSP/art/dex2oat/linker/oat_writer.h).

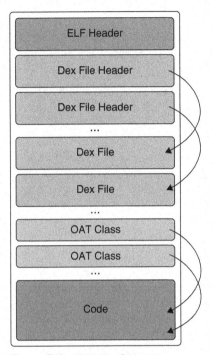

Figure 7.2   OAT File Structure

The point of embedding the complete, uncompiled DEX code in the OAT file is that doing so allows incremental compilation. Bits in the file header indicate which methods have been compiled and which have not.

The ART runtime is not only compiled to native code but, in the normal uses of the term, it is *linked*. The dex2oat compiler refers, during the process of compiling a .dex file, to the output of the previously compiled Android system libraries and compiles references to symbols defined in those libraries to their absolute locations. In other words, the compiled OAT file must be loaded into memory at exactly the location for which it was compiled and depends on having an image of the compiled libraries at exactly the locations at which they were found during the compilation process.

The process of loading independently compiled binaries into memory and resolving the references from one to the other is normally called *linking*. Linking can be an expensive process. Even the earliest versions of Android pre-linked many portions of the system libraries as an optimization: doing it once to save the cost of doing it each time it was necessary.

Of course, the consequence of pre-linking binary libraries is that those libraries cannot, once linked, be versioned independently. For instance, after a symbolic reference to the code that activates the haptic feedback device is linked as a reference to a specific location in memory, updating the haptic feedback library and changing its location would be disastrous.

On current mobile devices, however, this is not a significant issue. System libraries are never updated individually. Updates to the system software always involve updating the entire system as a unit, and all affected components are updated together.

In the Android system, building the pre-compiled, pre-linked image of the ART runtime is part of building the system image. The directory /system/framework contains the .jar files produced by compiling the Android libraries. In the Dalvik era, these .jar files were loaded into an application image and the code within them executed by the DVM.

For ART, those libraries are recompiled with dex2oat into a new subdirectory named for the device architecture (for example, arm). The two most significant files in this directory are boot.art and boot.oat. These two files—the first an image of initialized classes and objects, the second the ELF file containing the code and linking information—are loaded into memory: .art first, and immediately below it, .oat. Together, they comprise the pre-linked, pre-initialized system library image. These two files are soft-linked into /data/dalvik-cache along with the .art and .oat files for installed applications.

And this brings us at last to the second, less common use of dex2oat. A system update will almost certainly mean a new boot.art and boot.oat. These new files cannot be used with the pre-linked .oat files that dex2oat created previously when it compiled new applications as they were installed. A system update requires the recompilation of every single application on the device.

This recompilation is the source of the often seemingly interminable "Android Is Optimizing Applications" dialog that followed system updates on KitKat devices. It was not a great experience; more recent versions of ART do better.

Hybrid ART

Recent versions of ART are smarter and lazier. Why take the time and energy to compile code that might never be used? In what might at first seem like a step backwards, the new hybrid ART contains a Dalvik-like interpreter complete with a JIT.

Most applications are executed at first in the interpreted environment. Although interpreted, this environment is not Dalvik. The interpreted ART environment, for instance, uses the same highly tuned garbage collection system that was introduced with ART in KitKat.

The interpreter collects profile information on the code it executes. It stores the data it collects, per application, in files in the directory /data/dalvik-cache/profiles/. A new system daemon, the BackgroundDexOptService, parses these files occasionally and uses dex2oat.to compile the "hot" methods—methods that are 90 percent of the calls in the application. It also recompiles a program if the list of methods that comprise 90 percent of the calls changes by more than 10 percent.

The most immediate effect of this new, hybrid ART is that a system update no longer requires recompilations of every application known to the system and the attending several-minute wait. In addition, though, hybrid ART saves the substantial cost of running dex2oat on applications or parts of applications that are never used.

Zygote

Before any code that has been compiled to the DEX intermediate language (and that includes about half of the Android framework) can run, the system must initialize the runtime: Dalvik or ART.

The simplest way to run Java code is to run the java program, the virtual machine, and tell it which code to execute:

```
java -cp MyApplication.jar net.callmeike.MyApplication
```

The java program initializes a VM and uses it to execute the intermediate language instructions for the class net.callmeike.MyApplication in the file MyApplication.jar.

Similarly, the Android system, as part of startup, must create virtual machines and the runtime environment for all the system services that are compiled to the DEX IL. It must also provide a way to start and initialize new runtime environments for new applications as they start. The Android solution for this necessity is a clever program called Zygote.

Zygote Memory Management

Zygote is the solution to one of the oldest problems with Java desktop applications: startup time. Starting a Java desktop application requires each of the following steps:

- The OS resources. The system must find resources for a new, large program. On any machine that has been running for a while, finding those resources might well require swapping some other running program to disk.

- Start the JVM. The JVM, normally a program called java, is a moderately large and complex C++ program. Although it starts fairly quickly, getting it fully initialized does take time.

- Load basic Java libraries. Java loads its libraries lazily from a very large file called rt.jar. Finding and loading the classes required for minimal functionality, though heavily optimized, does take time.

- Initialize the basic libraries. Java classes quite frequently require some initialization (assignments to static variables or static initializer blocks). As each class is loaded, its initialization code must be executed. At this point, on a typical laptop computer, even for a completely trivial application, it may now be several tenths of a second since the user started the application.

- Load the application. This is the first step toward executing the application that the user actually requested. Application classes are, most likely, in another .jar file from which they are, again, loaded lazily. To start executing the program, however, the VM must load the closure of references from the main class: all the things to which it refers; all the things to which any of the referents refer; all the things to which they refer, and so on, until no unresolved references exist. Note, first of all, that this recursive resolution of references may very well require loading many Java system libraries as well as application code. Also note that it does not, by any means, imply the loading of all of them either.

- Initialize the newly loaded classes. Again, some or all of the newly loaded classes may require initialization. Any initialization code in any of the newly loaded classes must be executed.

- At this point, it is entirely possible that the initialization process has used enough memory so that a minor garbage collection (GC) is necessary. Although minor GCs are fast, they do take time.

- After all necessary classes have been loaded and initialized, the VM can begin to execute the application's main method. For a moderately complex application, it is entirely possible that it has been nearly a minute since the user-initiated startup.

Although this delay is definitely annoying on a laptop computer, it would be devastating on a battery powered mobile device. Wading through the preceding list of initialization procedures each time a new application started would drain a battery in no time. Add to that the idea of waiting for a full minute for a phone application to start up so that you could answer an incoming call. The Android OS had to address this problem to be viable. The answer is the Zygote application.

As mentioned earlier, Zygote is to Android what init is to Linux: the parent of all applications. init starts Zygote as part of bringing up the system. Zygote initializes itself by pre-loading the entire Android framework. Unlike desktop Java, it does not load the libraries lazily. It loads all of them as part of system startup. When completely initialized, it enters a tight loop, waiting for connections to a socket.

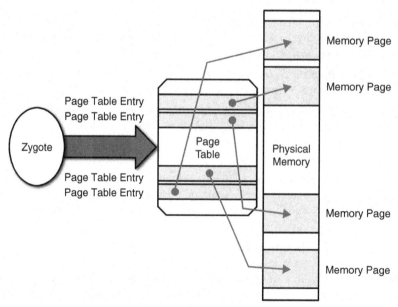

Figure 7.3   Zygote

Zygote makes use of an important feature of the Linux OS, copy-on-write paging, to eliminate nearly all the items in the Java initialization list. Figure 7.3 is a simplified illustration of how the operating system lays out virtual memory for applications; in this case, Zygote. Memory is organized into uniformly sized **pages**. When the application refers to memory at a particular address, the device hardware reinterprets the address as an index into a **page table** and an offset into the associated page to which the index points. It is entirely possible, as shown in Figure 7.3, that an address that points at the top of an application's virtual memory space refers to a location that is actually near the bottom of physical memory.

When the system needs to create a new application, it connects to the Zygote socket and sends a small packet describing the application to be started. Zygote clones itself, creating a new kernel-level process. Figure 7.4 illustrates the memory layout of a new application cloned from Zygote. The new application has its own page table. Most of the new page table is simply a copy of Zygote's page table. It points to the exact same pages of physical memory. Only the pages the new application uses for its own purposes are not shared.

The new process is interesting in that it shares memory with Zygote, its parent, in a mode called copy-on-write. Because the two processes are using *exactly* the same memory, starting the child process is nearly instantaneous. The kernel does not need to allocate much memory for the new process, nor does it need to load the Android framework libraries. Zygote has already loaded everything.

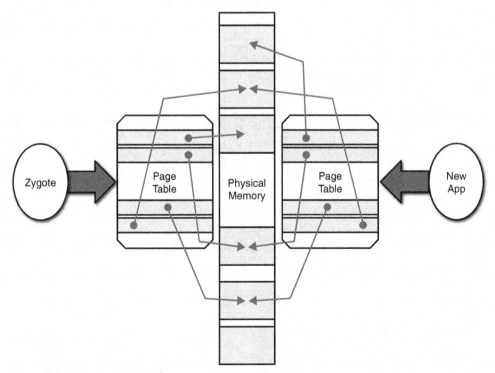

Figure 7.4   Zygote Clone

Because both processes have mapped exactly the same physical memory into their virtual address spaces, if either changed the contents of the memory by writing to it, the other would be affected. That would be *very* bad.

To avoid the problem, the system copies pages on write. The hardware notifies the kernel when either process attempts to write to a shared page. Instead of allowing the write, the kernel allocates a new page of memory and copies the contents of the original page—the page to which a process is writing—into it. After the two processes have separate copies of the page, each can freely modify its own copy. Figure 7.5 represents the state of memory after a new application spawned from Zygote attempts to write to a shared page.

Copy on write is a tremendous savings. In addition to the fast startup, there is only one copy for *all* processes of any pages that are unaltered by any process (all the library code, for instance). Even if some child process were to write on every single memory page (something that quite literally never happens), the cost of allocating the new memory is amortized over the life of the process. It is not incurred at initialization.

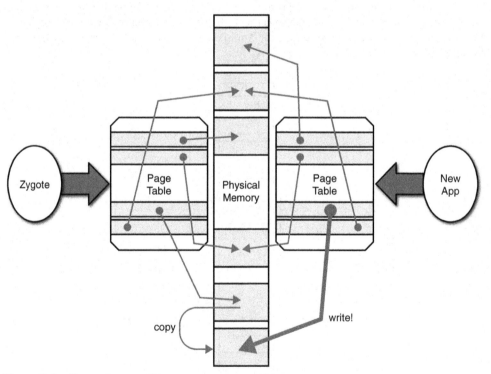

Figure 7.5   Zygote Copy on Write

Zygote Startup

As mentioned, Zygote is started by `init`. Recent Androids typically start multiple copies of Zygote. Depending on the chipset architecture or OEM preference, platform developers use the system variable, `ro.zygote`, set at platform at build time, to control which of four types of Zygotes are started and which one is "primary." Most modern Android devices start two zygotes—one for 32-bit applications and one for 64-bit apps—and default to 64-bit version.

> **Note**
>
> At the time of this writing, Zygote startup is still accurately described at https://elinux.org/ Android_Zygote_Startup.

The base `init` script, `init.rc`, described in Chapter 6, includes the script that starts Zygote:

```
import /init.${ro.zygote}.rc
```

The sources for the startup scripts are found in the directory:

```
$AOSP/system/core/rootdir
```

Listing 7.1 shows `init.zygote32_64.rc` for an older system, on which 32-bit apps were the default. It provides an opportunity to revisit the `init` scripting language. Note that the service lines have been wrapped to fit the page. They cannot be wrapped this way in the actual script.

Listing 7.1 **Zygote init for 32-bit Default Applications**

```
service zygote /system/bin/app_process32 \
        -Xzygote /system/bin --zygote --start-system-server --socket-name=zygote
    class main
    priority -20
    user root
    group root readproc
    socket zygote stream 660 root system
    onrestart write /sys/android_power/request_state wake
    onrestart write /sys/power/state on
    onrestart restart audioserver
    onrestart restart cameraserver
    onrestart restart media
    onrestart restart netd
    onrestart restart wificond
    writepid /dev/cpuset/foreground/tasks

service zygote_secondary /system/bin/app_process64 \
        -Xzygote /system/bin --zygote --socket-name=zygote_secondary
    class main
    priority -20
    user root
    group root readproc
```

```
socket zygote_secondary stream 660 root system
onrestart restart zygote
writepid /dev/cpuset/foreground/tasks
```

Consider the definition of the `zygote_secondary` service, the 64-bit zygote. The actual application that is started as user `root` at the very highest priority by `init` is `/system/bin/app_process64`. The script requests that `init` create a stream socket for the process and catalog it as `/dev/socket/zygote_secondary`: This is the socket that the system will use to start new Android applications. The script also contains an `onrestart` directive that will restart the primary Zygote if the secondary zygote fails.

The definition of the primary Zygote service, `zygote`, is nearly identical. It uses a different socket and has a much longer list of other servers that will be restarted if it fails. Note, of course, that if `zygote_secondary` fails, all of these servers will be restarted as well.

Runtime Initialization

Zygote's first order of business when it is started is to initialize the ART runtime environment. While reading this, keep in mind that it happens only once; that is, Zygote is started only once, during system startup. Subsequent application startup simply clones the running Zygote.

The applications that `init` starts, `app_process64` and `app_process32`, are just small applications (source in `$AOSP/frameworks/base/cmds/app_process`) that parse their command line and then run either Zygote or the class whose name has been passed as an argument. These are the programs used to start all programs (not applications!) compiled to DEX: anything that requires either Dalvik or ART. They serve a purpose very similar to that served by the "`java`" command, which starts the Java runtime.

The `app_process` creates an instance of `AppRuntime`, a subclass of `AndroidRuntime`. It does a lot of bookkeeping, setting up any runtime parameters (`runtime.addOption(…)`), the name for the process (`runtime.setArgv0(…)`), and the name of the class to run (used only when not running Zygote: `runtime.setClassNameAndArgs(…)`), and then calls `AndroidRuntime.start()` to invoke the runtime.

The `start` method (source in `$AOSP/frameworks/base/core/jni/AndroidRuntime.cpp`) eventually invokes `startVM`. `startVM` again is mostly setup.

Starting the runtime has gotten significantly more complex since the advent of ART. It is especially difficult to read the code because nearly all the variables that contain "dalvik" in their names actually apply to ART. Nonetheless, a review of the VM configuration options controlled by this code can prove extremely helpful to a developer. Among the more interesting are `–verbose:gc` and the compiler option `–generate-debug-info`. The former logs information about system garbage collection, and the latter causes `dex2oat` to add debugging information to the system image it builds after a system update.

After processing the options, `startVM` invokes `JNI_CreateJavaVM`. Again, the name is confusing: The runtime environment that is about to be initialized has almost nothing to do with

Java. To be compatible with code written for Java, though—and that includes the Java JNI API, discussed in the next chapter—this method inherits its name from its JNI counterpart. It is, though, almost certainly not the case that an application that uses the JNI API to start an instance of the Java VM on, say, a desktop Linux system, could successfully initialize the ART runtime on Android without further modification.

The `JNI_CreateJavaVM` method is defined in `art/runtime/jni/java_vm_ext.cc`. It, in turn, calls `Runtime::Create`, defined in `art/runtime/runtime.cc`. Finally, `Runtime::Create` initializes the ART runtime, loading the system OAT files and the libraries they contain.

The Android VM is now ready to roll. The argument that `app_process` passed in its calls to start was `"com.android.internal.os.Zygote.Init"`. Its source is in `$AOSP/frameworks/base/core/java/com/android/internal/os/ZygoteInit.java`.

System Service Startup

Most of the code in `ZygoteInit`'s `main` method (the method the runtime calls, once initialized) is wrapped in a Java try/catch block. The obvious reason is to allow Zygote to attempt to clean up after a failure. There is a second, very clever purpose to which we will return in a moment.

Zygote has three major tasks, on startup:

- Register the socket to which the system will connect to start new applications
- Preload Android resources and libraries, if necessary
- Start the Android System Server

After it has completed these three tasks, it enters a loop, waiting for connections to the socket.

The first of the tasks, opening the socket, is handled in the `registerServerSocket` method. The method creates the socket using the name passed in the parameters, probably from the `init` script originally.

The second task is accomplished with a call to the `preload` method. Historically, Zygote was initialized aggressively. Modern Androids, however, support a minimal system that postpones the cost of preloading the framework until the first application is spawned.

The `preload` method loads everything it can think of: classes, libraries, resources, and even a very special case, the WebView (a web browser view that can be embedded in an Android application). Note that, when using the ART runtime, many of the preloads are already in memory because they are in the system OAT file.

At the completion of the `preload` method, Zygote is fully initialized and ready to clone new applications very quickly, sharing most of its virtual memory with them.

The last of the tasks, starting the System Server, is accomplished in the `startSystemServer` method. The `SystemServer` is the first application cloned from Zygote. Following the process is instructive.

The startSystemServer method fakes a connection to the Zygote socket (for subsequent application startup, the connection will be real). It creates a new ZygoteConnection object with the hard-coded content that it would have received over the canonical socket connection were the system trying to start the server. It passes the contents of the connection object to Zygote.forkSystemServer which, in turn, wraps a native method, com_android_internal_os_nativeForkSystemServer (source in $AOSP/frameworks/base/core/jni/com_android_internal_os_Zygote.cpp). The native method first calls ForkAndSpecializeCommon, which does the actual fork system call. There are now two execution paths, one for Zygote, in which the fork system call returned the process id (pid) of the new child process, and one for the newly spawned child process, in which fork returned a pid of 0.

In the parent process (pid > 0) control returns, eventually to ZygoteInit and immediately enters the ZygoteServer method runSelectLoop. This is the endless loop that processes incoming connections with almost the same code that just started the System Server. The call to ZygoteConnection.runOnce eventually calls forkAndSpecialize, the analog of forkSystemServer for the masses.

Perhaps of more interest is what happens to the child process (pid == 0), the process that will become the System Server. First, the method SpecializeCommon is called with a flag indicating that this process will become the System Server. SpecializeCommon in turn calls a series of additional setup methods that set the correct SE Linux context and process capabilities.

After the child process has been set up with the correct process options, it calls Zygote.callPostForkSystemServerHooks and Zygote.callPostForkChildHooks to load the specialized System Server class libraries and to start its application code. Both of these calls trigger calls to the ART runtime native code located in art/runtime/native/dalvik_system_ZygoteHooks.cc.

Next, the child process calls the handleSystemServerProcess method, which, in turn, calls ZygoteInit.zygoteInit, RuntimeInit.applicationInit (source $AOSP/frameworks/base/core/java/com/android/internal/os.RuntimeInit.java), and, finally, invokeStaticMain, which is where the magic happens.

The invokeStaticMain method finds the class whose name was given in the data transferred to Zygote through the socket (or, in the case of the System Server, faked in hard-coded data), and then obtains a reference to the public static void main method on that class. The very last thing it does is to create a new exception holding the method reference and throw it.

This clever trick is the second reason for wrapping the top-level ZygoteInit code in a try/catch block. This throw, from within invokeStaticMain, clears the entire Java stack back to its very top. At this point, the new instance of Zygote has closed all unneeded file descriptors; set its permissions, group, and user IDs correctly; has the entire Android framework loaded and warmed up; and now has an empty stack. The exception's run method, called in the catch block, runs the new application's main method in this fully initialized environment with an empty stack.

When Zygote starts the System Server, it is the class com.android.server.SystemServer (source in $AOSP/frameworks/base/services/java/com/android/server/SystemServer.java) whose main method is run. It is here that all the familiar Android services are started: the PackageManagerService, the ActivityManagerService, the PowerManagerService, and so on.

Summary

This chapter traces the initialization of the main component of the Android system—its runtime, ART, and its root program, Zygote—from its initialization from Linux init through the start of the System Server and the initialization of the standard Android managers.

Citations

Davis, B., A. Beatty, K. Casey, D. Gregg, and J. Waldron. "The case for virtual register machines." In *Interpreters, Virtual Machines and Emulators* (IVME '03), pages 41–49, 2003.

## 8

Getting to Android: The HAL

The Android's Hardware Abstraction Layer (HAL) is just an interface. It is a layer of abstraction that separates components by disconnecting the definition of the component's behavior from its implementation.

As is always the case, introducing an abstraction layer comes with a cost. So why use the HAL? There are several reasons.

Why a HAL?

The HAL is Android's interface to hardware. On most Linux systems, the interface to the hardware is a device driver. Device drivers, however, are usually device specific and sometimes proprietary.

Consider: The Android system will be installed on diverse hardware with, for instance, a wide variety of Wi-Fi chips. Although each Wi-Fi chip has its own kernel driver, at some point, they all provide a Wi-Fi service used by Android code. It would be very convenient if above some point in the stack, the Android code for all the different Wi-Fi hardware/driver combinations were the same.

The HAL is the lingua franca for a class of devices. A single set of C header files describes the functionality that a HAL provides to the Android system. HAL code for a particular device is the implementation of the API defined by those header files. The HAL code shims the hardware device driver behavior so that it looks to Android like a generic device of some particular type: Wi-Fi, Bluetooth, and so on. Adapting Android to use, for instance, an entirely new Wi-Fi device consists of writing the native code that implements the Android Wi-Fi HAL (as defined by the .h files) for the new device. The HAL layer means that no code above the HAL—most of it written in Java—needs to be changed to port Android to use the new device.

Another reason for the HAL is that one of the original goals for Android (a goal that it has clearly achieved) was to make putting it on a new device as frictionless as possible from both engineering and legal points of view. From the legal point of view, that meant navigating a thin line between the GPL (GNU Public License) and proprietary code.

The Android system is based on the Linux kernel, which is licensed under the notoriously viral GPL. The Android platform, on the other hand, is intended to support hardware manufacturers with devices that are strictly proprietary, right down to their APIs. The HAL provides an elegant way of keeping proprietary code away from the GPL.

Hardware developers who are concerned about getting their proprietary code anywhere near an open source, or, worse yet, GPLed codebase, can keep all of their proprietary code in the HAL. To do this, they first create a trivial device driver. It can be open source or even GPLed if there is any reason to do so. The driver does essentially nothing: It simply passes data to and from the hardware. The developer next creates a HAL. The HAL code runs in user space (as a library linked into the application) and may be completely proprietary. It does not run as part of the kernel and is not a device driver under the normal definition of that term. It is, however, the actual driver for the device. Because it is linked into the application as a library, there is no requirement of any kind that this code be public. It need never be available except in a binary form.

A third application for the HAL has arisen more recently. An additional problem that Google encountered as Android came of age was that it could not get vendors to update devices with the latest versions of Android.

In early Android, hardware vendors built the system images that they deployed to their devices. They got the base system source from Google, modified it as necessary, adding their proprietary software and extensions, built an image, and deployed it to their devices. When a new version of Android came along, they did it again—sometimes. From a vendor's point of view, a new version of Android is something to be sold: a reason for end users to buy a new device. It is not at all surprising that they tended to drag their feet releasing updates.

Google, on the other hand, is constantly increasing the number of pies into which it has a finger. It does not want to have to wait for a recalcitrant vendor or an entirely new generation of hardware to reap the benefits of some new feature. Google needed a way to completely remove the device update mechanism from the clutches of the vendors.

To do this, Google created Project Treble. Treble specifies and requires that HAL modules use Binder, Android's interprocess communication (IPC) system, to communicate with the Android stack. HAL modules are no longer binary libraries that are linked into the Android runtime. Instead, they are separate binaries that are stored on completely separate hardware volumes from the ones that hold the Android core and user applications. The new HALs are not called directly from Android but are, instead, invoked using highly optimized IPC calls.

Since Project Treble went live, an over-the-air (OTA) update can completely rewrite the file system containing the Android OS without disturbing the vendor's HAL. There is no longer any need for Google to wait for a vendor to build a new, hardware-specific version of its Android system. Google can update the Android OS on any device at pretty much any time, according to its own schedule. As long as they don't violate the HAL IPC contract, the HAL that worked with the old version of the OS will work with the new version.

Is a HAL Necessary?

A HAL is necessary only for products that need the Android label or want automatic updates. Developers creating a custom Android for an OEM device may not need a complicated HAL. As described in the preceding section, the HAL has exactly three purposes:

- It is the native code layer that shims Android onto specific hardware. At the very least, this means bridging code written in Java to native code, usually written in C or C++.

- It is an abstraction for the functionality provided by a class of devices, for example, Bluetooth, Wi-Fi, graphics, and so on. It makes it possible for Android to abstract away the differences between, for example, Broadcom and Qualcomm Wi-Fi chipsets.

- It is an abstraction that permits OTA updates that do not require linking a new version of Android to vendor-specific binaries.

Although the first of these purposes is obviously necessary, the second two may not be. A developer building a custom Android targeting a specific hardware device might just dive right in and modify core Android code, as necessary, to adapt it to the device. One might even make the argument that the Java code is easier to modify than the native code in the HAL. So why not?

Actually, there are some fairly strong arguments for keeping platform customizations in the HAL. One good reason, of course, is updates. Even if your business plan does not depend on updates, not having some kind of firmware update plan for an embedded device would be irresponsible.

No matter what version of Android you choose, either security issues are already known or security issues will be known. One need only look back to the massive DDOS attack on Dyn, Inc. in 2016. The attack was launched predominantly from IoT devices, many of which were manufactured by a single company, XiongMai Technologies. It is a cautionary tale that should convince anyone that releasing a programmable device with software that cannot be updated is careless and dangerous. No one wants to be the trampoline for the next cyberattack and, even worse, be unable to fix a security breach when it occurs.

One of the easiest ways to patch bugs, of course, is to take updates from the official AOSP codebase. If a customized fork of AOSP code has been modified to adapt it to a specific device, the fork of AOSP will be much more difficult to merge with the official sources.

Allowing your device to be updated automatically by Google might even be worth considering. Doing so might take the entire issue of security and liability off your plate. To do that, though, your custom Android must at a minimum comply with the Project Treble standards.

Another reason for using the HAL is that an implementation for a new device may already exist. If the hardware that your project uses is something that other Android developers have used—say, a motion or a temperature sensor—it is entirely possible that a complete HAL may already exist. If it does not, it is possible that a HAL exists that supports a similar device and that you can adapt that HAL to the new device with minimal effort.

Designing the HAL

The initial discussion of the Acme project introduced a simple hardware proximity sensor. Preceding chapters sketched the process of building a device driver for it. The next step up the Android layer cake is creating code that uses the driver to interact with the sensor.

By design, the Acme proximity sensor HAL is not only simple but includes a stub for the device driver. The focus here is on defining the HAL API and publishing it into Java; not the vagaries of the Linux USB system. Even though part of the actual code is a stub, the functionality that it represents is intended to be entirely realistic.

Recall that a HAL is an abstraction for a group of devices. A device driver is also an abstraction for the device. On the hardware side, device drivers are typically very specific: a particular driver probably works only with very specific hardware. (A USB driver is a bit of an exception; an intermediate layer for devices that support the USB interface.) From the application side, a device driver is very general. They abstract devices into one of only two groups: character and block.

HALs are more general on the bottom and more specific on the top. On top, there are quite a few HAL abstractions, each of which is the interface for a narrower category of devices: cameras, Wi-Fi, Bluetooth, and so on. On the bottom a HAL provides access to multiple hardware implementations, all of which have a specific, common purpose. The possibility even exists that a single HAL abstraction could integrate multiple hardware devices (and their drivers), exposing the combination of several hardware components as a single service.

When designing a HAL, understanding how the services provided by the hardware will be exposed to an application is absolutely essential. Although this book has generally approached the Android system as a series of layers, each built on the previous layer, designing a HAL requires looking far ahead and trying to predict the future. Even when you build a simple, proprietary device that doesn't need a real HAL, this boundary is a good place to pause for a moment of reflection. Because the HAL is Android's abstraction layer, it is a great place to hedge your bets.

First, consider the constraints from below (nearer the hardware). In a project in which the creation of a hardware device (or its driver) is part of a project, the kernel device driver and the API (its .h file) that it publishes are also part of the project. Project developers can modify the driver API as necessary to sensibly divide functionality across code modules.

That is not the typical case, however. The likelihood is higher that a hardware device manufacturer that provides a device will also provide its driver. When a third party—the device manufacturer—provides the device driver, its API is not under project control. That is a constraint.

To be concrete, if the Acme team created an entirely new type of proximity sensor, wrote a device driver for it, and that device was the secret sauce for a new product, then the Acme team would choose the API for the sensor device driver and adjust it to suit their needs. If, on the other hand (the more typical case), the Acme team's plan was a clever new use of the ability to sense proximity, and they sourced a sensor during a trip to Shenzhen, then the device driver for the sensor would most likely be provided by the third-party hardware engineers: possibly as source, possibly not.

In either case, the API of the device driver is the constraint for the bottom of the HAL. In the former case, that API is more malleable than it is in the latter.

Next, consider the requirements from above (nearer application code). The HAL is the first step toward building a service that will expose the hardware to an application. Now would be a great time for an app developer (preferably not the same person as the one who will write the HAL!) to write one of those applications. What feels like a natural interface in the application? Are the edge cases—initialization, configuration, application failure, and access control—all handled? When a new sensor with new capabilities comes along, will the API accommodate the changes with backward compatibility?

After application requirements are more or less clear, converting the application API into a set of operations required of the hardware should be a relatively straightforward task. Remember, of course, that most of the heavy lifting will be done by a Java service that actually exposes the hardware to the application. The HAL layer doesn't have to provide the service API that the application uses. It merely has to provide a clean, minimal set of hardware operations on which the service can be built.

The HAL for the Acme proximity sensor is sleek to avoid obscuring the process of building a HAL. Its design is simple. As is often the case, power is an important concern. A sensor may use power when it is running and pointlessly load the battery unless it can be turned off. The design of the HAL for the Acme proximity sensor assumes that it is exactly such a power hog: there are calls to turn it on and off.

The call that turns the sensor on takes one argument—an out parameter `struct`—that the driver will populate with the `min` and `max` values acceptable in the precision argument passed to the HAL when polling it. Similarly, it contains the `max` and `min` values that the device will return for the proximity data it will return when it is polled.

After the sensor is turned on, it can be polled for proximity values. The polling call takes a single argument: the desired precision for the proximity value it will return. The precision argument restricts the resources (perhaps time or battery) that the sensor will expend in obtaining the returned value. The poll returns a current value from the sensor.

When all client applications are done using the sensor, it can be turned off to save battery.

Building a HAL

This chapter and the next show how to create the code that connects native code into the Android framework in four steps:

1. Define the HAL: create the `.h` files that specify the API for the proximity service

2. Implement the HAL for the Acme proximity service: create layers of code that shim the device driver API for the proximity service to its HAL API

3. Create a native (C language) daemon that uses the HAL to access the proximity device

4. Create the JNI interface that publishes the new HAL into the Java language

> **Note**
>
> In pre-SE Linux versions of Android, it was possible to create and run a standalone Java dae-
> mon, a translation of the C-language daemon created in step 3. Although it may still be pos-
> sible, we abandoned the effort to create one after many hours of trying. Caveat developer.

Code Structure

The code in these next two chapters will implement both the HAL for the proximity device and
a simple daemon that uses the device through the HAL code. This simple daemon could replace
the one introduced as a startup service in Chapter 6.

Figure 8.1 illustrates the components and their relationships.

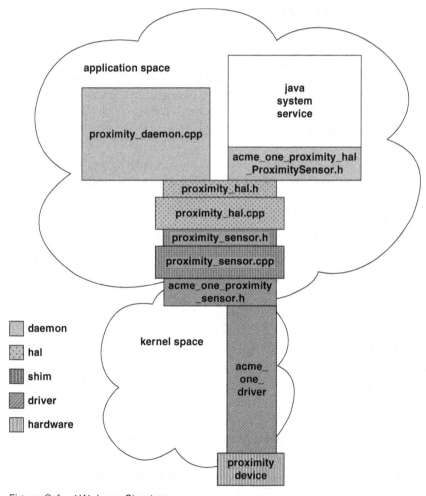

Figure 8.1   HAL Layer Structure

Note that all the code discussed in these chapters runs as part of an application (user space) and not as part of the kernel (kernel space). This is all just normal application code.

The code consists of four functional components, as shown in Figure 8.1:

1. **HAL code (dotted boxes):** This is the abstraction that separates the capabilities of hardware from its specific implementations. The .h file defines the HAL interface. The implementation (.cpp file) specializes the Android HAL API for the target hardware.

2. **Shim code (dashed boxes):** This is the glue code that connects the HAL to a specific device hardware/driver. This code adapts the Android HAL API to the device driver for the hardware.

3. **Daemon (blue/solid gray):** This is the stand-alone application that interacts with the hardware through the HAL.

4. **Java System Service (white):** This is the System Service that Android applications will use to access the custom hardware.

To build these components into the Acme One device, you must place their code in the Acme One device folder, as introduced in previous chapters. The new directories are organized as shown in Figure 8.2.

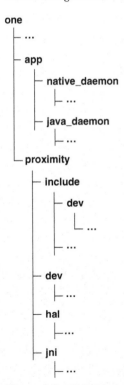

Figure 8.2   HAL Directory Structure

All the code implementing the HAL for the proximity sensor goes into a new subdirectory, proximity. If the Acme device had several HALs for several different devices, they might be further organized into an intermediate directory, perhaps hal, that contained separate subdirectories for each of the different device HALs. The Acme project contains only a single HAL so it is located directly in the project root directory.

Note that to be useful as a real HAL, the abstract definition of the interface—specifically the definition of the proximity HAL, proximity/include/proximity_hal.h—would have to be promoted from its current location inside the directory specifically for the One device, up into the Android source tree to a location that would make it visible to other code that needed to use it. If shared only by generations of Acme devices, it might be put into a subdirectory of the Acme device directory. If visible across devices from multiple vendors, it might even be promoted into the device directory itself.

Figure 8.2 also shows the locations in the source tree of the two daemons to be implemented in the next chapter. Although this organization is appropriate during the build process, it is entirely likely that applications—native daemons and system services—will be developed independently from the libraries on which they depend (the HAL); perhaps even by different developers. Facilitate this by separating the code bases into distinct git repositories and using the manifest to place them in the build tree in their required locations, as shown in Listing 8.1.

Listing 8.1   **Manifest Additions for the Acme HAL**

```
<!-- Acme Specific Projects -->
  <project path="device/acme/one-kernel" name="one-kernel" remote="acme" />
  <project path="device/acme/one/proximity"
           name="platform_device_acme_one_proximity"
           remote="acme" />
  <project path="device/acme/one/app/native_daemon"
           name="platform_device_acme_one_app_native_daemon"
           remote="acme" />
  <project path="device/acme/one/app/java_daemon"
           name="platform_device_acme_one_app_java_daemon"
           remote="acme" />
```

Implementing the HAL

The HAL is a line between two endpoints. The first of those two endpoints is the device driver. As noted previously, it is quite likely that the device driver interface for a specific piece of hardware is a given: that its API is not under project control. The device driver and its API are defined by a third-party hardware provider and whatever driver they supply with it.

Given the ubiquity of the universal serial bus (USB), it is also very likely that any new device will communicate with the processor via USB. Even a newly created device may not have its own driver. It may simply appear in the USB device tree and be accessed with generic USB commands. If it does have a distinct driver, that driver is likely to be a specialization of the USB interface.

Note

Contrary to the implications evoked by its name, USB is not really a bus. Instead, it is a tree containing a master device that polls one or more slaves. Masters and slaves behave quite differently and require very different implementations.

Linux USB core supports both modes, referring to the drivers for the master end as USB device drivers and those for the slave end as USB gadget drivers.

Although not discussed here, it is entirely possible that a small Android device will not be the bus master but, instead, a slave that is occasionally connected to a master. One can imagine, for instance, a tablet acting as master for the sensors plugged into it for data collection in the field. At night, though, when plugged into some kind of data aggregator, it would act as a gadget.

In its full generality, a USB device can be a very complex thing. Communicating with a single physical device, for instance, may require interacting with multiple virtual devices. A USB loudspeaker, for example, presents as both a keyboard—its controls—and a separate interface for the bulk transfer of sound data.

Entire books are available on the construction of USB drivers and the code that interacts with them. Those topics are well outside the scope of this book. Instead of accessing an actual USB interface (boxes with slanted lines in Figure 8.1) the shim code in this example (boxes with dashed lines in Figure 8.1) will be a stub. The "bottom" end of this example HAL does not actually connect to a device driver. In an actual HAL, the shim code would include the .h files for one or more device drivers. It would make read, write, and ioctl calls on the drivers they defined. Even though this example uses a stub, recall that Chapter 6 described the SE additions necessary to allow executables (applications) access to USB serial devices labeled as `proximityd_exec`. The SE additions in Chapter 6 illustrated creating the device-specific SE policy that is necessary to grant applications access to kernel-exposed interfaces.

Several resources can be quite helpful in building the HAL for a USB device. Most obviously, the Linux kernel contains an entire subsystem, USB Core, that does most of the heavy lifting.

Another important resource is *libusb* (https://libusb.info). Libusb is a portable, user-mode, and USB-version agnostic library for using USB devices. It supports Android. Even if the library is excessive and overly general for use in some specific applications, the code provides several excellent examples of how to use USB devices from application code.

HAL Declaration

The second of the two HAL endpoints is the definition of the HAL API. Visiting it next is another deviation from the strict bottom-to-top order in which we've been visiting components of the stack so far. It is, however, entirely realistic and appropriate. After the two endpoints are defined, writing the HAL is the straightforward (if not simple) task of drawing the line between them.

As noted earlier, the HAL definition should be more than just the simple reiteration of a hardware interface. A good HAL API will be flexible enough to support multiple related devices and friendly to the applications that use it. It is entirely prudent to define the interface as part of system and even application design, and then to do whatever is necessary to implement it.

As described previously, the HAL .h file *is*, in most senses, the HAL. It is the interface through which client code will interact with the device it represents.

The HAL for the proximity device is `proximity/include/dev/proximity_hal.h`. It is shown in Listing 8.2.

Listing 8.2 **Proximity HAL**

```
#ifndef PROXIMITY_HAL_H
#define PROXIMITY_HAL_H

#include <hardware/hardware.h>

#define ACME_PROXIMITY_SENSOR_MODULE "libproximityhal"

typedef struct proximity_sensor_device proximity_sensor_device_t;

struct value_range {
    int min;
    int range;
};

typedef struct proximity_params {
    struct value_range precision;
    struct value_range proximity;
} proximity_params_t;

struct proximity_sensor_device {
    hw_device_t common;

    int fd;

    proximity_params_t params;

    int (*poll_sensor)(proximity_sensor_device_t *dev, int precision);
};

#endif // PROXIMITY_HAL_H
```

Listing 8.2 first defines the constant ACME_PROXIMITY_SENSOR_MODULE. This is a unique string and the name that client code will use to find the proximity sensor's HAL.

Next, the code declares a struct that is best understood in the terms of object-oriented (O-O) design. Think of the `proximity_sensor_device` struct as the definition of a new O-O class. The first member of the struct, common, in O-O terms is its super class: it contains data and behaviors that are common to all HALs for all types of devices. This use of the term "super class" and the function of the common struct member will become clearer in the examination of the HAL implementation.

> **Note**
>
> The definitions of the device in hardware.h, hw_module_methods_t, really is a kind of raw version of inheritance. The HAL structs that represent device instances are hw_module_ methods_ts. That means that the open method, for instance, is at the same offset relative to the pointer to the HAL struct for every HAL for any device: hw_module_methods_t.open. Individual HALs, however, "subclass" the hw_module_methods_t struct by defining a new struct whose first element is an hw_module_methods_t but which allocate extra space at the end of that struct, containing pointers to methods with device-specific functionality. The resulting struct can be cast as the "super class" struct, an hw_module_methods_t, because the pointer to the subclass struct is *also* a pointer to the super class struct. It can also be cast as the device-specific struct by code that needs the device-specific functionality.

Next in Listing 8.2 are more of the struct's members. To continue the object-orientation analogy, these are the class's data members (fields). The first is the file descriptor for the open device driver that the HAL will hold. Next are the four values that all proximity sensor devices will provide: min and max for precision and proximity. Each individual hardware device and its driver will populate these fields with information about the behavior of that particular device.

The last member of the struct is a pointer to a function, poll, which takes the struct itself as its first argument. This is the O-O idiom for a method call.

> **Note**
>
> Object-oriented languages bundle data (fields) with the operations that may be performed on that data (methods). The standard way of implementing this is that an operation on a particular data type takes, as an implicit first argument, a reference to an instance of the data on which it will operate. Each call to the operation mutates only the specific instance passed in the call.

Note that nothing in the declaration of the HAL refers in any way to the actual hardware or driver to which the HAL provides access. In particular, the HAL definition file does not refer to the driver or even the shim code's .h file (see Listing 8.9). The isolation is complete.

This HAL, now completely described, defines what it is to be a proximity device. This is the bottleneck through which all information must pass, moving up or down the stack between any proximity device driver and Android Java code. With the definition of the top and bottom endpoints, the implementation should be simply a matter of programming.

HAL Definition

At last, we arrive at the definition of the HAL: its implementation. The implementation of the proximity HAL for the Acme proximity device is in proximity/hal/proximity_hal.cpp.

The most important resource for implementing a HAL is the AOSP source file `hardware/libhardware/include/hardware/hardware.h`. It defines the types needed to implement a HAL and, in its comments, describes how a HAL is implemented. It largely determines the structure of the code in `proximity_hal.cpp`.

The documentation in `hardware.h` outlines a three-step process for creating a HAL. The first step in the process consists of defining a HAL **module**. The HAL module contains metadata about a device and is also the factory for instances of the HAL. Listing 8.3 shows the module definition for the Acme One Proximity Sensor.

Listing 8.3   **Proximity HAL Module Definition**

```
// …
hw_module_t HAL_MODULE_INFO_SYM = {
        .tag = HARDWARE_MODULE_TAG,
        .module_api_version = HARDWARE_HAL_API_VERSION,
        .hal_api_version = 0,
        .id = ACME_PROXIMITY_SENSOR_MODULE,
        .name = "Acme Proximity Sensor",
        .author = "Acme Team",
        .methods = &proximity_sensor_methods
};
```

Several of these fields, `tag`, `module_api_version` and `hal_api_version`, are required and must be bound to the values specified for them in `hardware.h`. After the required fields are several fields that identify a specific HAL. The value of the field `.id`, for instance, is the constant defined back in this HAL's `.h` file.

The most interesting of the fields is `.methods`. The `.methods` field must hold a reference to an `hw_module_methods_t`. Listing 8.4 quotes—again from `hardware.h`—the declaration of `hw_module_methods_t`.

Listing 8.4   **HAL Methods Definition**

```
typedef struct hw_module_methods_t {
    /** Open a specific device */
    int (*open)(const struct hw_module_t* module,
                const char* id,
                struct hw_device_t** device);
} hw_module_methods_t;
```

In other words, the `hw_module_methods_t` is a struct that contains a pointer to a function that all HAL implementations have but that each will implement differently. In object-oriented terms, it is an abstract method in the HAL class, the super class for all HALs (including the proximity sensor HAL).

What method will all HAL implementations have but that each HAL will implement differently? Well, in O-O terms, it is the class's constructor, of course! In the realm of the HAL, the constructor is named .open.

The .open method takes a reference to the HAL module struct itself as its first parameter. As noted earlier, this is the O-O design idiom for a method call.

As its second argument, it takes the device ID. This allows the code for a single open method to specialize its behavior for several similar devices: a single implementation might have slightly different behaviors for each of several devices with different IDs. This is the mechanism that allows a single HAL to support multiple implementations.

Finally, down to business: It is the job of each HAL's implementation of the abstract .open method to allocate and initialize the hw_device_t object returned in the third parameter of the call.

Listing 8.5 shows the hw_module_method_t implementation for the proximity sensor.

Listing 8.5   **Methods Definition for the Proximity HAL**

```
// …

static hw_module_methods_t proximity_sensor_methods = {
        .open = &open_proximity_sensor_module
};

// …
```

The hw_module_t struct for the proximity sensor is now complete. Its .methods.open field contains a reference to a method that opens the underlying device for use: open_proximity_sensor_module. That method will be defined in a moment.

Although there is now a way (incompletely implemented) to create an instance of the proximity sensor HAL, as yet, there is no way use it. There is no way to poll it or to close it when it is no longer needed. This is the purpose of the struct created, initialized, and returned by the .open method, the hw_device_t. In O-O terms, it is roughly the equivalent of an instance of the HAL. The Acme proximity sensor device needs an extension of hw_device_t that declares the two needed methods, poll and close.

> **Note**
>
> Be careful not to confuse hw_module_t and hw_device_t. The hw_module_t is the HAL's description and factory. It has an open method that returns instances of extensions of hw_device_t that define the behavior of a class of devices.

Finally, Listing 8.6 is the complete definition of the HAL (located at device/acme/one/proximity/hal/proximity_hal.cpp). As one would expect in an O-O architecture, the subclass instance contains references to subclass methods.

Listing 8.6   **Proximity HAL Implementation**

```
#include <errno.h>
#include <string.h>
#include <malloc.h>
#include <log/log_system.h>

#include "proximity_hal.h"
#include "dev/proximity_sensor.h"

#define LOG_TAG "PROX"

static int poll_proximity_sensor(proximity_sensor_device_t *dev, int precision) {
    SLOGV("Polling proximity sensor");

    if (!dev)
        return -1;

    return poll_sensor(dev->fd, precision);
}

static int close_proximity_sensor(proximity_sensor_device_t *dev) {
    SLOGV("Closing proximity sensor");

    if (!dev)
        return 0;

    close_sensor(dev->fd);
    free(dev);
    return 0;
}

static int open_proximity_sensor_module(
        const struct hw_module_t *module,
        char const *name,
        struct hw_device_t **device) {
    SLOGV("Opening proximity sensor");

    auto *dev = static_cast<proximity_sensor_device_t*>
      (malloc(sizeof(proximity_sensor_device_t)));
    if (!dev)
        return -ENOMEM;

    memset(dev, 0, sizeof(*dev));

    int fd = open_sensor(dev->params);
    if (fd < 0) {
```

```
        SLOGE("Failed to open proximity sensor: %s", strerror(errno));
        free(dev);
        return -1;
    }
    dev->fd = fd;

    dev->common.tag = HARDWARE_DEVICE_TAG;
    dev->common.version = 0;
    dev->common.module = (struct hw_module_t *) module;
    dev->common.close = (int (*)(struct hw_device_t *)) close_proximity_sensor;

    dev->poll_sensor = poll_proximity_sensor;

    *device = reinterpret_cast<hw_device_t *>(dev);

    return 0;
}

static hw_module_methods_t proximity_sensor_methods = {
        .open = open_proximity_sensor_module
};

hw_module_t HAL_MODULE_INFO_SYM = {
        .tag = HARDWARE_MODULE_TAG,
        .module_api_version = HARDWARE_HAL_API_VERSION,
        .hal_api_version = 0,
        .id = ACME_PROXIMITY_SENSOR_MODULE,
        .name = "Acme Proximity Sensor",
        .author = "Acme Team",
        .methods = &proximity_sensor_methods
};
```

Note that, so far, this HAL implementation is completely device agnostic. This same code could be used for nearly any proximity sensor device, depending on the definitions of three methods: open_sensor, close_sensor, and poll_sensor.

There are a few ways of specializing this generic implementation for a specific device. A HAL implementation might be specialized at compile/bind time by statically assigning the reference to a method implementation appropriate for the specific device to each of those three symbols. In fact, that is how this example will work: That is what we do here. There will be a single shim that will define those three functions.

The choice could also be runtime, though. Multiple definitions of hw_module_t might all use a HAL implementation very similar to this one. An extension of the implementation might use the value of hw_module_t.id to choose among several device-specific function implementations to be assigned to the proximity_sensor_device_t's .common.close and poll_sensor methods.

The HAL must be added to the build system. The build file is shown in Listing 8.7 and is located at `device/acme/one/proximity/Android.bp`. The HAL is a shared library named "libacmehal" and is built from the source "proximity_hal.cpp." That source file, of course, includes the file "proximity_hal.h," which defines the HAL and which was shown in Listing 8.2.

Listing 8.7   **Acme HAL Build Blueprint File**

```
cc_defaults {
    name: "vendor.acme.one.proximity.defaults",
    relative_install_path: "hw",
    cflags: [
        "-g",
        "-OO",
        "-Wall",
    ],
    vendor: true,
}

cc_library_shared {
    name: "proximityhal.default",
    defaults: [
        "vendor.acme.one.proximity.defaults",
    ],
    srcs: [
        "hal/proximity_hal.cpp"
    ],
    header_libs: [
        "liblog_headers",
        "libhardware_headers",
    ],
    local_include_dirs: [
        "include"
    ],
    shared_libs: [
        "liblog",
        "libhardware",
    ],
    static_libs: [
        "libacmeproximityshim",
    ]
}
```

Understanding the Shim

The final step in connecting the proximity driver to its HAL is the shim that actually implements the three device methods, open_sensor, close_sensor, and poll_sensor, for the Acme Proximity Sensor device. The definition of the shim interface is in the file proximity/ include/dev/proximity_sensor.h. This is the "bottom" of the HAL. It is the API for the proxy to which the HAL code will delegate calls for one, specific type of proximity sensor device to which the proximity HAL provides access.

Because this example is quite simple and the HAL is responsible for only one actual hardware device, these multiple layers of abstraction may seem excessive. Indeed, in this specific context, they may be. Consider, though, that in this specific pedagogical exercise, the whole notion of a HAL may be excessive.

The shim API is not part of the HAL. It is not included by proximity_hal.h, the definition of a proximity sensor's HAL. The implementations of the device HAL (there may be more than one) is probably the only code in the entire system that uses it. It completely encapsulates the details of a specific device and should certainly never be needed by code that uses the HAL. Listing 8.8 shows the shim API.

Listing 8.8   **Proximity Sensor Shim API**

```
#ifndef ACME_PROXIMITY_SENSOR_H
#define ACME_PROXIMITY_SENSOR_H

#include "proximity_hal.h"

int open_sensor(proximity_params_t &params);

int poll_sensor(int fd, int precision);

int close_sensor(int fd);

#endif //ACME_PROXIMITY_SENSOR_H
```

No surprises here. These are exactly the services described earlier and used by the HAL: The sensor can be turned on and off to optimize battery use; while it is on, it can be polled. A poll takes as arguments the device file descriptor, a requested precision (a number between precision.min and precision.max), and returns a proximity value that is between proximity.min and proximity.max. These bounds are populated in the params struct passed to the shim when turning the sensor on.

It is worth restating that although the device driver for a given device may run at least partially as part of the kernel, none of the HAL code does. All the code in this chapter runs in user space. Although its use may be restricted to privileged applications, HAL code runs exclusively as part of some application.

Implementing the Shim

Finally, Listing 8.9 shows the actual implementation of the shim that connects the HAL to the device driver. It is in the file proximity/dev/proximity_sensor.cpp. In this example, it is just a stub. It just mocks the code that would actually talk to a device driver. Instead of the hardwired values returned here, a real proxy would interface with the hardware device, probably through its USB driver, to perform the actions required by the HAL.

Listing 8.9   **Proximity Sensor Glue Code Stub**

```
#include "dev/proximity_sensor.h"

// This is stub, mocking actual glue code.
// If this were a real thing, it would talk to a device driver,
// presumably for a USB device

int open_sensor(proximity_params_t &params) {
    params.precision_min = 0;
    params.precision_range = 100;
    params.proximity_min = 0;
    params.proximity_range = 100;

    return 0; // a completely fake fd
}

int poll_sensor(int fd, int precision) {
    if (precision < 0) {
        return -1;
    } else if (precision < 70) {
        return 60;
    } else if (precision < 100) {
        return 63;
    } else {
        return -1;
    }
}

int close_sensor(int fd) {
    return 0;
}
```

Now that the shim is defined, it must also be added to the build. Because it is used by the HAL as well as the simple daemon and the binderized HAL covered in Chapter 12, it is built as a library. The extension of the Android.bp shown in Listing 8.10 shows the additions necessary to build the library as well as expose its headers to other components of the system.

Listing 8.10   **Proximity Sensor Shim Additions to Android.bp**

```
cc_library {
    name: "libacmeproximityshim",
    defaults: [
        "vendor.acme.one.proximity.defaults",
    ],
    srcs: [
        "dev/proximity_sensor.cpp",
    ],
    header_libs: [
        "libhardware_headers",
    ],
    local_include_dirs: [
        "include",
    ],
}

cc_library_headers {
    name: "libacmeproximityshim_headers",
    defaults: [
        "vendor.acme.one.proximity.defaults",
    ],
    header_libs: [
        "libhardware_headers",
    ],
    export_header_lib_headers: [
        "libhardware_headers",
    ],
    export_include_dirs: ["include"],
}
```

Summary

This chapter introduced the Android HAL. A HAL is the interface between Android and a class of similar hardware devices: cameras, audio, sensors, and so on. The primary purpose of a HAL is to provide a single API for all devices that provide a similar service. A HAL abstracts device specifics so that Android code that uses the device need not change to accommodate a specific device.

Because they are both abstractions and APIs, designing HALs requires careful thought and a pretty good crystal ball. Especially when a team does not have a lot of experience with either Android or a new device, designing a HAL may bog down development and not prove future-proof anyway. Good reasons exist for creating a HAL. Good reasons also exist for planning to throw one away.

It is even possible to make an argument for C glue code that is extremely simple and hoisting any complexity up into Android Java. If the project scope already includes modification of the Android code, a Java device shim may be the most effective plan. On the other hand, for devices that will get OS updates—especially if those updates will come from an external source or that will need to adapt to multiple hardware implementations—a HAL is just the thing.

The implementation of the Acme Proximity sensor HAL in this chapter is a representative basic HAL: It is realistic, complete, and it compiled and ran at the time of this writing. It is, however, a stub. It does not actually use a USB driver to communicate with a physical device as it almost certainly would were it more than pedagogical.

The next chapter demonstrates using this HAL in a daemon written in C. Chapter 11 demonstrates converting this legacy HAL to a Binderized (Treble) HAL.

9

Getting to Java: The JNI

The previous chapter detailed the process of creating a HAL, an abstract interface between the Android framework and a novel bit of hardware.

That is only halfway there. Although a HAL is the canonical way of plumbing hardware into Android, it is not sufficient to make the device useful from Android Java programs. To do that, we need the Java's Native Interface, the JNI.

The goal for this chapter is to cross the boundary into Android's implementation language, Java. We'll cross that boundary by coding a Java language application that connects to the proximity sensor using its HAL and that logs its status once every minute or so. We'll achieve that goal in three steps:

1. We'll create a simple native application that talks directly to the proximity sensor. This application is a simple extension of the one discussed at the end of Chapter 6.

2. We'll refactor that application to use the HAL we built in the last chapter. A native application that uses the HAL is a useful artifact: The only significant distinction between a native application and the corresponding Java application is, exactly, the implementation language. The choice of environments depends entirely on the preferences of the team that will build and support it.

3. We'll implement an application in Java using Java's Native Interface (the JNI) that uses the native HAL from code running inside the Android's bytecode interpreter.

> **Note**
>
> It was our intention to run the last example, the Java application, also as a daemon. Unfortunately, we were unable to construct SE rules that allowed it to run in ART under `init`. Instead, the Java application shown here must be run as a system service started by Zygote (as described in Chapter 7).

Code Structure

The applications described in this chapter are complete and freestanding. Therefore, each goes into its own subdirectory of "app" directory in the Acme One source structure. Figure 9.1 shows the structure (with the code from the previous chapters elided).

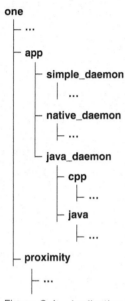

Figure 9.1   Application Code Layout

Although the code for each of the applications is nested inside the "app" folder in the Acme One device file structure, there is no need for all the code to be a fixed part of the Acme One source code repository. As usual, creating a new git repo for each separate application and using repo to add them at checkout time to the workspace makes sense.

It is possible to do even better, though. Notice that, as described, each of the applications has exactly the same function: periodically logging proximity data to the console. There is no reason ever to build all three for a single given device. All three implementations might exist—perhaps as legacy implementations or specialized versions required for some specific device—but having all three in the workspace at once would be useless, at best.

The repo tool not only supports this scenario—three different versions of the same application—but a nifty feature called groups (first described in Chapter 2) makes it very convenient. Listing 9.1 shows the additions to the manifest.

Listing 9.1   **Manifest Additions for the Proximity Applications**

```
<!-- Acme Applications -->
  <project path="app/simple_daemon"
           name="simple_daemon" remote="acme"
           groups="nodefault" />
  <project path=app/native_daemon
           name="native_daemon" remote="acme"
           groups="nodefault" />
  <project path=app/java_daemon
           name="java_daemon" remote="acme"
           groups="nodefault" />
```

Listing 9.1 demonstrates the use of this new workspace customization feature, the `groups` attribute. Annotating a project in the manifest with the group "nodefault" indicates to the repo tool that the annotated repository should not be downloaded as it normally would be when the workspace is synched. To pull the code for one (or more) of the applications into the workspace, use the repo tool -g flag to specify a group that includes the desired implementation.

One simple way to select a particular project is by its name. Every project belongs to a group whose name is "name:" followed by the value of the project's `name` attribute. For example, when used with the manifest shown in part in Listing 9.1, the following command will create a workspace that contains the simple-daemon application:

```
repo init -g name:simple_daemon …
```

Using the Device

The code for the first version of the application is almost trivial. It simply opens the device directly (no HAL), polls at a fixed interval, and logs the result. This is the trivial extension of the daemon from Chapter 6. Listing 9.2 shows the code for it.

Listing 9.2   **Simple Native Proximity Application**

```
#include <unistd.h>
#include <stdio.h>
#include <android/log.h>
#include "dev/proximity_sensor.h"

#define DELAY_SECS 60
#define ALOG(msg) __android_log_write(ANDROID_LOG_DEBUG, "PROXIMITY", msg)

int main(int argc, char *argv[]) {
    struct proximity_params_t config;
    char message[128];

    int fd = open_sensor(config);
```

```
    if (fd < 0)
        return -1;

    int n = 0;
    int precision;
    while (true) {
        sleep(DELAY_SECS);

        n++;
        if (n < 10) {
            precision = 40;
        } else {
            n = 0;
            precision = 80;
        }

        int proximity = poll_sensor(fd, precision);

        if ((proximity < config.proximity_min)) {
            close_sensor(fd);
            return 0;
        }

        snprintf(message,
                 sizeof(message),
                 "proximity @%2d: %4.2f",
                 precision,
                 (100.0 * (proximity - config.proximity_min))
                        / config.proximity_range);

        ALOG(message);
    }
}
```

This code polls the sensor once every minute with a precision of 40 and once every 10 minutes with a precision of 80. It logs the result to the console.

Listing 9.3 shows the blueprint file used to build the application. It appeared previously in Chapter 6 as Listing 6.11.

Listing 9.3 **Building the Simple Native Application**

```
cc_binary {
    name: "acmesimpledaemon",
    relative_install_path: "hw",
    init_rc: ["vendor.acmesimpledaemon.acme.one.rc"],
    header_libs: [
```

```
        "libacmeproximityshim_headers",
        "liblog_headers",
    ],
    srcs: [
        "acme-simple-daemon.cpp"
    ],
    shared_libs: [
        "liblog",
        "libcutils",
    ],
    static_libs: [
        "libacmeproximityshim",
    ],
    vendor: true,
    proprietary: true,
}
```

Using the HAL

The second version of the application is only slightly different from the first. The functional part of the code, the loop that logs proximity readings, is identical. The only differences between this code and that of the preceding application are that, instead of opening the device directly, it requests the device HAL by name from the OS and then uses the returned reference to invoke sensor methods through the HAL.

Listing 9.4 shows the code for the second version of the application (located at device/acme/ one/app/native_daemon/acme-native-daemon.cpp).

Listing 9.4 **HAL Native Proximity Application**

```
#include <unistd.h>
#include <stdio.h>
#include <android/log.h>
#include <hardware/hardware.h>

#include "dev/proximity_hal.h"

#define DELAY_SECS 60
#define ALOG(msg) __android_log_write(ANDROID_LOG_DEBUG, "PROXIMITYD", msg)

int main(int argc, char *argv[]) {
    const hw_module_t* module
    if (hw_get_module(ACME_PROXIMITY_SENSOR_MODULE, &module) {
        ALOG("Failed to load Acme proximity HAL module");
        return -1;
    }
```

```
    proximity_sensor_device_t* device;
    if (module->methods->open(
        module,
        nullptr,
        reinterpret_cast<struct hw_device_t**>(& device))) {
        ALOG("Failed to open Acme proximity HAL");
        return -1;
    }

    proximity_params_t config = device->params;
    char message[128];

    int n = 0;
    int precision;
    while (true) {
        sleep(DELAY_SECS);

        n++;
        if (n < 10) {
            precision = 40;
        } else {
            n = 0;
            precision = 80;
        }

        int proximity = device->poll_sensor(device, precision);

        if ((proximity < config.proximity.min)) {
            device->common.close(reinterpret_cast<hw_device_t *>(device));
            return 0;
        }

        snprintf(message, sizeof(message), "proximity @%2d: %4.2f", precision,
            (100.0 * (proximity - config.proximity.min)) / config.proximity.range);

        ALOG(message);
    }
}
```

The only thing worthy of particular notice, here, is that the second argument to the open method is null. It could have been used by the HAL to do runtime specialization. The simple Acme Proximity HAL described in the last chapter, however, ignores the parameter completely.

The build script for this second application is also nearly identical to that for the first native application. The acmenativedaemon must have the same SE label as that used for the simple version. That label allows it access to USB serial devices and to be started by init. The label is applied in file_contexts within the SE policy folder. Because these things are so similar, they are not included here. The only differences are the application name and the libraries it uses, as shown in Listing 9.5.

Listing 9.5   **HAL Native Proximity Application Build File**

```
cc_binary {
    name: "acmenativedaemon",
    relative_install_path: "hw",
    init_rc: ["vendor.acmenativedaemon.acme.one.rc"],
    header_libs: [
        "libacmeproximityshim_headers",
        "liblog_headers",
        "libhardware_headers",
    ],
    srcs: [
        "acme-native-daemon.cpp"
    ],
    shared_libs: [
        "liblog",
        "libcutils",
        "libhardware",
    ],
    vendor: true,
    proprietary: true,
}
```

Using the Java Native Interface

Most Android applications are written in interpreted languages. The source code for these applications—probably Kotlin or Java—is compiled to bytecodes. Bytecodes are not instructions that can be executed by any actual hardware. Instead, as discussed in Chapter 7, they are native instructions for a *virtual machine*. The virtual machine is an application that runs on the target device, interprets each of the bytecodes in the compiled app, and executes a set of native instructions necessary to perform the action described by the bytecode.

Most Android code, then, is executed as interpreted bytecodes. Clearly, the execution of those bytecodes can do only things that the virtual machine that interprets those bytecodes was built to do. In particular, because no virtual machine has compiled into it the ability to talk to the Acme proximity sensor, there is no way that interpreted code can use the sensor.

Fortunately, interpreted virtual machine instructions are not a running program's only interface to native instructions and the operating system. Since its creation, the Java language has defined a mechanism that allows an application to execute arbitrary native code uninterpreted and outside the virtual machine. The mechanism is as old as Java itself and is called the Java Native Interface (JNI). The Android virtual machines implement this mechanism.

> **Note**
>
> Although the JNI allows the execution of machine instructions that are not part of the virtual machine, JNI code is executed as part of the same **process** that is running the virtual machine. JNI code executes "outside the virtual machine" only in the sense that it is not executing instructions that virtual machine designers provided. It is still virtual machine methods that are below the JNI code in the call stack and to which control will return when the execution of the JNI code completes.

Executing Native Code

Figure 9.2 illustrates the ways in which native code can be used in an Android application.

Application code, as discussed earlier, is typically written in an interpreted language. It is represented in Figure 9.2 by the largest box at the top of the figure.

Android application code depends on a library of standard functions and classes in the `java.*` and `android.*` packages. The `java` packages have an API that is very similar to the Java 8 JRE. The `android` library defines the Android runtime environment. Both of these libraries are implemented largely in Java and, therefore, most of the code in each compiles into bytecodes that are executed by the virtual machine.

Beneath the interpreted code and shown in the center of Figure 9.2 is the virtual machine. It is, of course, written in a language (probably C and C++) that is compiled into machine instructions that are native to the target device.

To the left and right of the virtual machine in Figure 9.2 are two more pieces of code that are compiled directly (again, usually from C or C++) into instructions native to the target device. Although run as part of the application, these pieces of code are not compiled to bytecodes and are not interpreted by the virtual machine.

Nearly all Android programs make use of the native code represented by the block on the bottom right of the figure when they use the runtime libraries. Although, as mentioned earlier, much of the runtime environment code is implemented in Java, the implementations of certain functions that do specialized things—like interfacing with the kernel, file and network I/O or performing highly optimized functions like encryption and decryption—are all native (non-interpreted) code called from the Java.

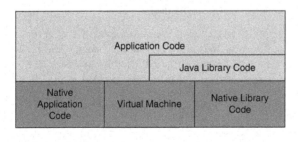

Figure 9.2   Interpreted and Native Code

The Java Native Interface (JNI) is the mechanism by which the interpreted runtime library code calls the device native code. It is also a well-defined, public API; is implemented by the Android virtual machine; and can be used directly by application code, just as it is used by the Java and Android runtime libraries. Any application can use the JNI to execute native code: While it is running, it can load an arbitrary native library and execute the code in it.

> **Note**
>
> A previous Java-based smartphone standard, J2ME, enforced security and controlled application access to hardware by preventing the use of native code. Applications could only execute instructions that were compiled into the virtual machine; access to instructions deemed "dangerous" was carefully controlled.
>
> Android has a much different security model and no such restriction. Applications can and do execute their own native code.

JNI: The Java Side

One more time, let's interrupt our strict up-the-stack journey through the Android landscape and look at the JNI starting from above, in code written in Java.

The Java side of the JNI is straightforward and quite simple. It consists of the keyword "native" and the system method, `System.loadLibrary`.

A method with the keyword `native` in its declaration—a **native function**—is similar to the declaration of a function in a Java interface: It declares the function prototype but not its implementation. Methods declared in an interface must be defined in the classes that implement the interface. Methods declared "native," to the contrary, are not defined in Java at all. Instead, the virtual machine expects to find their definitions as canonically named symbols in a library loaded with the `load` (or `loadLibrary`) method.

> **Note**
>
> Kotlin uses the keyword "external" to accomplish the same thing: declaring a function whose definition is elsewhere.

Listing 9.6 shows the declaration of the three methods that Java code will need to interact with the proximity device.

Listing 9.6 **Native Method Declarations**

```
package com.acme.device.proximity;
// ...

public class AcmeProximitySensor {
    // ...
```

```
    private static native long open();
    private static native int poll(long hdl, int precision);
    private static native void close(long hdl);
}
```

JNI: The Native Side

These three methods must now be defined in a linkable library. In this example, the library will be written in C.

The Android virtual machine will translate calls to these native methods into calls to canonically named functions in a native library. The definitions for the corresponding functions must have exactly the names that the runtime expects them to have. Fortunately, there is tool that is part of the Java Development Kit that will generate the C prototypes for the native definitions automatically: javah.

> **Note**
>
> javah has been deprecated as of Java 9. Even in Java 8, its functionality can be duplicated with the -h flag for the java compiler, javac.

Javah need not be part of the build process. Running it is necessary only when new native methods are introduced or when one of the signatures of an existing native methods changes: when the headers it generates will be different from the headers it generated last time it was run. Some shops decide to create the headers once and then check them in to source control like any other source file.

Because the process of generating the native prototypes can be automated, some shops do prefer to make it part of the build. When there are a lot of native methods and they are changing frequently, this is a very reasonable approach. Note, though, that javah only generates the header files and the function prototypes! If the corresponding function definitions (presumably in a .c file) do not match, the build will fail with native compiler errors.

Running javah by hand is quite simple. It takes as arguments:

- The classpath identifying the directory (or jar) that is the top of the package tree containing the compiled Java .class files. The classpath is specified using the -cp command line option.

- Either a -d or -o argument indicating the directory or file (respectively) into which the tool should put the generated output.

- The fully qualified name of the class containing native declarations for which headers are to be generated.

For instance, run from the root of the Java application package (device/acme/one/app/java_daemon), the following command will create a .h file from the binary generated by compiling the code in Listing 9.6:

```
javah -cp java \
 -o cpp/com_acme_device_proximity_AcmeProximitySensor.h \
  com.acme.device.proximity.AcmeProximitySensor
```

Javah will search the directory "java" for the class file containing the class com.acme.
device.proximity.AcmeProximitySensor, (probably java/com/acme/device/
proximity/AndroidProximitySensor.class) and create C prototypes for any native
methods it finds there. The prototypes will be written to the file cpp/com_acme_device_
proximity_AcmeProximitySensor.h. Listing 9.7 shows the generated file.

Listing 9.7   **Proximity HAL JNI Function Prototypes**

```
/* DO NOT EDIT THIS FILE - it is machine generated */
#include <jni.h>
/* Header for class com_acme_device_proximity_AcmeProximitySensor */

#ifndef _Included_com_acme_device_proximity_AcmeProximitySensor
#define _Included_com_acme_device_proximity_AcmeProximitySensor
#ifdef __cplusplus
extern "C" {
#endif
/*
 * Class:      com_acme_device_proximity_AcmeProximitySensor
 * Method:     open
 * Signature: ()J
 */
JNIEXPORT jlong
JNICALL Java_com_acme_device_proximity_AcmeProximitySensor_open
  (JNIEnv *, jclass);

/*
 * Class:      com_acme_device_proximity_AcmeProximitySensor
 * Method:     poll
 * Signature: (JI)I
 */
JNIEXPORT jint
JNICALL Java_com_acme_device_proximity_AcmeProximitySensor_poll
  (JNIEnv *, jclass, jlong, jint);

/*
 * Class:      com_acme_device_proximity_AcmeProximitySensor
 * Method:     close
 * Signature: (J)V
 */
JNIEXPORT void
JNICALL Java_com_acme_device_proximity_AcmeProximitySensor_close
  (JNIEnv *, jclass, jlong);
```

```
#ifdef __cplusplus
}
#endif
#endif
```

Note, especially, the `extern "C" { … }` directive. It is essential! It prevents a C++ compiler from mangling the names of the functions and making their definitions unrecognizable as the definitions for the corresponding Java `native` declaration.

> ### Note
>
> Canonically named methods are not the only way to link the native implementation of a method to its Java declaration. The `RegisterNatives` JNI function takes, as an argument, an array of `JNINativeMethod`, each of which identifies a Java method (by fully qualified signature) and includes a pointer to the native implementation. Used in the `JNI_OnLoad` method (called by the VM when it loads a native library), `JNINativeMethod` provides an alternative way of connecting Java and native methods.

Note also that these native definitions depend on the header file `jni.h`. The `jni.h` header file contains the definitions for the native type abstractions for Java's base types—int, `long`, [] (array), and so on—some macros (`JNIEXPORT`, `JNICALL`, and so on), but most importantly the definition of the JNI environment, a structure of opaque pointers to standard JNI functions. These functions allow native code to work with Java objects.

This chapter will conclude with a slightly deeper discussion of the JNI native environment. For the moment, though, let's just assume (as it is usually safe to do), that a `jint` is an int, a `jlong` is a `long`, and so on.

The next step is implementing the functions in native code. Stealing code from Listing 9.4 makes this a trivial task. Listing 9.8 shows the result.

Listing 9.8 **Proximity HAL JNI Implementation**

```
#include <jni.h>
#include <string>
#include <hardware/hardware.h>

#include "dev/proximity_hal.h"

JNIEXPORT jlong JNICALL Java_com_acme_device_proximity_AcmeProximitySensor_open
  (JNIEnv * env, jclass clazz) {
    const hw_module_t *module;

    if (hw_get_module(ACME_PROXIMITY_SENSOR_MODULE, &module))
        return -1;
```

```
    long device;
    if (module->methods->open(
            module,
            nullptr,
            reinterpret_cast<struct hw_device_t **>(&device)))
        return -1;

    return (jlong) device;
}

JNIEXPORT jint JNICALL Java_com_acme_device_proximity_AcmeProximitySensor_poll
    (JNIEnv *env, jclass clazz, jlong handle, jint precision);
    auto *device = reinterpret_cast<proximity_sensor_device_t *>(handle);
    return device->poll_sensor(device, precision);
}

JNIEXPORT jint JNICALL Java_com_acme_device_proximity_AcmeProximitySensor_close
    (JNIEnv * env, jclass clazz, jlong handle);
    auto device = reinterpret_cast<proximity_sensor_device_t *>(handle);
    return device->common.close(reinterpret_cast<hw_device_t *>(device));
}
```

This is a calculated and extremely simple example. Once again, though, the reader is cautioned! The JNI is extensive, complex, and easy to break. Entire books exist about this topic alone.

The alert reader will notice that the reference to the sensor, returned by the HAL, is cast as a `jlong` in both the `open` and the `close` methods. This is the introduction to a common and powerful JNI technique. Its purpose will become obvious when the corresponding methods are implemented in Java.

A Java Proximity Application

Having plumbed a path from Java code through the HAL and into the Acme Proximity Sensor, we can now implement an analog for the applications shown in Listings 9.2 and 9.4 that is written in Java.

The Native Shim

The first step will be to complete the `AcmeProximitySensor` class, shown in part in Listing 9.6. It is the shim that connects the Java environment to the native environment.

It is very much best practice that the shim code abstract away even the faintest whiff of native-ness. The API for the shim should follow all the best practices standard for any Java API. In particular, declaring the API in a mockable Java interface is a great way to make it possible to test client code without requiring access to any specific hardware.

Listing 9.9 shows a complete implementation of the `AcmeProximitySensor` class.

Listing 9.9 **Proximity HAL Java Implementation**

```java
public class AcmeProximitySensor implements AutoCloseable {
    static { System.loadLibrary("acmeproximityjni"); }

    private long peer;

    public void init() throws IOException {
        synchronized (this) {
            if (peer != 0L) { return; }
            peer = open();
            if (peer == 0L) {
                throw new IOException("Failed to open proximity sensor");
            }
        }
    }

    public int poll(int precision) throws IOException {
        synchronized (this) {
            if (peer == 0L) { throw new IOException("Device not open"); }
            return poll(peer, precision);
        }
    }

    @Override
    public void close() throws IOException {
        final long hdl;
        synchronized (this) {
            hdl = peer;
            peer = 0L;
        }
        if (hdl == 0L) { return; }

        if (close(hdl) < 0) {
            throw new IOException("Failed closing proximity sensor");
        }
    }

    @Override
    protected void finalize() throws Throwable {
        try { close(); }
        finally { super.finalize(); }
    }

    private static native long open();
```

```
    private static native int poll(long handle, int precision);

    private static native int close(long handle);
}
```

There are several things to note in this code.

The first is the use of the previously discussed System.loadLibrary method. It is called, as is frequently the case, from a static initializer that will be invoked when the class is loaded. This is a common strategy because the library must be loaded before any of the methods in the class can be used.

There are other strategies, though. A system that requires several native libraries may load them all at once, perhaps using some kind of registration system, as part of startup. Another possibility, especially in systems that require additional initialization, is loading necessary native libraries in an initialization method that client code must call explicitly before making any other use of the library.

Note, also, that System.loadLibrary loads the library named in its actual parameter in a system-dependent way. It modifies the name to conform to the platform library naming conventions and then attempts to load it from the library path. When run on a Linux OS, for example, the code in Listing 9.9 will load the libacmeproximityjni.so library. On a Windows system, though, it would load the acmeproximityjni.dll library.

The library path can be specified at JVM startup using the system parameter java.library.path or, on Android Linux, by setting the environment variable LD_LIBRARY_PATH. A second method, System.load, mentioned previously, will load a library from a specific file named in the fully qualified path passed as its argument.

Next, observe the use of the variable peer. In this code, the Java long variable peer contains the native reference to the HAL object as described in the discussion of Listing 9.8. Unlike C, in which a reference can be made opaque by declaring it void*, making a reference opaque in Java is fairly difficult. Nonetheless, it is crucial that the contents of a variable used in this way be treated as opaque. Any mutation of any kind by the Java code is almost certainly an error and probably a disastrous one. As usual, in situations like this, minimizing visibility and mutability is a useful strategy.

Together, Listings 9.8 and 9.9 illustrate the simplest form of a very common pattern. The responsibility for managing the Java use of specialized hardware is handled through the coordination of two objects, one Java and one native. The two objects are the two ends of a bridge—one end in the native code and the other in the Java code—through which all interactions take place. Client code instantiates the Java object and the Java object manages the native object, frequently called a native peer, or a companion object. The Java code holds a reference to the native object. The native code's awareness of the Java code is kept minimal.

The Native Shim: Opaque Peer

Another example of this pattern attempts to enforce the opacity of the native reference in the Java variable by using reflection in the native code to set the value of the reference held in the Java variable. Listings 9.10 and 9.11 illustrate this technique.

Listing 9.10 **Opaque Peer: Native**

```
JNIEXPORT int
JNICALL Java_com_acme_device_proximity_AcmeProximitySensor_open
    (JNIEnv *env, jclass klass, jobject instance) {

    if (hw_get_module(ACME_PROXIMITY_SENSOR_MODULE, &module))
        return -1;

    hw_device_t *device;
    if (module->methods->open(module, nullptr, &device)))
        return -2;

    jfieldID peer = env->GetFieldID(klass, "peer", "J");
    if (!peer)
        return -3;

    env->SetLongField(instance, peer, reinterpret_cast<jlong>(mem));

    return 0;
}
```

Listing 9.11 **Opaque Peer: Java**

```
public class AcmeProximitySensor implements AutoCloseable {
    /...

    private long peer;

    /...

    public void init() throws IOException {
        synchronized (this) {
            int status = open(this);
            if (status != 0) {
                throw new IOException(
                    "Failed to open proximity sensor: " + status);
            }
        }
    }
```

```
/...

private static native int open(AcmeProximitySensor instance);

/...
}
```

Two new JNI methods are used here without introduction: `GetFieldID` and `SetLongField`. Their names, though, are fairly self-explanatory (they return a reference to a Java field and assign the field value, respectively) so that the concept the listing introduces should be clear.

The `open` method in Listing 9.11 could, as easily, be an instance method instead of a static method. In JNI, the difference between the implementations of a static and an instance method is the second argument to the method. The second argument to a static native function is a reference to the class to which the function belongs. The second argument to an instance native function is a reference to the instance to which the function belongs. Holding a reference to the instance means that the native code can access the instance's fields, exactly as the example code does.

In this case, however, we also need a reference to the object's class (for the call to `GetFieldID`). Because both are needed, using a static method (which provides the reference to the class object) will work just as well. We pass the instance reference (`this` in the call to `open`, in Listing 9.11) explicitly. The native implementation then has both of the references that it needs.

Although somewhat more complex, the strategy illustrated in Listings 9.10 and 9.11 has advantages. In this implementation, any Java use of the variable `peer` is now clearly an error. Distinguishing between appropriate and inappropriate use of the stored pointer is not necessary: *Any* use is an error. Another advantage is that the `open` method's return value is now, unambiguously, a status code. No need exists to partition returns into legal values and illegal values.

The Native Shim: Finalization

Returning to Listing 9.9, one more issue is worthy of note: the management of the lifecycle of the companion object.

Although the garbage collector manages Java's memory, native memory usually must be allocated and deallocated explicitly. An `AcmeProximitySensor` object allocates its companion in its "open" method. So how does it free it? There are several possible answers to that question.

The first and best is "explicitly." For reasons that will be discussed momentarily, the most effective way to handle explicitly managed memory is explicitly. Ideally, an object with a native peer that must be freed explicitly would be marked somehow so that clients would know that they should explicitly free it.

That is exactly the purpose of Java's `Closeable` interface. An object that implements `Closeable` is hinting to its user that it needs to be closed explicitly when the user is through with it. The `AcmeProximitySensor` implements `Closeable`'s sub-interface `AutoCloseable` and uses it to free its companion.

> **Note**
>
> The `AutoCloseable` interface, introduced in Java 7, extends `Closeable`: Prefer it, where possible. Most significantly, instances of a class that implements `AutoCloseable` can be used with the *try-with-resources* statement. They can also throw exceptions, other than an `IOException`, as appropriate to their specific failure modes.
>
> The contract for the `AutoCloseable`'s `close` method is also different: idempotency is not a requirement. Rather, developers are strongly encouraged to mark closed instances and to prevent their use after closing.

A second strategy is a finalizer. A Java finalizer is a method with the specific signature, `protected void finalize() throws Throwable`. If an object has a method with that signature, it is called by the Java runtime just before the garbage collector frees the object's memory. This seems perfect: with one small method, when the `AcmeProximitySensor` goes away, so does its companion.

Unfortunately, however, there's no such thing as a free lunch. Finalizers are quite difficult to get right and, even when correct, have problems. Correctness first.

There is no guarantee about the order in which objects are finalized after they become eligible for garbage collection. The example code in Listing 9.12 has several problems, not the least of which is that it may get a `NullPointerException` in its finalizer. There is no guarantee that the list referenced by `objects` has itself not already been finalized when the finalizer for an instance of `BrokenFinalizer` is run. Its contents might well have been finalized first!

Listing 9.12 Broken Finalizer: Don't Do This!

```
public class BrokenFinalizer implements Closeable {
    @NonNull
    private final List<NativeObject> objects

    // …

    @Override
    protected void finalize() throws Throwable {
        for (NativeObject obj: objects) { obj.close(); }
    }
}
```

In addition to being brittle and very difficult to code, finalizers have two other problems. The first is that they impose a considerable inefficiency on the garbage collector. Because a finalizer can do all kinds of weird stuff (including "resurrect" the object being garbage collected by storing a reference to it somewhere!), the garbage collector has to do checks that are not necessary for an object that does not have a finalizer. These checks slow the collector down, cause it to place a heavier burden on the application, and mean that the lag between last use and deallocation gets longer.

The second problem, though, hinted at in the last sentence, is even worse. Although Java promises that it will run the garbage collector before it runs out of memory, there is no way to predict how long an object that is eligible for collection will sit around in memory before Java needs space and schedules it for collection. Furthermore, Java cannot guarantee that all finalizers will be run before an application runs out of memory. Finalizers are run in a platform-dependent way: almost universally on a single Java thread. If an application allocates and then frees a hundred large objects every second, each of those objects is scheduled for finalization, and each finalization takes a half a second to complete, the application is doomed. An application with native companion objects can build up a considerable backlog of dead objects before a garbage collection takes place. Instead of being freed incrementally, all of those objects are put on the finalization queue suddenly and all at once.

Despite these problems, finalizers can be a reasonable part of a "belt and suspenders" policy, as shown in Listing 9.9. An AcmeProximitySensor is Closeable: Client code is expected to explicitly close each instance when it is done with it. If the client code fails to do so, however, the finalizer will prevent a native memory leak.

The Native Shim: Reference Queues

The last and most complex way of managing native object lifecycles are **reference queues**. In return for somewhat more complicated code, reference queues remove many of the problems that finalizers have. They do not interfere with garbage collection, and they allow ordered freeing of objects.

As of Java 9, finalizers have officially been deprecated in favor of Cleaners. As part of Java 9, Cleaners are not available in Android. There is good news, though: PhantomReferences and ReferenceQueues, the technologies underlying Java 9's Cleaner, are available in Android. The message to Android developers should be clear, even if Cleaners themselves are not available in the Android runtime environment.

The combination of a reference queue and a phantom reference works like this: The constructor for an instance of the PhantomReference class (or one of its subclasses) takes two arguments: an object and a reference queue. When the object whose reference is the first parameter to the constructor becomes eligible for garbage collection, the phantom reference (itself) is enqueued on the reference queue that was the second parameter to the constructor.

Calls to PhantomReference.get *always* return null: The referenced object itself is unreachable via the phantom reference and the existence of the reference cannot affect its reachability. What the reference can do, though, is provide a way to remember that there is unfinished business, when the object to which it is a reference no longer exists.

The implementation of a reference queue solution is somewhat difficult. Let's take it in four parts. First, Listing 9.13 is the machinery that manages the lifecycle of an AcmeProximitySensor object and its peer.

Listing 9.13   **Reference Queue: Native Companion and Its Lifecycle**

```java
public class AcmeProximitySensor implements AutoCloseable {

    // …

    static final Map<AtomicLong, Reference<?>> CLEANERS = new HashMap<>();

    static { System.loadLibrary("acmeproximityjni"); }

    // …

    @NonNull
    public static AcmeProximitySensor getSensor() {
        synchronized (CLEANERS) {
            final AtomicLong peerRef = new AtomicLong(open());
            final AcmeProximitySensor sensor = new AcmeProximitySensor(peerRef);
            CLEANERS.put(peerRef, new SensorCleaner(peerRef, sensor));
            return sensor;
        }
    }

    static void cleanup(AtomicLong peerRef) {
        final long peer = peerRef.getAndSet(0);
        if (peer == 0) { return; }

        synchronized (CLEANERS) {
            CLEANERS.remove(peerRef);
            close(peer);
        }
    }

    // …

    @GuardedBy("CLEANERS")
    private static native void close(long handle);

    @GuardedBy("CLEANERS")
    private static native long open();

    @GuardedBy("CLEANERS")
    private static native int poll(long handle, int precision);
}
```

The static method getSensor is the factory method for instances of the class
AcmeProximitySensor. Client code will call this method instead of the class constructor to
create new instances. The class constructor is private, ensuring that this is the only way to
create new instances: All new instances come from this method.

The method does four things:

1. It creates the native companion object and stashes the reference to it in an `AtomicLong`.
2. It creates the Java instance, passing the peer reference. The Java object now has access to its native peer.
3. It creates a `SensorCleaner`. This is the object that will be responsible for cleaning up the native peer if the user fails to do so.
4. It stores the `SensorCleaner` in a map.

The last step is important and yet easy to forget. Like any other Java object, the `SensorCleaner` is eligible for garbage collection as soon as there are no more references to it. Unless something, somewhere, remembers it, it will be garbage collected and will not be around to clean up after the `AcmeProximitySensor` instance with which it is associated.

The static method `cleanup(AtomicLong)` is the bottleneck at the end of the lifecycle of every `AcmeProximitySensor` instance. It simply undoes what the `getSensor` method did: It frees the native companion object and removes the `SensorCleaner` from the map so that it can be garbage collected.

It also ensures that the native `close` method will not be called more than once. The `getAndSet` in its first line ensures that the rest of the method will be executed no more than once for a given native peer, no matter how often it is called. The method is idempotent.

These two methods are the bookends for the `AcmeProximitySensor` lifecycle. The `getSensor` method is the only way to get one. All we have to do is make sure that the `cleanup(AtomicLong)` method is called at least once for every native companion.

As mentioned earlier, the best way to do this is explicitly. Listing 9.14 shows the implementation of the `AcmeProximitySensor` and, in particular, its implementation of the `AutoCloseable` interface.

Listing 9.14   **Reference Queue: Explicit Close**

```java
public class AcmeProximitySensor implements AutoCloseable {

    // …

    private final AtomicLong peerRef;

    private AcmeProximitySensor(AtomicLong peerRef) { this.peerRef = peerRef; }

    public int poll(int precision) throws IOException {
        synchronized (CLEANERS) {
            final long peer = peerRef.get();
            if (peer == 0) { throw new IOException("Device not open"); }
            return poll(peer, precision);
        }
    }
}
```

```
    @Override
    public void close() { cleanup(peerRef); }

    // …
}
```

This code is similar to the equivalent code in Listing 9.9. The only significant difference, really, is that it delegates the call to close, required by the AutoCloseable interface, to cleanup(AtomicLong). Well-behaved client code will fulfill the outstanding condition: at least one call to cleanup(AtomicLong) via AcmeProximitySensor.close.

What happens, though, when client code is not well behaved? Listing 9.15 shows the backstop.

Listing 9.15 **Reference Queue: Service Task**

```
public class AcmeProximitySensor implements Closeable {
    private static final class SensorCleaner
        extends PhantomReference<AcmeProximitySensor> {
        private final AtomicLong peerRef;

        SensorCleaner(AtomicLong peerRef, AcmeProximitySensor sensor) {
            super(sensor, REF_QUEUE);
            this.peerRef = peerRef;
        }

        void cleanup() { AcmeProximitySensor.cleanup(peerRef); }
    }

    static final ReferenceQueue<AcmeProximitySensor> REF_QUEUE
        = new ReferenceQueue<>();


    @NonNull
    public static ScheduledTask getScheduledTask() {
        return new ScheduledTask(AcmeProximitySensor::cleanup, 100);
    }

    private static void cleanup() {
        Reference<? extends AcmeProximitySensor> ref;
        while ((ref = REF_QUEUE.poll()) instanceof SensorCleaner) {
            ((SensorCleaner) ref).cleanup();
        }
    }

    // …
}
```

The two functions in Listing 9.15, `getScheduledTask` and `cleanup()`, manage the native companions objects left behind by ill-behaved clients. They also illustrate the biggest downside of using reference queues: scheduling cleanup.

Typically, finalizers are run on a special thread, maintained by the runtime, whose sole purpose is running finalizers. The finalizer thread receives notification for objects that need finalization and schedules their finalizer methods.

When using reference queues, however, scheduling object cleanup is not handled by the runtime. The application must poll the reference queue occasionally and schedule any work that it finds there.

There are good and bad aspects of this requirement. The bad parts are probably obvious: An application that uses reference queues must be able to schedule a job to service the reference queue, and it must be able to schedule any work that the job finds on a robust execution service. If the execution service fails for any reason, managed objects will no longer be freed correctly. That is likely to be disastrous.

Note, by the way, that reference queues do not change the indeterminate scheduling of object cleanup. Objects are only enqueued for cleanup when the garbage collector needs space and only processed when the application program gets around to scheduling a cleanup task.

The good aspects may be a little less apparent. Consider: Finalizers are problematic because it is possible to overwhelm the finalizer thread. As noted previously, freeing hundreds of finalizable objects quickly might very well add those objects to the finalizer's queue faster than it can take them off for processing. Because the finalizer's queue is difficult to access programmatically, little opportunity exists for an application to gauge whether or not its doom is impending.

Using a reference queue, however, the application controls the cleanup mechanism; it can scale the object recovery process to the need. A multi-threaded, high-priority execution service might be able to stay ahead of object allocation.

Better yet, though, suppose that the same thread processes both the application-specific tasks that cause memory allocation and the reference queue that cleans them up. If the thread is busy managing the reference queue, it cannot allocate new objects. Allocation is naturally limited to creating no more than it can free. Governing the object allocation rate in this way makes for extremely robust apps.

Listing 9.15 posits a scheduling mechanism elsewhere in the system that registers new periodic tasks by calling a class's `getScheduledTask` method. The method returns the task to be run and the interval (in milliseconds) between runs. Surely, many other ways exist for accomplishing something similar: This particular implementation simply illustrates that the method `cleanup()` must be called periodically.

The `cleanup()` method polls the reference queue and calls the `cleanup(AtomicLong)` for each instance of the `SensorCleaner` object (whose associated `AcmeProximitySensor` has now been garbage collected) that it finds there. Recall from Listing 9.13 that each `AcmeProximitySensor` had a `SensorCleaner` associated with it in the factory method `getSensor`. This is the guarantee that, even if client code fails to close the sensor object, the `cleanup(AtomicLong)` will be called to free the native companion object.

There are a couple subtleties to be aware of. First, note that it is important that there are several references to the `AtomicLong` that contain the handle to the native peer. If the `AcmeProximitySensor` held the only reference, then when it became unreachable, the `AtomicLong` might be freed even before the sensor object itself. The `SensorCleaner` cannot depend on being able to find the native object unless it itself keeps a reference.

Second, notice that when a well-behaved client explicitly closes a sensor object, its `SensorCleaner` is removed from the map! That means the cleaner object is now unreachable and that the `AcmeProximitySensor` object holds the only reachable reference to the peer handle. It is entirely possible that the cleaner will be garbage collected first; thus, it will never be queued or scheduled. That's perfectly okay because there's nothing left for it to do.

Because the `AtomicLong` that is the reference to the native peer is in the map, a `SensorCleaner` is guaranteed that it will have access to it when the cleaner runs and that either it is the first attempt to free the native companion or that it will not try to do so.

JNI: Some Hints

As discussed earlier, entire books exist on the subject of writing JNI code. A comprehensive discussion is well outside the scope of this one. However, in our experience, some practices can make your code more robust and easier to maintain. Here are a few of them.

Don't Break the Rules

It is entirely possible to break Java's rules using native code. For instance, using native code, it is relatively easy to change the content of `String` or, indeed, any immutable object. Although JNI methods make some attempt to enforce visibility (`public` versus `private`) and mutability (`final`) constraints, sidestepping nearly any of them is quite possible. Java developers are used to being able to make assumptions about the environment in which their code runs. Changing the rules is asking for trouble.

Clearly and Without Exception, Document Native References to Java Code

Always and without exception, document any native use of Java code. If a native method refers to a class member by name, document that reference in a comment on the field. If native code calls a Java method, be certain that the Java method has a comment that indicates the fact. The same goes for native code that creates new instances of some Java class or other. As a related suggestion, be sure that any code that looks up Java identifiers—fields, classes, or methods—fails immediately and clearly if it cannot find its target. Failure to do these things will lead to bizarre crashes when some well-meaning developer does some small refactor.

Pass Simple Types to Native Code

The rest of the hints in this chapter have a single theme: When possible, don't put the burden of dealing with Java constructs on native code. Whenever possible, Java code should deal with Java data structures and should communicate with native code using only primitive types, Strings and arrays of those types. This may mean violating other general rules. For instance, passing the information in a complex data structure to its native companion as primitive types may mean that the native method has an uncomfortably large number of arguments. That is the lesser evil. Somewhere, code will have to extract the information. Keep that code on the Java side.

Make Native Methods Static, When Convenient

This tip is more a corollary to the previous hint than a new suggestion. Native instance methods are passed references to the calling Java instance. Cases surely exist in which that may be useful. In general, though, avoiding it is best. Pass the data that the native method requires and pass it to a static method instead of passing the whole object to an instance method.

Beware the Garbage Collector

This is probably the most important and most easily forgotten of the hints. Remember that as your native code runs, the garbage collector daemon is also running. It may move data to which you have a native pointer. Worse yet, it might deallocate it.

To keep the garbage collector from freeing an object, the object must appear to the collector as "reachable": There must be some way that running Java code can obtain a reference to it. Consider, however, a Java object that is created by native code. There are no references anywhere in the Java environment to this new object. Because there are no references, it is eligible for immediate garbage collection! The JNI provides two solutions to this problem: the LocalRef and the GlobalRef.

A LocalRef behaves as if a reference to an object had been put into the call stack of the nearest (in the stack) calling Java method. It creates a reference to the object that is visible to the garbage collector, making it reachable and thus ineligible for deallocation.

Many JNI methods that return references to Java objects also create a LocalRef to the returned object (be sure to verify this for specific calls). In general, if there is the potential for an object to disappear while native code is using it, a JNI call that returns a reference will create a LocalRef for it. Parameters to JNI method calls have LocalRefs as well. There is no danger that an object passed to a native method through the JNI will suddenly vanish.

LocalRefs are managed. They are automatically deleted (popped off the stack) when a native method returns to its Java language caller. Unfortunately, however, implementations of the JNI support only a limited number of LocalRefs: typically a few hundred but perhaps only a handful. As a rule of thumb, immediately deleting a LocalRef when it is no longer needed is best practice.

In fact, several circumstances exist under which deleting them explicitly is absolutely essential. Consider the example in Listing 9.16: native code that creates new objects of some kind and then adds them to a Java array.

Listing 9.16 **Filling an Array**

```
jobjectArray ds = env->NewObjectArray(arraySize, klass_MyObject, nullptr);
for (int i = 0; i < arraySize; i++) {
    jobject d = createNewObject(env, array[i]);
    env->SetObjectArrayElement(ds, i, d);
    env->DeleteLocalRef(d);
}
```

The JNI creates a `LocalRef` for the array created in the first line of the code. It also creates a `LocalRef` for each new object to be inserted into the array. After a new object is inserted into the array, it is reachable via the array. The individual `LocalRefs` for the new objects can (and should) be deleted. If the array is large, it is entirely possible that failing to delete the `LocalRefs` will exhaust the local ref pool.

Another, somewhat trickier condition is one in which the calling code never returns to a Java method. This can happen when a native thread, for instance, calls into Java code. Imagine, for example, a native thread—perhaps a thread servicing network connections—that uses a Java logger. The native code might create a Java `String`, log it, and then go back about its business. The `LocalRef` to the `String` will never be released because the calling code never returns to a Java caller.

The second kind of reference in the JNI toolbox is a `GlobalRef`. `GlobalRefs` are the way that native code holds a reference to a Java object across call boundaries. A `GlobalRef` behaves as if a reference to the object to which it refers had been added to a permanent static array. The ref prevents the garbage collector from recovering the referenced object's memory until the reference is deleted explicitly. Native developers, who are used to explicit memory management, will find this completely normal.

A common example of the need of a `GlobalRef` is native creation of a Java object, as shown in Listing 9.17.

Listing 9.17 **Native Object Creation**

```
jclass klass_MyObject = env->FindClass("my/project/MyObject");
if (!localClass)
    return nullptr;

method_MyObject_ctor = env->GetMethodID(
    klass_MyObject,
    "<init>",
    "(I)V");
if (!method_MyObject_ctor)
    return nullptr;

return env->NewObject(klass_MyObject, method_MyObject_ctor, (jint) param1);
```

If this call is used frequently, optimizing it might be possible. Both `klass_MyObject` and `method_MyObject_ctor` are references to Java objects: the class named "MyObject" and a constructor in that class with a single integer parameter, respectively. Using JNI methods to look up those references for every call to this code will take a substantial proportion of its execution time. To optimize it, an initialization method might be to look up the two references once and then hold them. Such an optimization requires a `GlobalRef` for each.

Use `GlobalRefs` with care. Although the limit on the number available (typically 65535) is usually much larger than the limit on the number of `LocalRefs`, they are memory leaks. Treat them as you would any other unmanaged memory.

Note that neither a `LocalRef` nor `GlobalRef` affects the garbage collector's ability to move an object in memory. Although such movement is completely invisible from Java code, a native reference can become a pointer to garbage, quite literally, in the middle of a line of code. This is not a tolerable situation and JNI calls have two strategies for handling it: copying and pinning. When using JNI methods that allow access the contents of a Java object—as with methods that created implicit `LocalRefs`—be sure to verify which of these two strategies a specific call uses.

Copying is just what it sounds like: An atomic JNI call copies the contents of a Java object into native-managed memory. The native code is free to do anything it likes with the copy, including, at some point, atomically copying it back into the Java object.

When an object is pinned, on the other hand, the garbage collector is not allowed to move it. Native code can access the contents of the pinned object directly, perhaps without the overhead of the copy. Pinning an object, however, means that memory in the Java heap is no longer under the control of the garbage collector. This can easily lead to fragmentation and premature out-of-memory errors. Best practice is to pin objects only if necessary, and then for as short a time as possible.

Use Weak Refs When Native Code Must Hold a Reference to a Java Object

A significant portion of this chapter is devoted to the discussion of how a Java object can hold a reference to a native companion object. What happens, though, when a native object needs to be able to find a particular Java object?

Consider, for instance, a native network management library. Suppose that client code creates a new Java `Connection` object for each of several network connections. The `Connection` object in turn creates a native companion object that actually handles socket connections. Finally, suppose that the native object calls back into Java code for each of the various events in the connection lifecycle.

Clearly, the callbacks from the native companion object must be calls to the specific Java `Connection` instance that created it and not to any other instance. The native code must, therefore, hold a reference to its Java companion.

This is, certainly, possible. As we've just seen, the native companion object might hold a GlobalRef to its Java companion: the Java code now has a reference to the native object and the native object has a reference to the Java object.

The problem with this, of course, is that a GlobalRef to the Java object will make it ineligible for garbage collection. Unless there is some explicit means of freeing it (and that explicit mechanism is carefully used for *every* instance), its referent will never be freed, will never be finalized (or added to a reference queue), and will never free its native companion. The belt still works but the suspenders are gone. Unless a clear architectural reason exists for doing the aforementioned, a good practice is to leave the management of native objects to their Java companions, not vice versa.

There are two ways around this issue. The first is a special global reference, a WeakGlobalRef. A WeakGlobalRef is similar to a GlobalRef, except that (like a Java WeakReference) it does not prevent the garbage collection of the Java object to which it refers. It is different from a raw native reference in that it will never point at garbage: It will always either point at the intended object or be null.

It is important to note that the referent in a WeakGlobalRef can disappear at any time, even between two native instructions, causing intermittent failures. Listing 9.18 illustrates such a scenario: a snippet in which a native instance stores a reference to its Java companion.

Listing 9.18   Incorrect Use of a WeakRef: Don't Do This!

```
mCompanion = reinterpret_cast<jobject>(env->NewWeakGlobalRef(javaObj));
if (env->isSameObject(mCompanion, NULL)
    return;
jclass klass = env->getObjectClass(mCompanion) // mCompanion may be NULL!
// …
```

Fortunately, a WeakGlobalRef can be used as the argument to LocalRef (or a GlobalRef). Local and global refs protect their referents from garbage collection. Listing 9.19 illustrates a corrected version of Listing 9.18.

Listing 9.19   Obtain a LocalRef from a WeakGlobalRef

```
mCompanion = reinterpret_cast<jobject>(env->NewWeakGlobalRef(javaObj));
companion = reinterpret_cast<jobject>(env->NewLocalRef(mCompanion));
if (env->isSameObject(companion, NULL)
    return;
jclass klass = env->getObjectClass(companion) // safe!
// …
```

There is one other way of managing native handles in Java objects. In this architecture, references to Java objects are never passed to native code at all. Instead, they are kept as weak references in a map at the Java/native boundary. Think of it as a "hat check": Java hands native code a token, which can be redeemed for a Java object. The token, however, is completely opaque to the native code. Listing 9.20 shows a sample implementation.

Listing 9.20   **Native Reference "Hat Check"**

```java
public class NativeRef<T> {
    @NonNull
    @GuardedBy("this")
    private final Random rnd = new Random();

    @NonNull
    @GuardedBy("this")
    private final Map<Integer, WeakReference<T>> refs = new HashMap<>();

    public synchronized int bind(@NonNull T obj) {
        int ref;
        do { ref = rnd.nextInt(Integer.MAX_VALUE); }
        while (refs.containsKey(ref));
        refs.put(ref, new WeakReference<>(obj));
        return ref;
    }

    public synchronized void unbind(int key) { refs.remove(key); }

    @Nullable
    public synchronized T getObjFromContext(long lref) {
        if ((lref < 0) || (lref > Integer.MAX_VALUE)) {
            throw new IllegalArgumentException("Ref out of bounds: " + lref);
        }

        final Integer key = (int) lref;
        final WeakReference<T> ref = refs.get(key);
        if (ref == null) { return null; }

        final T obj = ref.get();
        if (obj == null) { refs.remove(key); }
        return obj;
    }
}
```

This architecture has many of the same features that made WeakGlobalReferences attractive. Because the reference map holds weak references, native objects cannot force their Java companions to stay in memory. Perhaps an advantage, this architecture does not use the size-limited LocalRef pool.

Note that the implementation uses only positive integers for tokens. For most applications, this provides plenty of space and avoids problems that arise from sign extension.

Summary

This chapter, at last, brings us to Android's implementation language, Java. In it, we meet and use Java's JNI, the API through which Java language code invokes native code.

The chapter uses the Proximity Sensor project introduced in previous chapters to show three different implementations of a long-running daemon that logs proximity:

1. A naïve native implementation

2. A native implementation using the HAL (introduced in Chapter 7)

3. A Java app, also using the HAL

The third implementation, the Java application, provides the basis for a discussion of one of the key issues for code at the Java/native interface: lifecycle management and how to handle unmanaged native memory in Java's garbage-collected environment.

We recommend a "belt and suspenders" approach: Java objects with native companions should implement Java's `Autoclosable` interface. This makes it clear that client code should explicitly inform the object that it is ready for disposal.

In addition, we recommend the use of a finalizer or reference queue to guarantee the proper handling of objects that evade explicit release.

## 10

Project Treble: Binderized HAL

The Android system and its use of the HAL received a major overhaul starting with Android 8.0. Internally, this was called Project Treble and its goal was not only to provide a standard abstraction to the underlying hardware, but to do it in a way that allowed vendors to upgrade the core OS without requiring a rebuild of HAL libraries and the system image. This means Google can roll out OS updates without requiring modifications to the vendor proprietary components. Binderized HALs must be used for Android 8.0 and newer. This new, extremely flexible, and forward-looking approach to the HAL requires some knowledge of Android's Binder subsystem.

The platform vendor–supplied HAL is no longer a set of shared libraries following a specific naming convention and binary API. Instead, the vendor exposes a set of binder interfaces to the system and one or more backing services that host the HAL implementation. The HAL interfaces are defined using HIDL (pronounced "hide-l"), a language similar to the AIDL, used to define binder service interfaces.

This chapter explores the architecture of the binderized HAL and examines how Android uses it. We'll dig into an existing binderized HAL definition from the platform and explain how the pieces fit together.

> **Note**
>
> Unless otherwise noted, the remainder of this chapter uses HIDL when referring to the binderized HAL architecture, not just the interface definition language.

HIDL Architecture

The HIDL-based system is built upon the same concepts as Android's system services model. Each HAL implementation is backed by a service, running in user-space, that exposes a HIDL-defined interface. The HIDL services, usually native processes, are started at system startup and register with the system. Each HIDL interface is versioned so the system understands what is available at runtime. This allows the platform to support one or more interface versions for a specific hardware component, which is important for devices being upgraded to new versions of the OS.

The key feature of this architecture is that the vendor-provided HIDL components are separated from the core Android system, allowing the core OS to be updated without requiring the vendor to provide new custom libraries. The end result is a robust system that allows vendors to adopt new releases of Android for existing hardware with minimal friction.

Just like the Android system service architecture, the HIDL framework includes a hardware service manager, appropriately named hwservicemanager. This system daemon acts as the registrar of all HIDL-based HALs in the system. It can be thought of as the name server for HIDL-defined interfaces in the system. Each HIDL component initializes and registers its Binder-based interface(s) with hwservicemanager, making them available to other components in the system. Other processes in the system find the HIDL binders by making requests to hwservicemanager for a specific HIDL. Figure 10.1 shows the overall architecture.

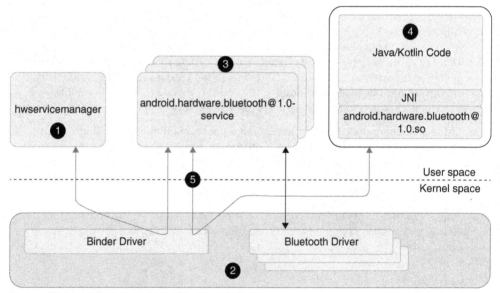

Figure 10.1   HIDL High-Level Architecture

In Figure 10.1, the numbered components are defined as follows:

(1) hwservicemanager, the central registrar of HIDL services in the system

(2) The Linux kernel with the Android Binder IPC driver and other hardware drivers within it

(3) The HIDL services in the system, providing the HAL implementation(s) for their respective hardware components

(4) The client application process that utilizes the Binder-exposed HIDL services

(5) The binder that connects the client and backing HIDL service processes

Although Android 8.0 and newer requires the use of HIDL, a small handful of exceptions exist: some HALs are provided in what is called "passthrough" mode or are specialized same-process HALs (SP-HALs). The passthrough HALs are effectively HIDL wrappers around legacy or conventional HAL libraries that allow those libraries to be used in the same process. Other SP-HALs may not even expose HIDL-defined interfaces.

Note

Google strictly controls which HALs are SP-HALs, and there are no exceptions for new devices rolling out Android 8.0 or newer. This includes vendor extension HALs. Devices that are upgrades to Android 8.0 are given some leniency with vendor extensions. Otherwise, all other Android-defined binderized HALs must be binderized for Android 8 or newer running on the platform.

You can find more details about the HIDL architecture at https://source.android.com/devices/architecture/hidl.

hwservicemanager

As previously stated, `hwservicemanager` is a central component of the HIDL architecture. Similar to the system services Binder subsystem's registrar, `servicemanager`, this component keeps a registry of active HIDL components in the system by HIDL interface, version, an optional name, and the backing binder interface/object exposed by the component. This binder object can then be found and requested by clients for making IPC calls into the HIDL component.

`hwservicemanager` leverages SE policies and the SE Linux kernel to ensure only components in the system that are assigned the proper SE context can register as a HIDL-defined HAL or ask to use one.

HIDL Services

HIDL services expose a binder to the system, which implements a HIDL-defined interface. This acts as the glue between the HIDL-defined contract and the hardware it is intended to control.

Note

"Hardware" in this context may or may not be actual underlying hardware. The interface being exposed may have its implementation entirely in software. For example, it may be possible to have a coarse-level location device using nothing more than geolocation information retrieved from a public Internet server.

HIDL Client Applications

As has already been discussed with the traditional Android HAL, the processes using the HIDL-based HAL are not typical Android applications. These are typically core system framework components, native processes/daemons, or vendor-specific add-ons that support the specific hardware.

Hardware Interface Definition Language (HIDL)

Each of the binderized HAL interfaces is defined using definition files written in HIDL, just as AIDL is used to define Binder-based service interfaces. HIDL syntax is somewhat different, though, adapting the features available from the underlying Binder subsystem to make it extremely efficient. This is important for low-latency communication with hardware.

HIDL is a mix of C/C++ and Java syntaxes, including support for Javadoc style comments and Java-like annotations. Like other Binder-based interfaces, HIDL interfaces are defined and implemented in a way that allows two separately compiled codebases to communicate with each other.

HIDL definitions are stored in `.hal` files and are located in specific directories within the platform source tree. Each HIDL defines an interface as part of a module within a package and is versioned. This combination of namespace and strict versioning is required because the HIDL package needs to remain compatible with both current and future software that may use the interface. For example, at the time of this writing, the latest HIDL interface for utilizing a fingerprint reader is `android.hardware.biometrics.fingerprint@2.1`.

Generally speaking, HIDL package namespaces fall into one of two categories:

- `android.hardware`: The core HIDL packages defined by Android
- `vendor.VENDOR.hardware`: OEM/ODM-defined HIDL packages

Android does define some additional package namespaces for other internal interfaces, but these are the two primary namespaces when dealing with hardware-related features. In the fingerprint HIDL shown in the preceding paragraph, the HIDL package is part of the `android.hardware` package, the `biometrics` module, and the `fingerprint` submodule. It is version 2.1 of the interface. The hierarchical nature of the package naming is also relevant when building the HIDL, as we will see in Chapter 11 when building a custom HIDL for Acme.

Like other source file types, HIDL files can import other interfaces as well as their types. Interfaces define one or more methods exposed by the HAL. Recall that HIDL is Binder-based, meaning that the client and backing HIDL service will almost always be in two separate processes. Thus, each HIDL method call is an interprocess communication (IPC) call, which involves transferring data and control between the processes. By default, methods are synchronous: The caller will block until the IPC call returns. For efficiency and clarity, data is always passed to the called method and is not copied back. This is the equivalent of the in keyword for arguments in AIDL-defined interfaces. In other words, any input arguments to a HIDL API call are passed by value.

You can find the HIDL grammar definition on the AOSP source site: https://source.android.com/devices/architecture/hidl#grammar.

Rather than drill down into every aspect of the HIDL language definition, walking through an example will illustrate the basics. For this example, let's look at the sensors HIDL definition, `android.hardware.sensors@2.0`. You can find the HAL in the source tree at `hardware/interfaces/sensors/2.0`. There are several files in this directory, as shown in Listing 10.1.

Listing 10.1 **Sensors 2.0 HIDL Files**

```
$ ls -l hardware/interfaces/sensors/2.0
total 56
-rw-r--r--  1 aosp  staff     404 Oct 13 09:31 Android.bp
-rw-r--r--  1 aosp  staff   12946 Oct 13 09:31 ISensors.hal
-rw-r--r--  1 aosp  staff    1778 Oct 13 09:31 ISensorsCallback.hal
drwxr-xr-x  2 aosp  staff     374 Oct 13 09:31 default
-rw-r--r--  1 aosp  staff    1596 Oct 13 09:31 types.hal
drwxr-xr-x  3 aosp  staff     102 Oct 13 09:31 vts
$
```

- `Android.bp`: This is the Android build blueprint file.
- `ISensors.hal`: This is the primary HIDL interface definition for the sensors binderized HAL.
- `ISensorsCallback.hal`: This is an additional HIDL-defined interface, provided by clients to the sensors binderized HAL and will be called when data is available.
- `default`: This subdirectory contains a default implementation of the binderized HIDL service.
- `types.hal`: This file is used to define any data structures that may be needed by the HIDL-defined interface. Unlike AIDL, there is no mechanism to declare a structure/object "parcelable" so it may be used across the binder interface. Instead, HIDL requires the types to be declared in a .hal file for use by the HIDL interface.

The complete sensors 2.0 interface illustrates the HIDL syntax and capabilities well. Let's walk through the `ISensors.hal` in pieces, starting with Listing 10.2.

Listing 10.2 **Sensors 2.0 Interface Definition, Part 1**

```
package android.hardware.sensors@2.0;

import @1.0::Event;
import @1.0::OperationMode;
import @1.0::RateLevel;
import @1.0::Result;
import @1.0::SensorInfo;
import @1.0::SharedMemInfo;
import @2.0::ISensorsCallback;
```

The start of `ISensors.hal`, as shown in Listing 10.2, will look somewhat familiar to Java developers. Each HIDL-defined interface is defined as a package and is versioned using the `@major.minor` syntax. HIDL interfaces are defined to be part of packages that follow a hierarchical namespace like in Java or C++. Android defines several internal packages for HAL and framework interfaces, as shown in Table 10.1.

Table 10.1   **Android-Defined HIDL Packages**

Package Prefix	Location	Interface Type
`android.hardware.*`	`hardware/interfaces`	HAL
`android.frameworks.*`	`frameworks/hardware/interfaces/*`	Android Framework Related
`android.system.*`	`system/hardware/interfaces/*`	Android System Related
`android.hidl.*`	`system/libhidl/transport/*`	Core HIDL
`vendor.VENDOR.interfaces.*`	`vendor/VENDOR/interfaces/*`	Vendor (OEM/ODM) Defined

As illustrated, vendors (ODMs/OEMs) may define their own HIDL interfaces. These may be completely custom HIDL interfaces or extensions to existing interface definitions. All interfaces are always versioned using a major and minor number.

After a HIDL interface is "published" (for example, in use on a platform) at a specific version, the interface is locked down and may not change for that specific version. This is enforced at build time using a hash of the HIDL interface definition at a specific version. Once the interface has been "published," any attempt to change the definition without changing the version will result in a build error.

After the package declaration, note the series of import statements. Just like Java or Kotlin, these statements are used to pull in other HIDL-defined interfaces or types. However, like AIDL definitions, types or other interfaces must be imported, even if they are defined in the same package, as shown with `@2.0::ISensosCallback` here.

The type of import depends on the file in which the `import` statement is located. In this example, the import statements are in the `ISensors.hal` file, making them interface-level imports. If, instead, these import statements were in the `types.hal` file for sensors, they would be package-level imports. The difference between the two is subtle, but important to understand. An interface-level import is an import statement located within a specific interface `.hal` file, making the `import` available to only that HIDL interface. On the other hand, a package-level import is an import statement located in a `types.hal` file for a given package/module/submodule hierarchy. The net effect of this type of import is that the imported type(s) are available to all interfaces within the package/module/submodule.

Note how each of the `import` statements in Listing 10.2 starts with the version declaration. This means the imports are types or interfaces that are defined within the current package, `android.hardware.sensors`. The sensors HIDL clearly shows how one interface version can build upon a previous version. In this case, the sensors HIDL version 2.0 builds upon the 1.0 definition by leveraging types/interfaces defined in both. Three other forms of import statements can also be used, all of which start with the fully qualified package name (FQPN) of the import, before the version specifier, as shown in Listing 10.3.

Listing 10.3   **Additional HIDL Import Syntax**

```
import FQPN@MAJOR.MINOR
import FQPN@MAJOR.MINOR::INTERFACE
import FQPN@MAJOR.MINOR::types
```

The first form would include all interfaces and types from the specified package version. The second form imports a specific interface and all types from a package. The third form is used to import just the types from another package, but none of the interfaces.

Continuing further into the sensors HAL example, the interface declaration comes next, a portion of which is shown in Listing 10.4.

Listing 10.4   **Sensors 2.0 Interface Definition, Part 2**

```
interface ISensors {
    /**
     * Enumerate all available (static) sensors.
     *
     * The SensorInfo for each sensor returned by getSensorsList must be stable
     * from the initial call to getSensorsList after a device boot until the
     * entire system restarts. The SensorInfo for each sensor must not change
     * between subsequent calls to getSensorsList, even across restarts of the
     * HAL and its dependencies (for example, the sensor handle for a given
     * sensor must not change across HAL restarts).
     */
    getSensorsList() generates (vec<SensorInfo> list);

    /**
     * Place the module in a specific mode. The following modes are defined
     *
     *   SENSOR_HAL_NORMAL_MODE - Normal operation. Default state of the module.
     *
     *   SENSOR_HAL_DATA_INJECTION_MODE - Loopback mode.
     *     Data is injected for the supported sensors by the sensor service in
     *     this mode.
     *
     * @return OK on success
     *     BAD_VALUE if requested mode is not supported
     *     PERMISSION_DENIED if operation is not allowed
     */
```

```
setOperationMode(OperationMode mode) generates (Result result);

...

@entry
@callflow(next = {"getSensorsList"})
initialize(fmq_sync<Event> eventQueueDescriptor,
           fmq_sync<uint32_t> wakeLockDescriptor,
           ISensorsCallback sensorsCallback)
    generates
           (Result result);

...

registerDirectChannel(SharedMemInfo mem)
           generates (Result,
                      int32_t channelHandle);
```

The code in Listing 10.4 defines the interface `android.hardware.sensors@2.0::ISensors` and the methods it exposes.

Each HIDL file contains a single interface definition and may also contain types the interface requires. Interfaces may also inherit from other interfaces using the `extends` keyword, similar to the way Java interfaces are inherited. However, just like Java, HIDL does not support multiple inheritance. Interfaces that do not explicitly extend another interface implicitly extend from `android.hdl.base@1.0::IBase`.

The methods shown in Listing 10.4 illustrate standard types, custom types, and return values. Methods may return nothing, a primitive, a custom type, or multiple values. All the interface methods shown in Listing 10.4 show return values that include custom types. The `registerDirectChannel` method returns multiple values.

The syntax for returned data looks different than in Java or C/C++. Return data is specified with the `generates` keyword. When a primitive value is returned, the returned data is simply returned from the method. If the returned value is not primitive, however, the HIDL framework generates a synchronous callback function that the server side calls to return data.

The prototypes for the HIDL methods are exactly the same for client and server side, so the client must handle the return data via callback when the return type is non-primitive. In this case, the HIDL method call on the client blocks until the server side returns, but the return data is sent back to the client via the server invoking the provided callback, which runs in the client before the original method call returns. This makes for an interesting mix of error-handling code. Even methods that have no return value still return a `Return` object defined by HIDL. Using this, the client can check to see whether a low-level error of some kind occurred while making the method call.

From the client perspective, the interface methods are blocking methods by default. This is true, even if the method does not return any data. Just like AIDL-defined interfaces, HIDL interface methods may be declared as asynchronous using the `oneway` keyword. Unlike AIDL interfaces, though, all data is owned by the caller. This is akin to an AIDL interface where input arguments for a method are declared using the `in` keyword.

> **Note**
>
> Although HIDL does not enforce a strict per-transaction (for example, method call) data limit, keeping the size of the data less than 4KB per transaction is considered a best practice. Remember, there may be multiple transactions from multiple processes in flight to a given HIDL simultaneously. If an interface's method(s) use more than this in a single transaction, the interface should be re-architected.
>
> Just like AIDL-defined interfaces, HIDL is built on top of Android's Binder framework, which has a 1MB limit for all concurrent transactions. Exceeding this limit will result in hard-to-debug failed transactions that are not directly related to the specific method throwing a `TransactionException`.

HIDL Types

Data types in HIDL look similar to Java and C++, with some subtle differences. In fact, the syntax used is a mix of both Java and C++:

- `struct` and `union` declarations follow C++ syntax and must be named.
- `typedef` is allowed and follows C++ syntax.
- C++-style comments may be used and are copied to generated header files.
- Package namespaces follow Java style syntax. Generated C++ headers convert the namespace to C++ style. For example, `android.hardware.sensors` in HIDL becomes `android::hardware::sensors` in C++.
- Comments may include documentation via Javadoc format.
- Java-style annotations may be added to type declarations.
- Forward declarations are not allowed. Structures may not refer to themselves.
- The concept of a pointer does not exist in HIDL.
- Arrays follow Java-style array usage, as shown in Listing 10.5.

Listing 10.5   **HIDL Array Syntax**

```
struct Point {
    int32_t x;
    int32_t y;
};
Point[3] triangle;
```

HIDL includes a number of pre-defined types, some of which are only available in C++ code. This is in large part because HALs generally deal with underlying hardware and need to be extremely fast and efficient. Although HIDL servers can be implemented in Java (for most things), implementing hardware driver HIDL servers in Java is not recommended. Table 10.2 provides a high-level view of HIDL types and their equivalent in C++ and Java.

Table 10.2   **HIDL-defined Types**

HIDL Type	C++ Type	Java Type
enum	enum class	final Class (with static constant fields)
uint8_t..uint64_t	uint8_t..uint64_t	int..long[†]
int8_t..int64_t	int8_t..int64_t	int..long
float	float	float
double	double	double
vec<T>	hidl_vec<T>	ArrayList<T>[††]
T[S1][S2]..[Sn]	T[S1][S2]..[Sn]	T[S1][S2]..[Sn]
string	hidl_string	String[†††]
handle	hidl_handle	N/A
safe_union	(custom)struct	N/A[††††]
struct	struct	Java Class
union	union	N/A[††††]
fmq_sync	MQDescriptorSync	N/A
fmq_unsync	MQDescriptorUnsync	N/A
memory	hidl_memory	N/A
bitfield<T>	Bitwise OR of underlying type	N/A

[†] Java does not have unsigned integer types. The unsigned data is placed into signed integer types, without conversion. Any Java code using this must treat the signed data as if it were unsigned.

[††] Java primitives are converted to the wrapped type (for example, vec<int> becomes ArrayList<Integer>).

[†††] Java String is converted to UTF-8 as the common HIDL type during transport and may never be null when passed into HIDL. Note that character set translation from Java's default UTF-16 to UTF-8 can result in different encodings.

[††††] Available starting with Android 11.

You can find more details on HIDL data types as well as how they are used in C++ and Java on these pages:

https://source.android.com/devices/architecture/hidl/types

https://source.android.com/devices/architecture/hidl-cpp/types

https://source.android.com/devices/architecture/hidl-java/types

Each HIDL package may define types that are relevant to it. This is accomplished via the file types.hal in the package module directory. Looking at the android.hardware.sensors@2.0 package again, the types.hal file is small because the 2.0 interface builds upon the 1.0 interface (see Listing 10.6).

Listing 10.6 **Sensors 2.0 `types.hal`**

```
package android.hardware.sensors@2.0;
enum SensorTimeout : int32_t {
    /**
     * The maximum number of seconds to wait for a message on the Wake Lock FMQ
     * before automatically releasing any wake_lock held for a WAKE_UP event.
     */
    WAKE_LOCK_SECONDS = 1,
};


enum EventQueueFlagBits : uint32_t {
    /**
     * Used to notify the Event FMQ that events should be read and processed.
     */
    READ_AND_PROCESS = 1 << 0,

    /**
     * Used by the framework to signal to the HAL when events have been
     * successfully read from the Event FMQ.
     *
     * If the MessageQueue::writeBlocking function is being used to write sensor
     * events to the Event FMQ, then the readNotification parameter must be set
     * to EVENTS_READ.
     */
    EVENTS_READ = 1 << 1,
};


enum WakeLockQueueFlagBits : uint32_t {
    /**
     * Used to notify the HAL that the framework has written data to the Wake
     * Lock FMQ.
     */
    DATA_WRITTEN = 1 << 0,
};
```

Note how the `types.hal` file uses the same package declaration as the interface files(s) for the package. Custom structures (classes) may be defined in the `types.hal` file as well as custom enums, typedefs, and so on.

HIDL Services

HIDL Services provide the implementation of a specific HAL definition. Although HIDL Services may be implemented in C++ or Java, the framework is geared more toward C++-based implementations. A handful of Java-based HIDL service implementations are in the Android framework, but they are more the exception than the rule. Because of this, the remainder of this section will only cover C++ implementations.

HIDL services, like their Android Binder service counterparts, run in standalone processes. These processes are started by the `init` daemon at startup, like other native processes. The HIDL service implements the HIDL-defined interface, communicating with whatever hardware or other component necessary to implement the defined interface.

To make itself available to HIDL client processes, each service is responsible for registering itself with the Android HIDL system and processing requests as they arrive.

Listing 10.7 contains the main entry point for the default sensor service implementation. This is found at `hardware/interfaces/sensors/2.0/default/service.cpp`. Note how this `main` is short and simple: It configures the thread pool, creates an instance of the `Sensors` class, and joins the thread pool. Each of these steps is important and ties the whole thing together.

Listing 10.7   **Default Sensors 2.0 Service Entry Point**

```
using android::hardware::configureRpcThreadpool;
using android::hardware::joinRpcThreadpool;
using android::hardware::sensors::V2_0::ISensors;
using android::hardware::sensors::V2_0::implementation::Sensors;

int main(int /* argc */, char** /* argv */) {
    configureRpcThreadpool(1, true);

    android::sp<ISensors> sensors = new Sensors();
    if (sensors->registerAsService() != ::android::OK) {
        ALOGE("Failed to register Sensors HAL instance");
        return -1;
    }

    joinRpcThreadpool();
    return 1;  // joinRpcThreadpool shouldn't exit}
```

The HIDL support library allows HIDL services to configure the number of threads used to handle requests via the `configureRpcThreadpool` method. In this case, the default sensor service implementation limits requests to being handled by a single thread. This is setting up the internal thread pool to be managed and used by the underlying Binder framework, similar to what is done for Android services.

The implementation of the sensors 2.0 HIDL is provided by the Sensors class, located in the same directory as the service code from Listing 10.7. The HIDL build tools automatically create the registerAsService method, called in the code in Listing 10.7. This method registers the backing binder object, exposed through the kernel, for the ISensors interface with the hwservicemanager process.

Finally, the joinRpcThreadpool method is called, making the main thread of this process one of the threads in the thread pool from which services requests. This results in the process servicing incoming requests forever. This method should never exit, as shown from the comment in the code.

When a client calls a specific API method defined in ISensors.hal, the Binder and HIDL framework calls the matching method in the instance of the Sensors class. The method will perform its required action, returning a primitive result or executing a callback.

Listing 10.8 shows a portion of the C++ prototypes for the ISensors interface that were shown in Listing 10.4. As previously mentioned, this file is autogenerated by the build system, which can make it a little difficult to track down! In the AOSP build tree for Android 10, the soong build system places the generated files into an intermediates directory tree based on the type of generated file. Because this is an AOSP-defined hardware interface, the base of the generated files is ./out/soong/.intermediates/hardware/interfaces; we'll call it HW_IFS for brevity. The resultant directory hierarchy is still quite lengthy, even with this substitution:

HW_IFS/sensors/2.0/android.hardware.sensors@2.0_genc++headers/gen/android/
➥ hardware/sensors/2.0/ISensors.h.

Note

Sometimes a line of code will be too long to fit on one line in this book. The code continuation symbol (➥) indicates that the line continues from the previous line.

Listing 10.8 ISensors C++ Definition

```
struct ISensors : public ::android::hidl::base::V1_0::IBase {

    ...

    using getSensorsList_cb = std::function<void(const ::android::hardware::hidl_vec
➥ <::android::hardware::sensors::V1_0::SensorInfo>& list)>;

    ...

    virtual ::android::hardware::Return<void> getSensorsList(getSensorsList_cb
➥ hidl_cb) = 0;

    ...

    virtual ::android::hardware::Return<::android::hardware::sensors::V1_0::Result>
➥ setOperationMode(::android::hardware::sensors::V1_0::OperationMode mode) = 0;

    ...
```

```
    virtual ::android::hardware::Return<::android::hardware::sensors::V1_0::Result>
➡ initialize(const ::android::hardware::MQDescriptorSync
➡ <::android::hardware::sensors::V1_0::Event>& eventQueueDescriptor,
➡ const ::android::hardware::MQDescriptorSync<uint32_t>& wakeLockDescriptor,
➡ const ::android::sp<::android::hardware::sensors::V2_0
➡::ISensorsCallback>& sensorsCallback) = 0;


    ...


    virtual ::android::hardware::Return<void> registerDirectChannel(const
➡::android::hardware::sensors::V1_0::SharedMemInfo& mem,
➡ registerDirectChannel_cb_hidl_cb) = 0;


    ...
}
```

Wow, that is tough to read! However, stripping down the namespaces a bit makes them easier to understand. For example, the extremely long method definition for initialize is shown in Listing 10.9 when using the namespaces in the C++ code. This is what the default implementation of the 2.0 sensors HAL does.

Listing 10.9   `ISensors` C++ **Service Implementation**

```
using ::android::hardware::sensors::V1_0::Event;
using ::android::hardware::sensors::V1_0::OperationMode;
using ::android::hardware::sensors::V1_0::RateLevel;
using ::android::hardware::sensors::V1_0::Result;
using ::android::hardware::sensors::V1_0::SharedMemInfo;
using ::android::hardware::sensors::V2_0::SensorTimeout;
using ::android::hardware::sensors::V2_0::WakeLockQueueFlagBits;

...

Return<void> Sensors::getSensorsList(getSensorsList_cb _hidl_cb) {
    std::vector<SensorInfo> sensors;
    for (const auto& sensor : mSensors) {
        sensors.push_back(sensor.second->getSensorInfo());
    }

    // Call the HIDL callback with the SensorInfo
    _hidl_cb(sensors);

    return Void();
}

...
```

```
Return<Result> Sensors::setOperationMode(OperationMode mode) {

    ...

    return Result::OK;
}

Return<Result> Sensors::initialize(
    const ::android::hardware::MQDescriptorSync<Event>& eventQueueDescriptor,
    const ::android::hardware::MQDescriptorSync<uint32_t>& wakeLockDescriptor,
    const sp<ISensorsCallback>& sensorsCallback) {

    ...

}
```

That is much better! Previously, in the HIDL definition of each method, the generates keyword declared the data to be returned. Note how depending on the return data, it may actually be returned directly or via an embedded callback. The getSensorsList method returns data (a list of SensorInfo) by executing the provided callback with the data. Both setOperationMode and initialize return Result, which is defined to be an int32_t so it can be returned directly.

HIDL Clients

HIDL clients utilize the interface exposed by the underlying service implementation. Unlike the Android Binder-based clients used at the system/framework level, the HIDL client code does not have to look up the binder for the backing service directly. The necessary functionality is built into the code generated when the HIDL interface is compiled. Each interface implementation has a getService method that returns an instance of the interface or a proxy to it. For example, Listing 10.10 shows the prototype for version 2.0 of the ISensors implementation.

Listing 10.10 ISensors Prototype for getService()

```
static ::android::sp<ISensors> getService(
  const std::string &serviceName="default",
  bool getStub=false
);
```

The getService method communicates with hwservicemanager to retrieve the backing binder from the HIDL service implementation. The interface type (for example, ISensors) and service name are used to look up the HIDL service that was registered with the system. The client leveraging this method uses the smart pointer to the interface (for example, ::android::sp<ISensors>), as defined by the prototype in Listing 10.10. However, behind the scenes, this may be direct access to the backing service implementation (for example, pass-through), or it may be a binder proxy instance. The calling semantics are exactly the same: The methods of the interface are called via the smart pointer.

An example of this is shown in Listing 10.11, taken from `SensorsWrapperBase` used within the AOSP framework (see `frameworks/native/services/sensorservice/SensorWrapper.h`).

Listing 10.11   **Calling the `ISensors` Interface**

```
Return<void> getSensorsList(ISensors::getSensorsList_cb _hidl_cb) override
    return mSensors->getSensorsList(_hidl_cb);
}
```

It is worth reiterating that HIDL interfaces that return non-primitive data accomplish it via callback to the client. In the implementation shown in Listing 10.11, the caller of this wrapper method must provide the callback function defined by the HIDL, an instance of `ISensors::getSensorList_cb`. In Listing 10.4 where this HIDL method was defined, the method does not return data, but *generates* it. Closing the loop, the code in Listing 10.8 defines `ISensors::getSensorsList_cb` to be a function that receives a vector of `SensorInfo` objects—the type that the HIDL interface generates.

Summary

This chapter examined the revised hardware abstraction layer architecture introduced in Android 8: binderized HAL using HIDL. Internally called Project Treble, the binderized HAL is a complete overhaul of the HAL concept. Prior to Android 8, vendor/OEM HALs were provided as a set of shared libraries customized for the specific target that were built into the system image. With HIDL, the HAL is now based on Android's IPC mechanism, Binder. The primary goals of such a radical change were isolation of vendor-specific components so the AOSP framework (system) can be updated without requiring a rebuild of the vendor components; better interoperability between components; better data movement efficiency; and more intuitive calling semantics with respect to memory usage/ownership.

Similar to the traditional Android HAL, the platform defines the abstractions to be implemented by the platform components or the vendor/OEM. Unlike the traditional HAL, though, the abstractions are now defined via HIDL `.hal` files, which are cousins to the AIDL file used in Binder-based services. Although HIDL and AIDL files have some things in common, they are different in their syntax with HIDL placing stricter syntax rules and form into place. This allows for much of the server and client "boilerplate" code to be autogenerated or provided via helper library—leaving the vendor/OEM to focus on the functionality of the HIDL implementation rather than the nuts and bolts of the underlying HIDL/Binder interactions.

11

Creating a Custom Binderized HAL

In Chapter 10, we introduced Project Treble, or the new binderized HAL architecture rolled out with Android 8.0. The new binderized HAL, or HIDL, is required for all devices running Android 8.0 and newer. Now it is time to apply the HIDL concepts on a custom platform, making it clear how a new HIDL-based HAL can be created and utilized.

This chapter demonstrates replacing the legacy HAL for Acme's custom proximity device, making it HIDL based. We'll see how the system can be customized to pick up new, custom hardware for unique devices like those used in the IoT space.

Acme Custom HIDL

As mentioned in Chapter 10, vendors are free to define their own HIDLs as well as vendor-specific customizations of AOSP/Google-defined HIDLs. Unlike traditional HAL shared libraries, these components will live within the vendor area of the platform: the /vendor or /odm filesystems. This clean separation allows the core Android system to be updated without requiring the OEM's involvement; this is one of the primary goals of the HIDL architecture.

To illustrate this, let's define a new HIDL for the Acme One, building upon our previous work in Chapter 8 with a custom proximity HAL. Because this proximity support is custom and is not part of the standard AOSP sensors API, our custom HIDL is needed and is called aproximity. To keep things simple, the HIDL implementation will not require modifications to the kernel—it will leverage the same shim library used in Chapter 8 to access the underlying device. The HIDL will illustrate both simple as well as more complex return data.

> ### Note
>
> This chapter utilizes a tool from the AOSP build results, hidl-gen. This tool is built at the same time as a given target. If you have not previously built a platform, this tool will not be found in your build tree. Please see Chapter 2 for building the platform. Alternatively, if the build system is set up and lunch has been run, the tool may also be built by executing the command m hidl-gen.

HIDL Definition

The `aproximity` HIDL definition is similar to the traditional HAL API covered in Chapter 8. In addition to the `poll` API, you can use a couple of new APIs to retrieve the proximity details for the underlying sensor as well as some details about the HIDL's usage. Listing 11.1 and Listing 11.2 define the `IAproximity` HIDL (`IAproximity.hal`) and its corresponding types (`types.hal`), respectively.

Listing 11.1 `IAproximity` **HIDL Definition**

```
package vendor.acme.one.aproximity@1.0;

/**
 * The Acme specialized proximity support, providing simple APIs to
 * illustrate vendor custom HIDL.
 */
interface IAproximity {
    /**
     * Retrieve the latest proximity value for the specified precision
     * value.
     *
     * @param precision contains the precision requested by the caller.
     *    Valid values may be retrieved using the get_details method.
     * @return the proximity value returned by the sensor
     */
    poll(int32_t precision) generates (int32_t proximity);

    /**
     * Get the details about the underlying sensor.
     *
     * @return the details for the underlying sensor, containing the
     *    supported precision values and the range of proximity values.
     */
    get_details() generates (ProximityDetails details);

    /**
     * Retrieve usage summary information about the backing HIDL service.
     *
     * @return a summary of usage information for the HIDL service.
     */
    summarize() generates (ProximitySummary summary);
};
```

Listing 11.2 `aproximity` HIDL `types.hal` **Definition**

```
package vendor.acme.one.aproximity@1.0;

struct ValueRange {
    int32_t   min;
    int32_t   max;
};

struct ProximityDetails {
    ValueRange   precision;
    ValueRange   proximity;
};

struct ProximitySummary {
    uint64_t   pollCallCount;
    int64_t    lastPollCalledMs;
};
```

Create these files in the location `vendor/acme/one/interfaces/aproximity/1.0` within the
AOSP source tree. The AOSP build contains a tool to help generate build files and boilerplate
code to get started with a service implementation. After the preceding files have been created
in the tree, execute the following command in the AOSP build shell to generate an `Android.bp`
file for building the HIDL (see Listing 11.3).

Listing 11.3 **Create the HIDL** `Android.bp` **File**

```
hidl-gen -L androidbp \
    -r vendor.acme.one:vendor/acme/one/interfaces \
    vendor.acme.one.aproximity@1.0
```

The new `Android.bp` file will be located alongside the `.hal` files. This file instructs the build
system to generate interface headers and boilerplate code needed for the implementation and
client(s). Listing 11.4 shows the generated content.

Listing 11.4 `Android.bp` **for the** `aproximity` **HIDL**

```
// This file is autogenerated by hidl-gen -Landroidbp.

hidl_interface {
    name: "vendor.acme.one.aproximity@1.0",
    root: "vendor.acme.one",
    product_specific: true,
    srcs: [
        "types.hal",
        "IAproximity.hal",
```

```
    ],
    interfaces: [
        "android.hidl.base@1.0",
    ],
    gen_java: true,
}
```

Before the AOSP build system will recognize the new HIDL, the top-level `interfaces` directory within the vendor tree for the device needs an `Android.bp` file. This informs the build system that the directory is the root location for HIDL packages. Create a new file, `vendor/acme/one/interfaces/Android.bp`, with the content of Listing 11.5.

Listing 11.5 **`Android.bp` for the Acme One HIDL Interfaces**

```
hidl_package_root {
    name: "vendor.acme.one",
}
```

HIDL Service Implementation

Now that the `aproximity` HIDL is defined, the platform needs the actual implementation. As previously mentioned, this is typically handled by a separate service process, particularly for HIDLs that are "drivers" for hardware. Because `aproximity` is an example of such a HIDL implementation, a native (for example, C++) implementation is needed. Fortunately, `hidl-gen` comes to the rescue here and can generate boilerplate code as a starting point. Listing 11.6 shows the commands to execute at the top level of the build tree to generate the boilerplate code for a C++ implementation of the HIDL.

Listing 11.6 **Create `aproximity` Service Boilerplate**

```
mkdir -p device/acme/one/hidl/aproximity
hidl-gen -L c++-impl -o device/acme/one/hidl/aproximity
    -r vendor.acme.one:vendor/acme/one/interfaces vendor.acme.one.aproximity@1.0
```

You can find the resultant files, `Aproximity.cpp` and `Aproximity.h`, in `device/acme/one/hidl/aproximity`. Similar to the way the `javah` or `javac -h` tools are used to help create JNI boilerplate code, `hidl-gen` is invaluable for creating a starting point for the service implementation. These two files will be built into a library that is then used by the service process to host the HIDL. First things first: The files need to be modified to remove unnecessary boilerplate code and provide the implementation for Acme One. The details of the methods and the special `Return` type will be covered shortly while working through the implementation. Listing 11.7 shows the updated header file.

Listing 11.7   `Aproximity.h` **Implementation**

```
#pragma once

#include <vendor/acme/one/aproximity/1.0/IAproximity.h>
#include <hidl/MQDescriptor.h>
#include <hidl/Status.h>

namespace vendor {
namespace acme {
namespace one {
namespace aproximity {
namespace V1_0 {
namespace implementation {

using ::android::hardware::hidl_array;
using ::android::hardware::hidl_handle;
using ::android::hardware::hidl_memory;
using ::android::hardware::hidl_string;
using ::android::hardware::hidl_vec;
using ::android::hardware::Return;
using ::android::hardware::Void;
using ::android::sp;

struct Aproximity : public IAproximity {
    Aproximity();
    ~Aproximity();

    // Methods from ::vendor::acme::one::aproximity::V1_0::IAproximity follow.
    Return<int32_t> poll(int32_t precision) override;
    Return<void> get_details(get_details_cb _hidl_cb) override;
    Return<void> summarize(summarize_cb _hidl_cb) override;

    // Methods from ::android::hidl::base::V1_0::IBase follow.
    Return<void> debug(const hidl_handle &handle,
                       const hidl_vec<hidl_string> &options) override;

private:
    uint64_t            pollCallCount;
    int64_t             lastPollCalledMs;
    int                 fd;
    proximity_params_t  params;
};

}  // namespace implementation
}  // namespace V1_0
}  // namespace aproximity
```

```
}  // namespace one
}  // namespace acme
}  // namespace vendor
```

Now for the actual implementation of the IAproximity methods for the HIDL. Remember that for a hardware-based HIDL (for example, driver HIDL), this is where access to the kernel via a /sys or /dev interface would be performed (or connected via a secondary library that performs the actual kernel I/O). For our trivial HIDL implementation, we will leverage the shim library that was created as part of the traditional HAL in Chapter 8, as shown in Listing 11.8.

Listing 11.8 **Aproximity.cpp Implementation**

```
#include <chrono>
#include "Aproximity.h"

using namespace std::chrono;

namespace vendor {
namespace acme {
namespace one {
namespace aproximity {
namespace V1_0 {
namespace implementation {

static int64_t now() {
    time_point now = system_clock().now();
    milliseconds nowMs =
        duration_cast<milliseconds>(now.time_since_epoch());
    return static_cast<int64_t>(nowMs.count());
}

Aproximity::Aproximity() {
    this->fd = open_sensor(this->params);
    if (this->fd < 0) {
        this->params.precision.min = -1;
        this->params.precision.range = -1;
        this->params.proximity.min = -1;
        this->params.proximity.range = -1;
    }
}

Aproximity::~Aproximity() {
    if (this->fd >= 0) {
        close_sensor(this->fd);
        this->fd = -1;
    }
```

```
    this->pollCallCount = 0;
    this->lastPollCalledMs = 0;
}

// Methods from ::vendor::acme::one::aproximity::V1_0::IAproximity follow.
Return<int32_t> Aproximity::poll(int32_t precision) {
    this->pollCallCount++;
    this->lastPollCalledMs = now();

    if (this->fd < 0) {
        return -1;
    }

    int shimPrecision = static_cast<int>(precision);
    int32_t result =
        static_cast<int32_t>(poll_sensor(this->fd, shimPrecision));

    return result;
}

Return<void> Aproximity::get_details(get_details_cb _hidl_cb) {
    ProximityDetails  result;

    result.precision.min = static_cast<int32_t>(this->params.precision.min);
    result.precision.max = static_cast<int32_t>(this->params.precision.range);
    result.proximity.min = static_cast<int32_t>(this->params.proximity.min);
    result.proximity.max = static_cast<int32_t>(this->params.proximity.range);

    _hidl_cb(result);
    return Void();
}

Return<void> Aproximity::summarize(summarize_cb _hidl_cb) {
    ProximitySummary  result;

    result.pollCallCount = this->pollCallCount;
    result.lastPollCalledMs = this->lastPollCalledMs;
    _hidl_cb(result);
    return Void();
}

Return<void> Aproximity::debug(const hidl_handle &handle,
                               const hidl_vec<hidl_string> & /*options*/) {
    if (handle == nullptr || handle->numFds < 1 || handle->data[0] < 0) {
        return Void();
    }
```

```
    int fd = handle->data[0];
    dprintf(fd, "HIDL:\n");
    dprintf(fd, "  Poll call count: %lu\n", this->pollCallCount);
    dprintf(fd, "  Last poll call: %ld\n", this->lastPollCalledMs);
    fsync(fd);
    return Void();
}


}  // namespace implementation
}  // namespace V1_0
}  // namespace aproximity
}  // namespace one
}  // namespace acme
}  // namespace vendor
```

Notice how the methods get_details and summarize each use a HIDL callback function
provided by the caller to return data. This must be done before the method returns: it is how
the service "generates" the non-primitive data returned to the client, which is waiting synchro-
nously. What makes this particularly confusing is both methods do return something: an
instance of a special class, Void! If you look carefully at the generated C++ code, each of the
HIDL methods returns a special Return class instance. The HIDL framework uses the Return
class along with the help of the backing Binder framework to determine that the HIDL call
succeeded or not. The aproximity clients, discussed in Chapter 12, will demonstrate how this
can be used.

The remaining method defined for the IAproximity interface is the poll method, which
generates an int32_t with the latest proximity value. However, unlike the other methods that
return more complex data types, this return value is provided as part of the Return object
rather than utilizing a synchronous callback method.

Most HIDL service implementations will build the backing HIDL calls into a static library that
is then linked with the service executable. The aproximity service is constructed in the same
manner, requiring a separate file containing the main service (daemon) entry point. The file
device/acme/one/hidl/aproximity/service.cpp provides the entry point for the service.
This is where the Aproximity class instance is created and registered as the HIDL service. It
then joins the RPC thread pool used by the HIDL subsystem. The RPC thread pool is utilized
by the HIDL framework (really, the backing Binder subsystem) to process incoming requests.
By joining the thread pool, the main thread of this service is added to the pool and will not
return—it will process incoming requests forever. The code for this is straightforward as shown
in Listing 11.9.

Listing 11.9 Aproximity Service Entry Point

```
#include <hidl/HidlSupport.h>
#include <hidl/HidlTransportSupport.h>
#include <utils/Errors.h>
```

```
#include <utils/StrongPointer.h>

#include "Aproximity.h"

using android::hardware::configureRpcThreadpool;
using android::hardware::joinRpcThreadpool;
using vendor::acme::one::aproximity::V1_0::implementation::Aproximity;
using namespace android;

int main() {
    configureRpcThreadpool(1, true);

    sp<Aproximity> aproximity = new Aproximity();
    status_t status = aproximity->registerAsService("default");

    if (status != OK) {
        return status;
    }

    joinRpcThreadpool();
}
```

After the HIDL service is built and present on the platform, it needs to be started by the system so the service is available for clients. This is done using an init run command (or rc) file for the service. Unlike other daemons in the system that require changes to a core platform script (such as init.hikey960.rc), the rc file for a HIDL service is kept alongside the service code and is pulled into the image based on build rules. Create the file device/acme/one/hidl/aproximity/vendor.acme.one.aproximity@1.0-service.rc with the content shown in Listing 11.10.

Listing 11.10   **The Aproximity Service rc File**

```
service vendor.aproximity-1-0 /vendor/bin/hw/vendor.acme.one.aproximity@1.0-service
    class hal
    user system
    group system
```

The rc file tells the (vendor) init process to start a service named vendor.aproximity-1-0 using the executable found at /vendor/bin/hw as part of the class of daemons labeled hal, and it is to be executed as the user system and in the group system.

The service code is ready! Time to pull it into the platform build. Create the file device/acme/one/hidl/aproximity/Android.bp with the content in Listing 11.11.

Listing 11.11 **Aproximity Service** Android.bp

```
cc_defaults {
    name: "vendor.acme.one.aproximity@1.0-defaults",
    defaults: ["hidl_defaults"],
    relative_install_path: "hw",
    shared_libs: [
        "libhidlbase",
        "libhidltransport",
        "libhwbinder",
        "libutils",
        "vendor.acme.one.aproximity@1.0",
    ],
    vendor: true,
    proprietary: true,
}

cc_library {
    name: "vendor.acme.one.aproximity@1.0-impl",
    defaults: ["vendor.acme.one.aproximity@1.0-defaults"],
    srcs: [
        "Aproximity.cpp",
    ],
    header_libs: [
        "libacmeproximityshim_headers",
    ],
    export_include_dirs: ["."],
}

cc_binary {
    name: "vendor.acme.one.aproximity@1.0-service",
    defaults: ["vendor.acme.one.aproximity@1.0-defaults"],
    init_rc: ["vendor.acme.one.aproximity@1.0-service.rc"],
    srcs: ["service.cpp"],
    header_libs: [
        "libacmeproximityshim_headers",
    ],
    static_libs: [
        "libacmeproximityshim",
        "vendor.acme.one.aproximity@1.0-impl",
    ],
    proprietary: true,
    vendor: true,
}
```

This blueprint file for soong lays out three different pieces: a set of default build options for C++ code, a C++ library containing the Aproximity.cpp implementation, and a C++ binary containing the service entry point and linked with the service library implementation.

The cc_defaults section builds on top of an existing hidl_defaults definition elsewhere in the platform and is named vendor.acme.one.aproximity@1.0-defaults. This type of section in a blueprint file sets up common things that can be applied to other blocks, such as building a library or executable binary. The defaults section in this file specifies the relative install path for any rule using these defaults as well as a set of shared libraries to be used. The HIDL library and service binary sections both apply these defaults. The net result is the service binary will be located at /vendor/bin/hw on the target.

The service helper library is static, so it is not installed on the running target. It is linked directly into the service binary along with the contents of the libacmeproximityshim library that provides access to the underlying device.

The final section pulls together the static libraries and the service entry point code to create an executable, vendor.acme.one.aproximity@1.0-service. This is what is executed by init via the rc file in Listing 11.10. Remember: It is a native Linux binary, not a runtime (for example, Java/Kotlin) Android application.

SE Linux for Android Changes

Before the new HIDL can be used, you must put some security-related settings into place. As discussed in Chapter 5, Android's use of SE Linux requires that binaries have the necessary access controls enabled. In this case, the aproximity service executable will need to have SE policies defined and applied to it before it will function.

Even though Acme One is built upon the HiKey960 device support, the SE policy changes are made in the overlay found in device/acme/one/acme_one/sepolicy. The changes are broken down into three different files: the policy file for the HIDL and two context definition files that utilize the context labels defined in the policy. The longest and most complex is the policy type enforcement file, because it defines several attributes and context labels needed for the HIDL service. As discussed in Chapter 5, crafting an SE policy file is non-trivial and also sparsely documented within AOSP. Often, the best documentation is examining existing SE policy files beneath system/sepolicy in the AOSP source tree. For example, the files system/sepolicy/public/hal_sensors.te and system/policy/vendor/hal_sensors_default.te were used as guideposts when creating the policy file for aproximity. Listing 11.12 shows the policy file, device/acme/one/acme_one/sepolicy/hal_aproximity.te.

Listing 11.12 **hal_aproximity.te Type Enforcement File**

```
hal_attribute(aproximity)

type hal_aproximity_hwservice, hwservice_manager_type;
```

```
###
# The HIDL aproximity attribute defines the _server and _client
#
binder_call(hal_aproximity_client, hal_aproximity_server)
binder_call(hal_aproximity_server, hal_aproximity_client)

hal_attribute_hwservice(hal_aproximity, hal_aproximity_hwservice)

####
# Create an execution domain for the service hosting the server side
#
type hal_aproximity_default, domain;
hal_server_domain(hal_aproximity_default, hal_aproximity)

type hal_aproximity_default_exec, exec_type, vendor_file_type, file_type;
init_daemon_domain(hal_aproximity_default)

allow hal_aproximity_default hal_aproximity_hwservice:hwservice_manager find;

# Allow the HIDL access to /dev/tty*, which would cover USB
# serial devices at /dev/ttyUSB*
allow hal_aproximity_default serial_device:chr_file rw_file_perms;
```

The file leverages a number of macros defined by the AOSP policy files, which makes the policy file shorter and consistent with other HIDL definitions. But those macros also obfuscate some very important details! Let's walk through the file in chunks to make it easier to digest.

The first chunk to look at is up through the hal_attribute_hw_service line. The hal_attribute macro at the start of the file does a number of things. First, it sets up new SE attributes hal_aproximity, hal_aproximity_client, and hal_aproximity_service. From there, it also declares some neverallow policies restricting processes that have these attributes from forking other processes. This lays the groundwork for definitions later in the file. Similarly, the hal_aproximity_hwservice type is defined to be an hwservice_manager_type. This ultimately allows the hwservicemanager to manage service interfaces labeled with this type. The new hal_aproximity attribute and hal_aproximity_hwservice are tied together via the macro hal_attribute_hwservice. This macro sets up allow rules for hal_aproximity_client to find interfaces labeled with hal_aproximity_hwservice via hwservicemanager. The client label will be used later in Chapter 12 when we create HIDL client apps. The hal_attribute_hwservice macro also sets up components running as hal_aproximity_server so they can add themselves and perform find operations with the hwservicemanager and use the base HIDL functionality. Finally, the binder_call macros are used to link the hal_aproximity_client and hal_aproximity_service processes via Binder, allowing the client to call the server as well as transfer references and files between the two. That is a ton of setup for just five lines!

The next chunk defines an execution domain for the HIDL service. Recall from Chapter 5 that Android SE policies require daemons to run in a well-defined execution domain. Further, the init process handling of vendor services will not even try to start up the service defined in the rc file shown earlier in this chapter, if the SE domain is not set up correctly! The new domain, hal_aproximity_default, is first defined then passed to the macro hal_server_domain with the previously defined attribute hal_aproximity as a type attribute of the domain. Additionally, the macro associates type attributes halserverdomain and hal_aproximity_server to the new domain. This effectively marks anything in the new domain as being an aproximity server and also within the scope of the existing halserverdomain. From here, a new type, hal_aproximity_default_exec, is used for describing files needed for the HIDL service execution. This new execution domain will be used to label the HIDL service binary shortly, in another SE file.

Now that the server side has an execution domain defined, the init process must be allowed to transition to it. This is a subtle, but critical nuance. After init has forked to create the new process for the service, it needs to be allowed to transition domains to the one defined for the HIDL service. This is accomplished via the init_daemon_domain macro. This macro sets up several allow policies for init to automatically transition to hal_aproximity_default when it forks and starts a process labeled as hal_aproximity_default_exec. Rounding out this chunk is an allow policy for processes within the hal_aproximity_default domain to find the hal_aproximity_hwservice.

The final allow rule specifies that any binary running in the hal_aproximity_default domain is able to access serial devices exposed by the kernel. Because this HIDL leverages the same shim library as the traditional HAL to access the underlying device interface(s), it needs the same SE access to the backing USB serial interface that connects the custom proximity device to the system on a chip (SoC). This is the same type of allow rule that is applied to the domain executing the daemon(s) leveraging the legacy HAL, discussed in Chapter 9.

All the various types defined and allow rules established in hal_aproximity.te are great, but by themselves they do not accomplish anything. Remember, with SE Linux, each process, file, socket, and so on is given a context for the kernel to understand what access it has to features within the system. In the case of our custom HIDL, the two "top" level points of concern are the HIDL service and the HIDL interface. The service is an executable binary that is stored on the file system. To apply the SE policies to the specific file, add the lines in Listing 11.13 to the end of device/acme/one/acme_one/sepolicy/file_contexts.

Listing 11.13 Aproximity Additions to file_contexts

```
# Acme One Specific Changes
/vendor/bin/hw/vendor\.acme\.one\.aproximity@1\.0-service
➡ u:object_r:hal_aproximity_default_exec:s0
```

The vendor.acme.one.aproximity@1.0-service executable is declared to be the hal_aproximity_default_exec type. This also marks it as a vendor-executable file and also establishes that it is a HIDL service for hal_aproximity_hwservice labeled interfaces.

This leaves the HIDL interface (the binder interface) to be defined. Create the file device/acme/one/acme_one/sepolicy/hwservice_contexts with the content shown in Listing 11.14.

Listing 11.14 `Aproximity-Specific hwservice_contexts`

```
vendor.acme.one.aproximity::IAproximity     u:object_r:hal_aproximity_hwservice:s0
```

This final piece brings all the SE policy definitions added for the HIDL together. The one inter-face the custom HIDL exposed, `vendor.acme.one.aproximity::IAproximity`, is declared to be of type `hal_aproximity_hwservice`.

Device Manifest

Now that the HIDL is defined and SE policy has been associated with it, the system needs to know that this HIDL exists and some of the details about it. The HIDL infrastructure requires devices to declare via a manifest which HIDL components are present and the details about them. Without the details in this file, `hwservicemanager` does not know how the HIDL can be registered and used (for example, the transport). Using this information, `hwservicemanager` can verify/impose correct SE policy and support for the transport. The possible values for transports are `hwbinder` and `passthrough`. Any other value, including a missing transport, is considered an error. Remember that any new devices running Android 8 or newer are allowed a very limited set of passthrough type HIDLs. Create the file `devices/acme/one/acme_one/manifest.xml` with the content shown in Listing 11.15.

Listing 11.15 `Aproximity` Additions to Device `manifest.xml`

```
<manifest version="1.0" type="device">
    <hal format="hidl">
        <name>vendor.acme.one.aproximity</name>
        <transport>hwbinder</transport>
        <version>1.0</version>
        <interface>
            <name>IAproximity</name>
            <instance>default</instance>
        </interface>
    </hal>
</manifest>
```

Because Acme One is derived from the `hikey960` device, the device manifest changes need to be picked up by the HiKey960 board configuration makefile. Edit the file `device/linaro/hikey/hikey960/BoardConfig.mk`, adding the content shown in Listing 11.16 immediately after the `BoardConfigCommon.mk` file is included.

Listing 11.16 `Aproximity` Additions to HiKey960 `BoardConfig.mk`

```
# Extend the device manifest file (for Acme One HIDL)
ifeq (acme_one, $(TARGET_PRODUCT))
$(warning Including Acme One HIDL manifest)
```

```
DEVICE_MANIFEST_FILE += device/acme/one/manifest.xml
endif
```

Build the HIDL into Acme

Just like adding a custom app or other component, you must add the HIDL service to the Acme build. Edit the file `device/acme/one/acme_one/acme_one.mk` and add the line shown in Listing 11.17.

Listing 11.17   **Acme One HIDL Updates to `acme_one.mk`**

```
PRODUCT_PACKAGES += vendor.acme.one.aproximity@1.0-service
```

Re-running the build for the target will result in updates to `system.img` and `vendor.img`. After these are flashed on to the HiKey960 board, the `aproximity` service will start at system startup, shown in bold in Listing 11.18.

Listing 11.18   **Running `aproximity` Service**

```
$ adb logcat -v time | grep -C 3 -i aproximity

01-01 00:07:12.519 I/ServiceManagement( 2453): Removing namespace from process name
android.hardware.configstore@1.1-service to configstore@1.1-service.
01-01 00:07:12.523 I/ServiceManagement( 2449): Registered
android.hardware.health@2.0::IHealth/backup (start delay of 70ms)
01-01 00:07:12.523 I/health@2.0/( 2449): health@2.0/backup: Hal init done
01-01 00:07:12.525 I/ServiceManagement( 2460): Registered
vendor.acme.one.aproximity@1.0::IAproximity/default (start delay of 56ms)
01-01 00:07:12.525 I/ServiceManagement( 2460): Removing namespace from process name
vendor.acme.one.aproximity@1.0-service to aproximity@1.0-service.
00:07:12.532 I/netdClient( 2443): Skipping libnetd_client init since *we* are netd
01-01 00:07:12.533 I/ServiceManagement( 2458): Registered
android.hardware.memtrack@1.0::IMemtrack/default (start delay of 65ms)
01-01 00:07:12.534 I/ServiceManagement( 2458): Removing namespace from process name
android.hardware.memtrack@1.0-service to memtrack@1.0-service.

<CTRL-C>

$ adb shell
hikey960:/$ ps -A | grep -i aproximity
system    2460    1   37068   4652 0       0 S vendor.acme.one.aproximity@1.0-service
```

Locking Down the API

Just like a publicly released SDK or library, defining a new, custom HIDL is a non-trivial effort. It requires careful consideration of the API details. Creating an API just to turn around and change or remove it would be obnoxious as well as a nightmare to support. These public interfaces are not the same as internal codebase APIs, which may be constantly refactored. After they are "published," HIDL-defined interfaces have to be considered frozen: "stable" and always available. This ensures that clients using the HIDL will work on any target that provides the interface, and that future devices that expose the HIDL are also compatible. The AOSP framework does not enforce this requirement at runtime—it really can't because it has no way of knowing what prior revisions of an API looked like. All is not lost, though. The AOSP build system has a mechanism that ensures that an interface at a specific API does not change. Recall that each HIDL defined by the AOSP framework, as well as the custom HIDL in this section, has a version number associated with it. This combination makes the HIDL interface unique. After an interface has been defined and is ready to be "locked down," a special hash is created for it. This hash is used both at build time and also when executing the Vendor Test Suite (VTS) to verify the vendor's device build is compliant. You can find more details about interface hashing at:

https://source.android.com/devices/architecture/hidl/hashing

All HIDL interfaces, including the system-defined interfaces, must be locked down to pass VTS. For example, Listing 11.19 shows the first several lines of the AOSP HIDL interfaces for Android 10. It has been abbreviated for space considerations. You can find the actual file at `hardware/interfaces/current.txt`.

Listing 11.19 **AOSP HIDL Hashes**

```
# Do not change this file except to add new interfaces. Changing
# pre-existing interfaces will fail VTS and break framework-only OTAs

# HALs released in Android O

f219c3b5b8c...9ad090417a2 android.hardware.audio@2.0::IDevice
4d579cae1cd...9de5c1c7362 android.hardware.audio@2.0::IDevicesFactory
203e23f1801...624c2b0848a android.hardware.audio@2.0::IPrimaryDevice
aaf93123dee...ebe1ee86748 android.hardware.audio@2.0::IStream
0468c5723b0...27b04b766df android.hardware.audio@2.0::IStreamIn
7296f7064fd...178d063680a android.hardware.audio@2.0::IStreamOut
19d241d71c3...25e9a98b6c2 android.hardware.audio@2.0::IStreamOutCallback
c84da9f5860...774f8ea2648 android.hardware.audio@2.0::types
1305786c06e...54752b8566b android.hardware.audio.common@2.0::types
. . .
```

The Acme One `aproximity` HIDL is now "locked down" and ready for use. Because this is a vendor-specific HIDL, the hash details for it go into the vendor-specific interfaces directory. Thankfully, there is no need to know the exact algorithm used to generate the hash, the exact hash type (SHA-256), or to manually calculate it. The `hidl-gen` tool provides support for

generating interface hashes. Listing 11.20 shows how to generate the file vendor/acme/one/
interfaces/current.txt, which will contain the locked-down hashes for the aproximity
HIDL.

Listing 11.20   **Create Custom HIDL Hashes**

```
hidl-gen -L hash -r vendor.acme.one:vendor/acme/one/interfaces \
  -r android.hidl:system/libhidl/transport vendor.acme.one.aproximity@1.0 \
  >> vendor/acme/one/interfaces/current.txt
```

The content of the file will look similar to the AOSP framework's current.txt, shown in
Listing 11.19. However, only the custom HIDL interface and types are present in the file, an
abbreviated version of which is shown in Listing 11.21.

Listing 11.21   **Acme One HIDL Hashes**

```
3b78d426c04...8b4b19ef250 vendor.acme.one.aproximity@1.0::types
dff6991e375...976a938449f vendor.acme.one.aproximity@1.0::IAproximity
```

To demonstrate how changes to the HIDL are caught at build time, let's change a small aspect
of the HIDL definition. Edit the file IAproximity.hal and add a new API, reset, which can
be used to reset the underlying hardware (see Listing 11.22).

Listing 11.22   **Add the reset Method to IAProximity**

```
package vendor.acme.one.aproximity@1.0;

interface IAproximity {
...
    /**
     * Reset the underlying hardware
     */
    reset();
};
```

There is no need to provide an implementation of the new interface. Simply start a build and
notice how it fails. The hash for the interface does not match the hash for the same version of
the interface. An abbreviated output is shown in Listing 11.23, with the error set in bold.

Listing 11.23   **Failed Build After HIDL API Change**

```
$ m -j 1

...
```

```
[ 19% 7/36] HIDL c++-sources: vendor/acme/one/interfaces/aproximity/1.0/types.hal
vendor/acme/one/interfaces/aproximity/1
FAILED:
out/soong/.intermediates/vendor/acme/one/interfaces/aproximity/1.0/vendor.acme.
one.aproximity@1.0_genc++/gen/vendor/acme/one/aproximity/1.0/AproximityAll.cpp
out/soong/.intermediates/vendor/acme/one/interfaces/aproximity/1.0/vendor.acme.
one.aproximity@1.0_genc++/gen/vendor/acme/one/aproximity/1.0/types.cpp
rm -rf
out/soong/.intermediates/vendor/acme/one/interfaces/aproximity/1.0/vendor.acme.
one.aproximity@1.0_genc++/gen && out/soong/host/linux-x86/bin/hidl-gen -R -p . -d
out/soong/.intermediates/vendor/acme/one/interfaces/aproximity/1.0/vendor.acme.
one.aproximity@1.0_genc++/gen/vendor/acme/one/aproximity/1.0/AproximityAll.cpp.d -o
out/soong/.intermediates/vendor/acme/one/interfaces/aproximity/1.0/vendor.acme.
one.aproximity@1.0_genc++/gen -L c++-sources -
rvendor.acme.one:vendor/acme/one/interfaces -
randroid.hidl:system/libhidl/transport vendor.acme.one.aproximity@1.0
ERROR: vendor.acme.one.aproximity@1.0::IAproximity has hash
c270b98c7a304a5026ffd1c6e6cfb03bf01756efdcd45950758a87e604b108d7 which does not match
hash on record. This interface has been frozen. Do not change it!
ERROR: Could not parse vendor.acme.one.aproximity@1.0::types. Aborting.
09:55:15 ninja failed with: exit status 1

#### failed to build some targets (46 seconds) ####
```

Because we had locked down the HIDL interface (hashes were created), the build system will
not allow a new image to be created. There are three choices in this situation: do not modify
the API, bump the version number and provide the new API implementation, or provide the
new API implementation and re-generate the hash (safe because the HIDL API was not fully
released). Bumping the version number would require a new HIDL implementation that derives
from this 1.0 version and is beyond the scope of this book. See the AOSP sensors HIDL API
for an example of a multi-versioned HIDL API. To keep things simple, we will just add a no-op
implementation for the new API, regenerate the API hashes for our HIDL, and verify we can
build, as shown in Listing 11.24.

Listing 11.24 Regenerate Custom HIDL Hashes

```
$ hidl-gen -L hash -r vendor.acme.one:vendor/acme/one/interfaces \
  -r android.hidl:system/libhidl/transport vendor.acme.one.aproximity@1.0 \
  > vendor/acme/one/interfaces/current.txt
$ m -j 12


...


[100% 15/15] Target vendor fs image: out/target/product/hikey960/vendor.img

#### build completed successfully (10 seconds) ####
```

Summary

This chapter defined a new HIDL-based HAL for the Acme platform: `aproximity`. This HAL replaces the traditional HAL implementation defined in Chapter 8. The implementation leverages the shim library that was built as part of the traditional HAL, but exposes the functionality via Binder-based APIs. The binders are registered with the system by a simple service executable and processed by a service-side implementation of the `IAproximity` interface. Chapter 12 will round out the HIDL example by showing how to create client applications that can access the `aproximity` HAL.

## 12

Clients for a Custom Binderized HAL

Android's newer binderized HAL, HIDL, is a fundamental shift in the way that OEMs and vendors provide platform-specific support for a device. Not only does this impact the OEM/ vendor implementation of a custom HAL, the code that utilizes the backing HIDL is also different than a traditional HAL. Client apps may be written in native C/C++ or Java code but no longer require special vendor-provided libraries to be bundled with the system. Similarly, the platform automatically builds Java-side support, removing the need for a custom JNI layer to take advantage of the HAL implementation.

HIDL client executables are similar in function to pre-Android 8 daemons or Android services that leveraged traditional HAL libraries. Typically, daemons or services using a traditional HAL load the requisite HAL shared library and often expose functionality to other parts of the system that require the backing HAL library. This is central to the way Android manages access to scarce resources, such as hardware features. Exposing the HAL features is typically done via a binder interface, or other IPC mechanism such as a POSIX socket. Depending on the exact function of the HIDL, the same techniques may be used to expose the HIDL functionality to the rest of the system.

This chapter demonstrates HIDL client implementation using both C++ and Java/Kotlin code, tapping into the Acme proximity HIDL created in Chapter 11. Exposing the HIDL functionality to the rest of the system via daemon or service is device and feature specific, so it is beyond the scope of this chapter. The main takeaway from this chapter will be how to tap into the new custom HIDL via a client application that is built into the system. Remember, these are not third-party applications that are released to the Google Play or any other app store. Only system- or vendor-provided executables/apps will have the necessary security access to directly leverage HIDL interfaces.

Native C++ Aproximity Client

Conceptually, the HIDL client implementation is quite simple with regards to interfacing with the backing HIDL service: get the backing service then call the appropriate method as needed.

In fact, most of the C++ example code deals with input arguments and providing output to the caller!

As discussed in Chapter 10, when a HIDL's .hal file(s) are built with the platform, a shared library is created for the HIDL along with the necessary headers for both service and client. This shared library provides all the functionality for the client to find the backing HIDL service, connect with it, and call through to its methods. The Binder-specific bits are handled by the generated code, allowing the HIDL client developer to focus on the functionality being used.

Listing 12.1 contains a simple C++ client for the custom HIDL. This is a command line application that can be run to exercise the different HIDL features of aproximity. This file is located at device/acme/one/app/aproximitycl in the platform tree. The key section of the code is the portion near the end of main, which acquires a pointer to the backing service and calls the specific HIDL method (shown in bold.)

Listing 12.1   **Aproximity C++ HIDL Client**

```
#include <hidl/HidlSupport.h>
#include <vendor/acme/one/aproximity/1.0/IAproximity.h>
#include <vendor/acme/one/aproximity/1.0/types.h>
#include <utils/StrongPointer.h>
#include <getopt.h>

using vendor::acme::one::aproximity::V1_0::IAproximity;
using vendor::acme::one::aproximity::V1_0::ProximityDetails;
using vendor::acme::one::aproximity::V1_0::ProximitySummary;
using android::sp;

using namespace android::hardware;

static void detailsCb(const ProximityDetails& details) {
    printf("[details] precision min/max: %d/%d\n",
            details.precision.min,
            details.precision.max);
    printf("[details] proximity min/max: %d/%d\n",
            details.proximity.min,
            details.proximity.max);
}

static void summaryCb(const ProximitySummary& summary) {
    printf("[summary] poll call count: %lu, last poll call (ms): %ld\n",
            summary.pollCallCount,
            summary.lastPollCalledMs);
}

void printUsage(char *name) {
    printf("Usage: %s [-ds] [-g input_precision]\n", name);
```

```cpp
    printf("\td:  Display the details of the sensor\n");
    printf("\tg:  Get the latest proximity reading at the precision\n");
    printf("\ts:  Print the summary details of the service\n");
}

int main(int argc, char* argv[]) {
    if (argc < 2) {
        printUsage(argv[0]);
        return -1;
    }

    bool doDetails= false;
    bool doProximity = false;
    int precision = -1;
    bool doSummary = false;
    bool doDebug = false;
    int  currentOpt;

    // Parse the command line options, determine what to do
    while ((currentOpt = getopt(argc, argv, "dg:s")) != -1) {
        switch (currentOpt) {
            case 'd':
                doDetails = true;
                break;
            case 'g':
                doProximity = true;
                precision = atoi(optarg);
                break;
            case 's':
                doSummary = true;
                break;
            case '?':
                if (isprint(optopt)) {
                    fprintf(stderr,
                            "Unknown option: '%c'\n",
                            optopt);
                } else {
                    fprintf(stderr,
                            "Unknown option character: '\\x%X'\n",
                            optopt);
                }

                printUsage(argv[0]);
                return -1;

            default:
                abort();
```

```
        }
    }

    if (!doDetails && !doProximity && !doSummary) {
        doDebug = true;
    }

    //  Get the HIDL to use (IAproximity)
    sp<IAproximity>  client = IAproximity::getService();
    if (client == nullptr) {
        fprintf(stderr, "Unable to get aproximity service interface\n");
        return -2;
    }

    if (doDetails) {
        Return<void> result = client->get_details(detailsCb);
        if (!result.isOk()) {
            fprintf(stderr,
                    "Unable to get proximity service details. Err: %s\n",
                    result.description().c_str());
            return -1;
        }
    }

    if (doProximity) {
        Return<int32_t> retProximity = client->poll(precision);
        if (!retProximity.isOk()) {
            fprintf(stderr,
                    "Unable to get proximity for precision (%d). Err: %s\n",
                    precision,
                    retProximity.description().c_str());
            return -1;
        }

        printf("[proximity] %d\n", static_cast<int32_t>(retProximity));
    }

    if (doSummary) {
        client->summarize(summaryCb);
    }

    return 0;
}
```

After acquiring a smart pointer to the `IAproximity` service, `sp<IAproximity>`, the client can simply call the desired method. If the smart pointer is `nullptr`, it means the client could not connect with the backing service. This typically happens if the HIDL service is not present or there was a SE policy violation.

> **Note**
>
> Just like communicating with other binder-based services, if the HIDL framework is unable to start/find the service that provides the HIDL implementation, the client may block indefinitely. Under normal circumstances this will not happen, but during development can be a major source of confusion. If this happens to your client app, check the kernel logs (via `dmesg`) and `logcat` output for errors relating to starting the backing HIDL service.

One of the more confusing parts of HIDL interface APIs is the handling of returned values. Depending on the specific service method, the return results may be received in different ways. Primitive data (for example, `int32_t`, `int64_t`, `boolean`, and so on) are returned (almost) directly. However, as shown in the service-side code in Chapter 11, complex or multiple return types require the client side to provide a callback method to receive the return data. This can be seen in Listing 12.1 with the three different `IAproximity` methods.

All the exposed service methods return a `Return` object, which contains information about the service call and possibly some return data. The `Return` object contains status details for the method call. The result of the `Return.isOk()` method indicates whether the service call succeeded or not. If it did not, the `Return.description()` method can be used to get a log-friendly message.

Primitive return type handling is demonstrated with the return handling for the `poll` method. When `Return` indicates the call is successful for a primitive return value, the `Return` object is simply cast to the primitive type.

In the case of the complex return values `ProximityDetails` and `ProximitySummary`, there is no direct return data. Instead, the client must provide callback methods, `detailsCb` and `summaryCb`, to the HIDL `get_details` and `summarize` methods, as shown in Listing 12.1. These callback functions handle the different complex return values. Note that even though callback methods are used, the actual HIDL service call blocks, so the results will be received via the callback *before* the service call returns.

Building the `aproximitycl` client executable requires a small blueprint file. Create the file `Android.bp` in `device/acme/one/app/aproximitycl` with the content shown in Listing 12.2.

Listing 12.2 **`aproximitycl` Blueprint File**

```
cc_binary {
    name: "aproximitycl",
    srcs: ["aproximitycl.cpp"],
    vendor: true,
    shared_libs: [
```

```
    "libhidlbase",
    "libutils",
    vendor.acme.one.aproximitycl@1.0
  ]
}
```

The blueprint file instructs the build system to create a C++ binary based on the input file aproximitycl.cpp using the necessary HIDL libraries. Because the vendor field is set to true, the resultant executable will be in the vendor file system on the running device. Specifically, it will be located at /vendor/bin/aproximitycl. Before the new executable can be used, some new SE policy details must be added to the system.

SE Linux for Android Changes for aproximitycl

Just like when the HIDL service was added in Chapter 11, some new SE Linux policy changes are needed for aproximitycl to function. Because the Aproximity HIDL support has already been created, adding the client-side support is rather simple. Edit the file device/acme/one/ acme_one/sepolicy/hal_aproximity.te, adding the content from Listing 12.3 to the end.

Listing 12.3 **Additions to the hal_aproximity.te Type Enforcement File**

```
###
# Create an execution domain for aproximitycl which is able to access the service
#
type aproximitycl, domain;
hal_client_domain(aproximitycl, hal_aproximity)

type aproximitycl_exec, exec_type, vendor_file_type, file_type;

domain_auto_trans(shell, aproximitycl_exec, aproximitycl)
allow shell aproximitycl_exec:file { getattr open read execute map };

# Allow `adb shell /vendor/bin/aproximitycl` and also
# `adb shell` then `/vendor/bin/aproximitycl`
allow aproximitycl shell:fd use;
allow aproximitycl adbd:fd use;
allow aproximitycl adbd:process sigchld;
allow aproximitycl adbd:unix_stream_socket { getattr ioctl read write };
allow aproximitycl devpts:chr_file rw_file_perms;
```

This new content for the type enforcement file sets up a new domain and execution attribute for the HIDL client (aproximitycl). Because it builds upon the server setup described in Chapter 11, there is no reason to dig into each line. However, the end of this section is worth mentioning. Instead of init, the aproximitycl executable may only be run manually via the shell. To allow this, the domain_auto_trans macro is used, which sets up a policy to automatically transition anything in the shell domain to the new aproximitycl domain when the shell forks and executes a binary labeled with the aproximitycl_exec type. If that sounds familiar, it is because it is exactly what the service-side init_daemon_domain macro uses behind the scenes to allow auto-transition of init! The remaining lines of this policy file establish several "allow" policies needed to permit actual use of aproximitycl. These policies allow the shell to execute binaries labeled as aproximitycl_exec and also allow the aproximitycl domain executables to use file descriptors, UNIX domain sockets, virtual terminals, and to send child signals. All of that is required so aproximitycl can use standard input/ output when run via the shell manually or via the adb shell command.

The remaining SE change needed for the aproximitycl client is to set the label of the executable binary. Add the line in Listing 12.4 to the end of device/acme/one/acme_one/ sepolicy/file_contexts to place aproximitycl into the aproximitycl_exec domain.

Listing 12.4 **Addition to file_contexts for aproximitycl**

```
# Acme One Specific Changes
...
/vendor/bin/aproximitycl    u:object_r:aproximitycl_exec:s0
```

Build aproximitycl into Acme

Just like when adding a vendor app or other component to the Android OS build, you must add the HIDL client to the Acme build file. Edit the file device/acme/one/acme_one/ acme_one.mk and add the line shown in Listing 12.5.

Listing 12.5 **Add aproxmitycl to acme_one.mk**

```
PRODUCT_PACKAGES += aproximitycl
```

Re-running the build for the target will result in updates to system.img and vendor.img. After these are flashed on to the HiKey960 board, the service will start at system startup and can be leveraged via the aproximitycl executable (see Listing 12.6).

Listing 12.6 **Running aproximitycl**

```
$ adb shell
hikey960:/ $ aproximitycl
Usage: aproximitycl [-ds] [-g input_precision]
        d:  Display the details of the sensor
        g:  Get the latest proximity reading at the precision
        s:  Print the summary details of the service
255|hikey960:/ $ aproximitycl -d
[details] precision min/max: 0/100
```

```
[details] proximity min/max: 0/100
hikey960:/ $ aproximitycl -g -1
[proximity] -1
hikey960:/ $ aproximitycl -g 50
[proximity] 60
hikey960:/ $ aproximitycl -g 99
[proximity] 63
hikey960:/ $ aproximitycl -s
[summary] poll call count: 3, last poll call (ms): 1609601581478
```

Java/Kotlin `Aproximity` Client

Utilizing a HIDL directly in a Java (or Kotlin!) package is substantially easier than legacy HAL access. This is in part because HIDL leverages the power of Android's Binder framework, but also because the HIDL build support auto-generates Java libraries for use by Java-based components. In other words: No custom JNI code is required! That being said, it is important to remember that performance-critical features are generally better kept to native code rather than runtime-based code.

To keep things simple, there is a complete Java/Kotlin-based client for `IAproximity` in the platform tree at `device/acme/one/app/AproximityClient`. This section will not walk through setting up each file in that directory. The layout is a typical Android Studio project. Note, though, that the AOSP build tree does not support Gradle-based builds.

This example brings up a simple UI showing the details of the `aproximity` HIDL and allows the user to request the latest proximity data via the user-provided precision value. The result is shown along with summary information. The code for `MainActivity`, written in Kotlin, can be seen in Listing 12.7 and has been trimmed here for brevity.

Listing 12.7 `AproximityClient MainActivity`

```kotlin
package com.acme.one.aproximityclient

import ...

import vendor.acme.one.aproximity.V1_0.IAproximity
import vendor.acme.one.aproximity.V1_0.ProximitySummary
import java.lang.NumberFormatException

class MainActivity : Activity() {
    companion object {
        const val TAG = "MainActivity"
    }
    private lateinit var proxDetails: TextView
    private lateinit var proxSummary: TextView
    private lateinit var proxPrecision: EditText
    private lateinit var proxValue: TextView
```

```kotlin
private lateinit var pollButton: Button
private lateinit var proxHidl: IAproximity

override fun onCreate(savedInstanceState: Bundle?) {
    super.onCreate(savedInstanceState)
    setContentView(R.layout.activity_main)

    setupHalAccess()
    setupViews()
}

override fun onResume() {
    super.onResume()

    updateDetails()
}

@SuppressLint("SetTextI18n")
private fun setupViews() {
    ...
    pollButton = findViewById(R.id.get_proximity)
    pollButton.setOnClickListener {
        val precision = try {
            proxPrecision.text.toString().toInt()
        } catch (e: NumberFormatException) {
            null
        }

        precision?.also {
            val proximity: Int = proxHidl.poll(precision)
            Log.d(TAG, "Latest proximity: $proximity")
            proxValue.text = proximity.toString()

            // Also update summarize details
            val summary = proxHidl.summarize()
            val count = summary.pollCallCount
            val timeStamp = summary.lastPollCalledMs
            proxSummary.text =
                "Poll called $count times, last at $timeStamp"

        } ?: run {
            Toast.makeText(
                this,
                R.string.bad_precision,
                Toast.LENGTH_LONG
            ).show()
        }
```

```
        }
    }

    private fun setupHalAccess() {
        proxHidl = IAproximity.getService(true)
    }

    private fun updateDetails() {
        val details = proxHidl.get_details()
        val precMin = details.precision.min
        val precMax = details.precision.max
        val proxMin = details.proximity.min
        val proxMax = details.proximity.max
        val detailText =
            "Precision ($precMin / $precMax)," +
                    "Proximity ($proxMin / $proxMax)"
        proxDetails.text = detailText
    }
}
```

Gaining access to the HIDL service is accomplished in a helper method, `setupHalAccess()`, which is called `from onCreate()`. This method calls the static method, `IAproximity.getService()`, which internally communicates with `hwservicemanager` to retrieve the backing binder to the HIDL service and returns an `IAproximity` proxy instance. The proxy instance is saved in the member field, `proxHidl`.

The `onResume()` method calls another helper method, `updateDetails()`. This is the first time the proxy class is used to call to the HIDL service. The `get_details()` HIDL method is called to retrieve a `ProximityDetails` object. The data from this object, the min and max for precision and proximity values, are formatted and added to a text field onscreen.

Finally, a simple `OnClickListener` closure is hooked into the button object, `pollButton`. When the user clicks the button, the precision value the user has selected is retrieved, and the proxy is once again called. This time both the `poll()` and `summarize()` methods are called. The results of both calls are then formatted and displayed onscreen.

Acquiring access to the HIDL service and utilizing it is noticeably simpler here in the Java/Kotlin side. There are no thread pools to configure and join, nor are there any callback methods that need to be provided when calling through to the service. However, a couple of potential pitfalls exist that need to be mentioned because the example code is so simple.

First, this code gets access to the HIDL and makes all calls to it directly in the main thread of the app. For this simple example, that's fine. However, each of these operations is an IPC call, which means the main thread is blocked waiting on another process to handle the request and return data. Second, the code has no error handling with respect to the HIDL service calls. Just like binder-based services, anytime an IPC call is made, there is the possibility of encountering a `RemoteException` or `SecurityException`. These should be dealt with as appropriate for the app when in production release code. Finally, it may not be obvious because this code looks like run-of-the-mill Android app code, but this app must be a vendor- or platform-provided package in order to access the HIDL interfaces. Typically, an app package like this or special system service would expose the HIDL functionality via a binder interface. A great example of this is the Secure Element application, located at `packages/apps/SecureElement` in the AOSP tree.

SE Linux for Android Changes for `AproximityClient`

Fortunately, the necessary changes to allow `AproximityClient` to use the `aproximity` HIDL are very straightforward. This is, in part, because of the type of enforcement macros available in the AOSP SE definitions, but also because this app needs to be a system app and will be built as such. Listing 12.8 shows the additions needed to the `hal_aproximity.te` file.

Listing 12.8   **Adding `AproximityClient` to the `hal_aproximity.te` Type Enforcement File**

```
###
# Allow platform apps (AproximityClient) to find and use hal_aproximity
#
hal_client_domain(platform_app, hal_aproximity)
```

Build `AproximityClient` into Acme

Getting the `AproximityClient` package built and installed on the Acme One platform is similar to other executables we have created. As previously mentioned, the full AOSP build system does not support Gradle-based builds. Dropping a typical Android Studio–based project into the tree will not work. In fact, if we look at the bundled system packages in the AOSP tree (under `packages/*`), the projects that build APKs do not even follow the typical Android Studio source tree layout! This makes sense; these packages are not third-party packages to be built against the public SDK and released for any Android device. These packages are intended to be built for a specific Android target.

Instead, a `soong` blueprint file is needed to get `AproximityClient` built and included in the platform. The blueprint rule for creating an Android app package includes support for specifying the source, resources, and manifest location(s) as well as some other options. This allows a new project to still utilize the Android Studio project layout.

> **Note**
>
> Even though the `soong` blueprint file syntax supports a project layout like those used by Android Studio, it does not have feature parity with Gradle-based builds. There is no support for Maven dependencies, Android Gradle Plugin features, build variants/flavors, and so on. Any package created as part of the platform build would either need the dependencies built as part of the AOSP tree or dropped into the specific project as a JAR file. Building the same app via Gradle or Android Studio can be achieved, but the dependency setup when using platform-specific libraries can be involved.

Listing 12.9 shows the blueprint file for AproximityClient.

Listing 12.9 **Android.bp Blueprint File for AproxmityClient**

```
android_app {
    name: "AproximityClient",
    vendor: true,
    privileged: true,
    certificate: "platform",
    srcs: [
        "app/src/**/*.java",
        "app/src/**/*.kt",
    ],
    resource_dirs: [
        "app/src/main/res",
    ],
    static_libs: [
        "vendor.acme.one.aproximity-V1.0-java",
    ],
    manifest: "app/src/main/AndroidManifest.xml"
}
```

As we have seen before, you can specify the location of the sources via the srcs field, allowing the use of an Android Studio project layout. Similarly, the resource_dirs and manifest fields provide the mechanism to specify the locations of the package resources and manifest, respectively.

The static_libs field is used to pull in Java libraries, which are available in the build tree. This is where the HIDL client library for aproximity is specified as a dependency of this package. This library is auto-generated by the platform based on the .hal file(s) for a given HIDL. Oddly enough, it does not actually perform this auto-generation until something specifies the library as a dependency! When you build the platform after adding the HIDL service implementation and C++ native client, this library is nowhere to be found in the build output or intermediates. The build system will not create the library until the AproximityClient application package is built.

Two other fields in this blueprint file worth mentioning are the privileged and certificate fields. The privileged field is used to build the package into the platform as a special platform app. This ultimately places it into a different SE context, platform_app. This domain was configured in the previous section to be allowed to use the aproximity HIDL. The certificate field specifies which of the certificates known to the platform should be used to sign the APK. This goes hand-in-hand with the privileged field as the platform certificate is needed for the app to be placed into the platform_app SE context.

Summary

Creation of a customized HIDL API for an Android platform necessitates the use of a custom HIDL client application. This is analogous to the service- or daemon-side access to a traditional Android HAL, exposing the HAL functionality to the rest of the system. This chapter explored the creation of both native (C++) and runtime (Java/Kotlin)–based clients for the Acme One `aproximity` HIDL. Both types of clients are able to leverage the HIDL libraries that are generated by the platform. The libraries obfuscate most of the binder-based mechanics used by the HIDL architecture behind the scenes. However, both client implementations still require some knowledge of the backing architecture—specifically with the use of threads and context of execution. Regardless, the end result is a straightforward way to use API for accessing the underlying HIDL service created for the platform.

Index

C

G

H

I

J

S

Photo by izus

Register Your Product at informit.com/register

Access additional benefits and **save 35%** on your next purchas

- Automatically receive a coupon for 35% off your next purchase, valid for 30 days. Look for your code in your InformIT cart or the Manage Codes section of your account page.
- Download available product updates.
- Access bonus material if available.*
- Check the box to hear from us and receive exclusive offers on new editions and related products.

Registration benefits vary by product. Benefits will be listed on your account page under Registered Products.

InformIT.com—The Trusted Technology Learning Source

InformIT is the online home of information technology brands at Pearson, the world's foremost education company. At InformIT.com, you can:

- Shop our books, eBooks, software, and video training
- Take advantage of our special offers and promotions (informit.com/promotions)
- Sign up for special offers and content newsletter (informit.com/newsletters)
- Access thousands of free chapters and video lessons

Connect with InformIT—Visit informit.com/community

the trusted technology learning source

Addison-Wesley • Adobe Press • Cisco Press • Microsoft Press • Pearson IT Certification • Que • Sams • Peachpit Press

 Pearson